W9-CHI-451

# The Distinctive College

## Foundations of Higher Education
### Lionel Lewis, Series Editor

# The Distinctive College

## Burton R. Clark

### *With a New Introduction by the Author*

Transaction Publishers
New Brunswick (U.S.A.) and London (U.K.)

Second printing 1999
Copyright © 1992 by Transaction Publishers, New Brunswick, New Jersey.

All rights reserved under International and Pan-American Copyright Conventions. No part of this book may be reproduced or transmitted in any form or by any means, electronic or mechanical, including photocopy, recording, or any information storage and retrieval system, without prior permission in writing from the publisher. All inquiries should be addressed to Transaction Publishers, Rutgers—The State University, 35 Berrue Circle, Piscataway, New Jersey 08854-8042.

This book is printed on acid-free paper that meets the American National Standard for Permanence of Paper for Printed Library Materials.

Library of Congress Catalog Number: 91-30246
ISBN: 1-56000-592-0
Printed in the United States of America

Library of Congress Cataloging-in-Publication Data

Clark, Burton R.
    The distinctive college/Burton R. Clark.
    p.    cm. — (Foundations of higher education)
    Originally published: Chicago: Aldine Pub. Co., 1970. With new introd.
    Includes bibliographical references and index.
    ISBN 1-56000-592-0
    1. Education, Humanistic—United States—Case studies.  2. Swarthmore College.  3. Reed College (Portland, Or.)  4. Antioch College.  I. Title. II. Series.
LC1023—C53      1992
378.1'542'0973—dc20                                      91-30246
                                                            CIP

# Contents

# Introduction to the Transaction Edition

HOW ARE values firmly embodied in organizations, there to guide the thoughts and steer the actions of various participants? The research that led to publication of *The Distinctive College* in 1970 sought answers to this question by concentrating on three institutions in the private college sector of American higher education. Along with other enterprises, colleges and universities were assumed to develop particular personalities that holistically express what they value most deeply. They come to stand for something; they develop beliefs about themselves; they take up definable roles; their members have a certain outlook about their work. The organization accumulates a predisposition that arguably becomes the best predictor of its reaction to contemporary pressures and future trends.

Since organizational character develops over decades, its study requires historical exploration. It may be largely set during the initial years of an organization, which was the case at Reed College. Its current nature may be the outcome of radical transformation in a period of crisis in an old organization, which occurred at Antioch. It may also stem from evolutionary changes in an ongoing organization that is not in crisis but develops a desire to be something other than what it is, as was the case at Swarthmore, where ambition to become an academically superior college led to the 1920-40 evolution to which the name of Frank Aydelotte, president during those years, became attached. Hence the case studies found in the book became accounts of organizational development over long periods of time, emphasizing critical periods of character determination.

Organizational character can vary greatly in depth and richness. As for individuals, it may be vivid or colorless, strong or weak, one of a kind or a face lost in the crowd. Antioch, Reed, and Swarthmore had raised themselves to a position of preeminence among the hundreds of liberal arts colleges that dotted the landscape in the 1950s and 1960s. Each was highly distinctive, hence the title of the book.

The distinctiveness of these institutions, it turned out, was not based on programmatic features that we might think all leading liberal arts colleges necessarily possess. In courses and curricula, modes of student interaction and faculty activity, there was an Antioch way, a Reed way, and a Swarthmore way–as there undoubtedly is a special way at Amherst, Carleton, Pomona-Claremont, or any of a number of outstanding colleges. What could I then assert to be common ground for distinctiveness, for strong personality in a liberal arts college? The central component, I gradually realized, was how much a college believed in itself and in what it was doing. A coherent belief system proved central, one that was expressed in valued practices that ranged from certain types of seminars to student extracurricular traditions. The belief system had historical depth. It had passionate support: those who had saving faith told of intense commitment and hard struggle that had led to successful outcome. The most important step in my analysis–close to completion of the first draft!–was to sharply conceptualize this phenomenon. I toyed for several months with such likely labels as organizational doctrine, ideology, idea, myth, culture, story, legend. "Saga" finally turned out to have the most appropriate traditional meanings and overtones. Hence organizational saga became the concluding idea, the one for which the book is known.[1] A concept that caught on, it placed the study in the literature on organizations as well as in the writings on higher education.

Appearing at the beginning of the 1970s, the book has stood as an early contributor to certain conceptual and methodological developments that blossomed in the late 1970s and 1980s. Conceptually, the study became one of the intellectual roots of a field of thought and analysis increasingly known as "organizational culture." A citation analysis of thirty-two articles on organizational culture appearing in an anthology and two special issues of journals during 1983 listed the book as tied for second among the most frequently cited sources.[2] Among the top seven sources for this rapidly growing field, *Distinctive College* was the only empirical case study; the others were general statements, such as Clifford Geertz's 1973 classic, *The Interpretation of Culture*, and the noted books by William G. Ouchi (*Theory Z*, 1981) and Terrence Deal and A. Kennedy (*Corporate Cultures*, 1982). Methodologically, the study came to be viewed as a successful example of qualitative analysis rooted in sustained field interviewing, open-ended observation, and perusal of documents, a method that openly stresses interpretation. Hence, if the study were newly completed in the early 1990s, I undoubtedly would need to define it more explicitly as a study of academic culture, one that pointed to holistic institutional character. Given the advances in the methodology of qualitative analysis, I probably also would need to be more self-conscious about the nature of my research procedures. However, at the time of my fieldwork, 1958-63, and the years of writing in the mid- and late 1960s, an organizational sociologist could simply do a qualitative study of one or more organizations and not dwell very long on how it was done. Even now, of course, the proof of the value of an analysis lies in its substantive contributions rather than its methods, and there remains nothing particularly arcane about visiting colleges to talk with people, attend meetings, observe campus events, and read historical and contemporary documents.

*Distinctive College* was also about leadership. The preceding book that most shaped how I approached this study was Philip Selznick's classic, *Leadership in Administration*, which appeared in 1957.[3] In each of the three case studies that composed *College,* I stressed the interplay between college presidents and faculty, trustees, students, and alumni. In the concluding chapter on "the making of an organizational saga" I developed a section on charismatic leadership in order to stress its situational determination, pointing to how much it depends on nominal followers, such as faculty and students, who can attribute greatness to a leader at one point but sour on him or her a few years later and turn off the play of charismatic traits. Also at the heart of the matter were varying roles played by successive presidents in a college as well as those occasioned by different college contexts. When a vivid organizational saga exists, the odds are high that one or more strong presidents played a significant role in its initiation. But then we also find that the embodiment and persistence of a unifying belief system requires sustaining presidential successors, a devoted faculty core, an allied student culture, and a supportive external social base. Hence to highlight the book in the terms and concerns of the 1980s and early 1990s, I would like it to be clearly identified as a study of organizational leadership as well as an analysis of academic culture.

Since the research of *The Distinctive College* from the beginning took as a central issue the realization of holistic orientations, I would most of all like to have the book understood as a study of how values become concretely expressed. Discussions about values in higher education are notorious for softening minds and putting listeners and readers to sleep. Speakers and writers, to no avail, huff and puff about the "shoulds," "musts," and "oughts" of colleges and universities. In comparison, we attend to values in a serious and useful way when we seek to find how they are realized in the ongoing behaviors of individuals and practices of organizations. It is not easy to concretely express liberal education values in colleges; more institutions fail than succeed in this quest, or at best settle for very limited accomplishment. The success story told in *The Distinctive College* is how three colleges, each in its own way, came to strongly embody in their everyday practices an effective definition of the ideals of liberal education. These enterprises were indeed strongly value oriented. Values are finally what *The Distinctive College* is about, values made real, values brought alive, values realized in the ways of organizations and the actions of their devoted members.

Preparing this introduction to a new edition twenty years after the time of first publication brings to mind a problem faced in writing the book of attempting to transmit to readers the emotion, the passion, that professors, students, administrators, trustees, and alumni invest in an academic enterprise when they are in the grip of an organizational saga. I encountered people at Reed, Antioch, and Swarthmore who were positively in love with their college, who were happy when its affairs were going well and sad when it had hard days, who quietly believed that their college was the best of all possible places, who turned down considerably greater material rewards offered them to go elsewhere because their college had become the center of meaning in their lives. "True believers" was frequently not an inappropriate term to apply. To make readers feel the deep emotional involvement seemed to require terms that were themselves loaded with emotion. Thus as I attempted to explain how nominally rational organizations become emotion-laden ends in themselves, my writing at times slipped toward sentimentality. The risk was gushing prose that might well not appear as cool judgment.

The problem of how to depict and convey passionate commitment in such ordinary settings as the institutions of education has continued to interest me. A large fieldwork-based study of American academics carried out in the mid-1980s in a wide range of institutional and disciplinary settings convinced me again that deep passion is often found in the commitments of professors to their research and teaching and to the colleges and universities that provide favorable settings for these activities.[4] That passion is largely beyond the reach of questionnaires distributed in national surveys and hence goes largely unreported in analyses based on this common method. It is also downplayed by the norms of social science that emphasize hard-headed skepticism in confronting the extravagant exaggerations of organizational myths and the pretenses of academic cultures. And it is certainly the case that American colleges and universities, operating in competitive arenas, offer a steady diet of fanciful statements about their individual virtues. Who believes such embellished claims? Participants often do, and their believing becomes a social fact. It is then up to the investigator to capture and present that fact, even if necessary in emotion-laden terms. Luckily, this problem has been reduced in the 1980s by the rebirth of case study fieldwork and the new respect given to qualitative analysis. The interpretive power of results again becomes more important than adherence to certain canons of method, including the prose style of written presentation.

Among my publications, *The Distinctive College* has been a personal favorite. Its preparation took me deeply and richly into the academic life. I still like the institutional stories it tells and I am pleased with the contribution it has made to the thought of others. Yet it is the book of mine that disappeared most quickly from print, only a half-dozen years or so after publication. Hence I am doubly grateful to Transaction Publishers for this new edition. To have a beloved book again publicly available is ample reason for deep gratitude to the editors of a firm whose characterological passion lies so clearly in the publishing of good books.

**Burton R. Clark**

## Notes

1. The article that best highlighted the book was "The Organization Saga in Higher Education," Administrative Science Quarterly 17, 1972, 178-84. A second statement prepared for a college audience appeared as "Belief and Loyalty in College Organization," Journal of Higher Education 42, 1971, 499-515.
2. William G. Ouchi and Alan L. Wilkins, "Organizational Culture," Annual Review of Sociology 11, 1985, 457-83.
3. Philip Selznick, Leadership in Administration (New York: Harper & Row, 1957). Reprinted by University of California Press in a paperback edition, 1984.
4. See Burton R. Clark, The Academic Life: Small Worlds, Different World (Princeton: Carnegie Foundation for the Advancement of Teaching and Princeton University Press, 1987).

# Acknowledgments

I AM pleased to acknowledge the generous and patient support of the Carnegie Corporation for the research effort out of which this study developed. That support was expressed specifically in the granting of major research funds to the Center for the Study of Higher Education, University of California, Berkeley, of which I was a member from 1958 to 1966. I am indebted to the Berkeley Center and to its former director, T. R. McConnell, who, together with the Carnegie Corporation, gave me the unusual opportunity to spend a good share of a number of years visiting and otherwise acquainting myself with the colleges in this study.

I am naturally also deeply indebted to the faculty members, administrators, and students at Antioch, Reed, and Swarthmore who, on my visits between 1958 and 1963, gave me their versions of the development and character of their own college and steered me to useful historical and current information. The colleges were models of openness to inquiry. I wish to thank the many individuals in each college, here unnamed for practical reasons of simplicity and anonymity, who opened their doors again and again upon my request for advice, interview, or observation of college affairs.

An early draft of this volume benefited from a critical reading by several members of the colleges and by colleagues at the University of California and Yale University, particularly Wendell Bell, Kai T. Erikson, and

Sheldon L. Messinger. Many persons in the Department of Sociology at Yale assisted in the preparation of drafts of this study. Among them I would like to thank particularly Carol Cofrancesco and Phyllis Swift for managing the technical preparation and Janet Turk for editorial comment.

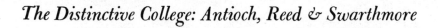

*The Distinctive College: Antioch, Reed & Swarthmore*

# Introduction to the Original Edition

THE PRIVATE liberal arts college is the oldest of the institutions for higher learning in America. Beginning with Harvard (1636), William and Mary (1693), and Yale (1701), this organizational form monopolized higher education until the development of university structures, public and private, in the last half of the nineteenth century. There were several hundred of these enterprises before the university, all small by present standards and nearly all close to a group of supporters, commonly a church denomination, who with much sweat and sacrifice had initiated and sustained a place of and for their own. It is little wonder that the liberal arts college has been long an object of sentiment and nostalgia. Daniel Webster surely represented the affection of many when in pleading the case of Dartmouth as a private entity before the United States Supreme Court in 1818, he presented the brief of this "humble institution" as "the case of every college in the land," went on to declare that "this little institution" would be destroyed if a public legislature were allowed "to turn it from its original use," and concluded with the memorable phrase, "It is, sir, as I have said, a small college, and yet there are those who love it. . . ."[1] The tears reputedly shed that day by Chief Justice John Marshall as well as by

1. Quoted in Frederick Rudolph, *The American College and University* (New York, Alfred A. Knopf, Inc., 1962), p. 210.

3

the eloquent attorney are symbolic of the deep sense of caring developed before and since that time. Still today, in an age of giant universities and mass higher education, these small places retain impressive status in American society and a hold on the hearts of many. The private liberal arts college is *the* romantic element in our educational system.

This organizational form is fascinating on more than the grounds of historical primacy and public affection. It is a device for higher education that most other major countries have managed to do without; its widespread development in the United States entailed the adaptation of an English model of higher learning to the peculiarly American conditions of nation-building, denominational zeal, and voluntary effort. After long development this educational form now exhibits not common style and national standards but great variety in performance and achievement. Its foremost representatives set a pace in the quality of undergraduate education matched, if at all, only by a few of the best endowed private universities. Its hindmost members offer a narrow religious and cultural fundamentalism and a mean spirit hardly duplicated in the rearguard of the public institutions. The present eight hundred liberal arts colleges, religious and secular, cover the whole spectrum of quality and sophistication, providing in themselves much of the extreme pluralism that characterizes American higher education.

As we contemplate this variety, we are led back toward questions of necessity and accident and of condition and effort in organizational achievement. Some colleges appear caught in a circle of perpetual mediocrity; others appear to have been blessed with luck in finding the road to academic acclaim. The conditions and the means seemingly have varied widely and for obscure reasons. Certainly many college staffs in any period have desired high quality, a gain in public respect, and the rewards of work well regarded. In recent years, when hundreds of small colleges have felt imperiled by the flow of money, students, and staff into public institutions and large private universities, they have often considered an improvement in performance the ground for survival. But the desire to be better regarded and the search for higher quality commonly bring little gain. The making of a first-rank liberal arts college appears clothed in difficulty, even hidden from view in the mysteries of personal magnetism and institutional aura. The insistent questions remain: How is it done? How has it been done?

Quite different perspectives in history and the social sciences can usefully guide us in pursuing answers to these questions. Here we see the issue as a sociological problem of formal organization. One basic concern in sociology is the fate of culture—values, norms, knowledge—at the hands of social conditions and social structures. In our time, broad social values are often neither self-preserving nor guaranteed by unstinting commitment across community and society but rather have their survival and strength bound up in the work of those specialized and deliberate social systems that we call organizations. Cultural stability and change, value strength and weakness, become in part specific issues of organizational purpose and organizational performance. A "crisis in education" is a crisis of the urban elementary school or of the teachers training college or of the university. From this general perspective, then, we first view the liberal arts college as an organized social system for reaching toward certain values.

What are the social values in question? When people speak of undergraduate education in the United States, they usually have ideas of broad liberal education somewhere in mind. The ideas are commonly ambiguous, are nearly always difficult to define, and are expressed in a time-worn rhetoric that muddles the mind. But the concern persists, being part of the fundamental tension between general and specialized education found in the middle and upper levels of advanced and modernizing educational systems. Early in this century, Max Weber portrayed this tension as the root of educational problems and struggles.[2] Although the positive value placed on the specialized expert is increasing, that placed on the generalist, even on the cultivated man, continues. In the United States the private liberal arts colleges (and the undergraduate colleges of a few of the private universities) are expected to devote themselves to the liberal arts and general education. The private colleges accept this expectation, seeing their own efforts concentrated on liberal education more than is possible at the universities, the state colleges, and the junior colleges, where occupational training and sometimes community services are part of the purpose and program. The terms of this expectation, however, have shifted somewhat through the years. Only a few places try to hold their students to the great books for four years. The others offer some specialized work and are proud when their graduates are technically well prepared for graduate school or professional performance. The expectation then is that the liberal arts college is better equipped than the other institutions, both in formal arrangement and in informal association, to provide a combination of general and specialized education.

One way to search for the organizational fulfillment of the values of such a college is to study intensely some colleges that are highly regarded —socially defined as successful and effective. This route allows our sociological problem to converge with the educational problem established earlier—how to make a college first rank. For several decades, back to the nineteen-thirties, Antioch, Reed, and Swarthmore have had reputations as institutions of quality. Their reputations continued to grow, placing them ever higher among American colleges. In important national rankings in the early fifties, based on the "production" of scholars and scientists, they

2. *From Max Weber: Essays in Sociology,* trans. by H. H. Gerth and C. Wright Mills, eds. (New York, Oxford University Press, Inc., 1946), p. 243.

appeared in the top ten colleges.[3] Each fascinating in its own right, these three colleges are our empirical subjects. To them we apply our general perspectives, and about them we ask specific organizational and educational questions; from them we attempt to gain insight and generalizations that may apply in other places, to other colleges, and even to some other kinds of organizations.

Within the broad sociological interest in values and organizations mentioned earlier, this study has been guided by an analytical perspective historical in nature as compared to those perspectives now commonly used in sociology or in the interdisciplinary field of organizational studies. Our wish is to study general organizational character, especially distinctive character, and to understand its initiation and development—much as certain psychologists attempt to study individual personality and its determinants. This interest entails temporal inquiry. We need to work back through the organizational history until we find the critical years when the basic present orientation was initiated. For that period we wish to know the conditions under which the orientation was introduced and precisely how it was managed. We then study ensuing years and decades to discover how the basic orientation, the expression of a certain set of values, became firmly fixed in the workings of the institution. Finally, if the organization has further history, we can look for the problems of fixed character in a changing environment. This approach to the study of organizations brings us quickly to central organizational problems. To go back to the time of critical change is to approach innovating leaders in the broad sense—influential men who affected the long-run nature of an entire organization. To study how the change was effected and then made durable is to identify the components that must be manipulated to change the character of the whole and then must be maintained in an interlocking way to sustain the newly won character. To pursue finally the later consequences of fixed character is to encounter some of the strains and adaptations occasioned by the effort to keep viable the old in the face of new demands in a new time.

The materials that follow on Antioch, Reed, and Swarthmore are therefore organized as historical studies. The three narratives in Parts I, II, and III follow in general the rhythm of each organizational development. Parallel sections have not been closely enforced; and unique events, special conditions, and unusual features are given their due. To structure each history tightly in the boxes of comparison and generalization would have prematurely torn apart the developmental story and underplayed the unique components of each institutional fabric. The three accounts

3. Robert H. Knapp and Hubert B. Goodrich, *The Origins of American Scientists* (Chicago, The University of Chicago Press, 1952); and Robert H. Knapp and Joseph J. Greenbaum, *The Younger American Scholar: His Collegiate Origins* (Chicago, The University of Chicago Press, 1953).

do, however, receive some guidance, and hence their selectivity, from comparative categories. Ideas brought to the study or developed in the course of research enter as tools of analysis and foci of discussion when appropriate in the historical story of the individual college.

Antioch College, in existence since the middle of the nineteenth century, was sharply transformed in the nineteen-twenties. Chapter 1 takes brief note of the early history and then concentrates on the ends and means of the transformation. These materials indicate the importance of charismatic leadership, new personnel, and altered public image in changing the character of this particular college. Chapter 2 follows Antioch into the thirties and early forties, concentrating on the cementing of changes in such parts of the institution as its distinctive curriculum and its unusual structure of authority. The third and concluding chapter on Antioch studies its evolution after World War II, attempting to identify the central tensions inherent in its character or produced by the relation of its character to a changing environment.

Reed College had no nineteenth century, having been founded in 1910. Chapter 4 concentrates on the early intentions of this unusual college and on the actions and practices meant to embody those intentions in its first fifteen years. Here, as at Antioch, we encounter strong personal leadership. We also note how organizational character was defined through such means as faculty recruitment, distinctive curriculum, and public reputation. Chapter 5 centers on the means by which the hard-won character was elaborated and defended in the ensuing decades, with faculty commitment and control the central structural elements. Chapter 6 looks at the persistence of fixed character in this institution in the years since World War II, as the college encountered deep tensions in its control and environmental relations.

Swarthmore, like Antioch, got under way in the middle of the nineteenth century. It, too, underwent a major change in the nineteen-twenties, but one not so disruptive of institutional history. Since Swarthmore was a viable institution before 1920 and its early character affected its later character, Chapter 7 is devoted to the early history. Here we see an initially provincial college come into the mainstream of liberal arts colleges in the country. Chapter 8 concentrates on the twenties and thirties as a period of great change. Here, again, we encounter the charismatic leader, and we watch him and his growing band of supporters alter one major feature of the college after another to produce a unified character supporting a new set of values. Chapter 9 examines the resulting structures that fully embodied, protected, and conserved the distinctive character of the college in the forties and fifties.

In each case, the historical account stops at the beginning of the sixties. (The field research out of which this study developed took place between 1958 and 1963; see Appendix 1). Thus the case studies, aside from the early periods at Antioch and Swarthmore, cover developments spanning forty to fifty years. The attempt has been made to round these accounts to the point where they are reasonably balanced statements of historical reality, despite the selectivity imposed by general categories, and thus they can stand on their own as organizational narratives. At the same time, the narratives provide the food for theoretical thought. We first see a given phenomenon, e.g., charismatic leadership, in the elaborate reality of a functioning organization, and then return to it in a more generalized fashion in the concluding section (Part IV).

As developed in that final section, the phenomenon of the organizational saga is the central ingredient in the making of the distinctive college (and here of the distinctively excellent college). This concept, which emerged late in the study, is explained by relating it to the ideas of organizational role and mission. All organizations have a social role, ways of behaving linked with defined positions in the larger society, but only some have seized their role in the purposive way that we can call a mission. Then, among those that have been strongly purposive, only some are able to sustain and develop the mission over time to the point of success and acclaim. The mission is then transformed into an embracing saga. We are able to speak then of colleges (and other organizations) that become legendary, even heroic, figures on the social stage.

The materials of the three college narratives suggest the bases for sagas. We note three conditions under which they begin as strong-willed efforts in institutional innovation: the new context—Reed as the case in point—where the effort is made in a new organization; the revolutionary context—Antioch as example—where deep crisis in an old organization opens it for radical and quick transformation; and the evolutionary context—as at Swarthmore—where the effort to effect major change takes place in a stable and secure setting. The contexts are likely to lead to somewhat different styles of leadership, particularly to different timings of innovative efforts. The new and revolutionary settings are the most dramatic, but the evolutionary situation is perhaps the most intriguing since reform is most often attempted (or at least contemplated) in ongoing organizations not in deep crisis. Here we can speculate on openness to change in established organizations.

Examination of the initiation of sagas brings us directly to the role of the individual leader since in each of the colleges the innovating effort was conceived, enunciated, and put in motion by a strong-willed man in the president's chair. Here we emphasize how much charisma, generally portrayed in terms of individual gifts of grace, depends on certain organizational conditions, and especially on the acceptance of followers, for its occurence and its strength. Organizations have a number of weapons against charismatically inclined individuals, and the fate of strong leaders in these three colleges suggests some of the interaction that diminishes, as well as that which makes possible, the influence of the man of unusual personal gifts.

Although Antioch, Reed, and Swarthmore differed in the context and style of the first days and years of the innovating effort, they converged on organizational elements that made the innovation durable and noteworthy and led finally to the sense of a saga. First, we emphasize the development of belief and power in a personnel core. In colleges this core is commonly the senior faculty, which comes on strong as a group after the leader has left or has had his influence diminished in a collegial web. Second, we look to the importance of the program of work—curriculum and teaching in a college—as an embodiment and expression of distinctiveness. Antioch, Reed, and Swarthmore each have had great success in convincing themselves and outsiders that their programs are special. Third, we point to the integral importance of an external social base, those small segments of the larger society that send students, money, moral support, and affection. Fourth, we review the special role of those transient participants that colleges call students. Finally, we highlight the force of organizational ideology, where doctrine defines a straight line that rules out the zigs and zags of opportunism and where the theme of the institution becomes reflected in a thousand and one bits of statue and sidewalk, story and song. These major elements interconnect and seemingly are inescapably the fundamental tools of the making of a college saga. Expressed in only slightly altered terms, they may, as theoretical categories, have wide applicability in enhancing the understanding of the development of organizational sagas in other institutional spheres.

The discussions of the concluding section attempt to face in two directions. One is to the perspectives of organizational theorists and researchers, emphasizing the analytical importance of historical inquiry and the use of the concept of the saga in understanding distinctive organizational character. The other is to the perspectives of those who administer or profess or otherwise play some part in deciding the character of colleges; here the emphasis is on the necessary tools of distinctiveness. In either case, I wish finally to convey how some colleges, and apparently some organizations in other realms, so elicit dedication and affection that the quality of life for those involved is significantly altered, often for a lifetime. Developing that capacity is no mean feat for what are purportedly rational formal organizations, places of work and career, and locales of transient participation. As we understand the emotional investment, we understand the very considerable contribution that some organizations make to individuals, even to those engaged for only a few years. The organization with a saga is only secondarily a social entity characterized by plan and reason. It is first of all a matter of the heart, a center of personal and collective identity.

# PART I
## *Antioch*

# *Chapter 1.* Transformation

COLLEGES are often somewhat unsure of their age since birth is commonly a prolonged affair, and such occasions as temporary bankruptcies, only partially hidden in the closets of history, cast doubt on continuity. Colleges also can change in character and even be reborn while continuing under the same title and charter. The longevity of Antioch is slightly clouded by early discontinuities. The college had reasonable claim to celebrate a centennial in 1953, for an entity named Antioch opened its doors in 1853. One can readily overlook the reshuffling of ownership papers that took place before the first decade was over and even the brief periods during which the doors of the college were closed, but to speak of the college as a century old is almost misleading because of a later major change. Those who know the college well often speak of two Antiochs, having in mind a sharp break in character in 1920. The first college, in existence for sixty-five years, was an obscure Ohio school attracting only local boys and girls. A largely unsuccessful venture, this small, struggling institution was never far from the extended graveyard in which so many colleges on the American landscape in those years of western movement found a quiet and honorable burial.[1] Of forty colleges established by

1. Of 516 colleges established (in sixteen states) before the Civil War, only 104, or 19 per cent, survived. Donald G. Tewksbury, *The Founding of American Colleges and Universities Before the Civil War* (Hamden, Conn., Archon Books, 1965 [originally published by Teachers College, Columbia University, New York, 1932]), pp. 27–28.

Protestant churches in Ohio by the time of the Civil War, only half have survived to the present, and Antioch could easily have numbered among those that perished. In character, the first Antioch did indeed die on the brink of bankruptcy in 1919. The second Antioch, born at that time amidst despair, is the institution of today—a college of national and international renown, a successful and fascinating experiment in American higher education.

## The First Antioch

The origin of Antioch was connected with the twilight of Horace Mann's notable career in American education. At the age of fifty-six, after twelve years as secretary of the Massachusetts Board of Education and four years in the United States Congress, the "father of the common school" was prevailed upon by members of the Christian Church, a Protestant sect, to become the first president of a college of which they had for some time dreamed, for which they had then planned, and which they were in 1853 about to open in Ohio. The Christians came late to college founding, for they were one of "those sects claiming to be closest to the people and least in need of the fancy obscurantist learning of scholars." [2] They finally conceded, however, the competitive necessity of a college in a time when religious revivalism had whetted denominational appetites. How else to keep one's flock intact while chasing members of other denominations? They named their college Antioch after the great Syrian city from which Paul, the apostle, had set out on his missionary journeys. After some competitive bidding by Ohio towns, they established it in Yellow Springs, a small resort center and railroad stop between Cincinnati and Springfield, which pledged twenty acres and thirty thousand dollars and boasted of life-giving water. [3]

The founding fathers, together with Mann, put the institution on the high road of idealism and reform by admitting dispossessed groups—women and Negroes—at a time when only Oberlin and a few other colleges engaged wholeheartedly in such radical action, but Mann found his pleasures at Antioch few and short lived. Its doors were hardly opened before trouble erupted.

The trustees who had persuaded Mann to leave civilized New England for the wilds of the West had assured him, among many other promises, that the college would be nonsectarian. Mann, a Unitarian with "the deepest aversion to sectarianism," found "the idea of maintaining a nonsectarian college" one of the "great ideas which win me toward your

2. Frederick Rudolph, *The American College and University* (New York, Alfred A. Knopf, Inc., 1962), p. 55.
3. Robert L. Straker, *Horace Mann and Others* (Yellow Springs, Ohio, The Antioch Press, 1963), p. 30.

plan." [4] But most influential persons in the Christian Church who were close to this, their first-born college, had no such intention. They wanted a Christian college that would keep out the dangerous doctrines of other groups. To have believed the nonsectarian promise was to have misjudged the temper of the church and of the whole state of Ohio, which at the time had twenty-six colleges "all small and all sectarian." [5]

Within a few months, the gloves were off. Mann's plan to present features of all religions was termed a "dark plot" that would "Unitarianize" the place and put it on a "thoroughly liberal basis." [6] The campus rang with charges, and pro- and anti-Mann factions split the faculty and the trustees. The biggest cannon shots to land in the midst of the Mann forces were fired by the Reverend Ira W. Allen, professor of mathematics, who, after dismissal, wrote a slashing account of campus affairs "in a large octavo volume" that circulated through the Christian churches. The violent tone of this tract earned it a place in literature as a "classic of sectarian vituperation." [7] The press of the church joined in claiming that the students were being turned away from "vital piety": "no revival season has ever been enjoyed in this College"; and "no conversions" had been made.[8] As the controversies of the campus fanned out through the congregations of the church, Mann came to feel that the "whole artillery" of Calvinism was "levied against us." "We take it broadsides, and work on." [9]

Doctrinal infighting was not unusual on college campuses in those days, but in Mann's case it took the somewhat unusual form of attempting to maintain a nonsectarian school under sectarian auspices. As a second major problem, the founders also managed to divide authority about as thoroughly as can be done: The trustees *and* a superintendent, as well as President Mann, made appointments to the faculty. But a third problem was worst of all: Despite the trustees' promise that they would see to the necessary funds, Mann found the college so badly financed that it was virtually bankrupt before it opened.[10] Money became the problem that overshadowed all others; by the time the first class went to its commencement, the principal supporter had been wiped out by the panic of 1857. Two years later the college itself had to go under the sheriff's hammer to

4. Mary Peabody Mann, *Life of Horace Mann* (Washington, D.C., National Education Association of the United States, 1937 [Centennial Edition. *in facsimile*; originally published by Walker, Fuller and Company, Boston, 1865]), p. 366.

5. Robert L. Straker, *The Unseen Harvest: Horace Mann and Antioch College* (Yellow Springs, Ohio, The Antioch Press, 1955), p. 12.

6. Straker, *Horace Mann and Others*, p. 22; and Ernest Earnest, *Academic Procession* (Indianapolis, Ind., The Bobbs-Merrill Company, Inc., 1953), p. 79.

7. Earnest, *op. cit.*, p. 79. The book was Rev. Ira W. Allen, *A History of the Rise, Difficulties and Suspension of Antioch College* (Columbus, Ohio, J. Geary & Son, 1858).

8. Earnest, *op. cit.*, p. 80.

9. Correspondence of May 18, 1858, reported in Mann, *op. cit.*, p. 519.

10. Joy Elmer Morgan, *Horace Mann at Antioch* (Washington, D.C., National Education Association of the United States, 1938), p. 74.

clear its debts. It was bought back by Mann and friends and staggered on, but the dream was gone. The price paid by Mann was the final one. He collapsed from exhaustion shortly after the commencement of 1859 and died before the summer was out.

Mann's years at Antioch were tragic in the malevolence of the forces that gathered against his marshaling of affairs. A few years after his death Mann's widow wrote in anguish that "the blood of martyrdom waters the spot." She was joined by Ralph Waldo Emerson, who lamented "what seems the fatal waste of labor and life at Antioch." [11] In the detachment of another century a historian of the liberal arts college concluded that Mann had been "crucified by crusading sectarians." [12]

Horace Mann clearly wanted Antioch to be an intellectual opening to the West. He had intended to cut a gap through the foothills of poor education and the rugged mountains of sectarianism, a gap through which would flow westward the best that the East—and he—could bring. He had fathered the common school in the East; he would now father nonsectarian college education in the West and in short order: "I do not expect . . . to remain connected with the institution for many years. My health and age denote this." [13] But the times were out of joint. The most generous interpretation that can be placed on this personal tragedy was that, for the institution, Mann had sown an "unseen harvest." [14]

The harvest was to remain unseen for a long time. The most compelling determinants of the character of the college after Mann's term of office were not his ideas but rather the financial and religious foundations of the college. The financial straits of the early days continued in only slightly modified degree for the next sixty years. To gain necessary funds that they could not raise within their own group, the Christians entered into a joint-control arrangement with Edward Everett Hale and fellow Unitarians in the East who raised $100,000 and put it into the college in 1865. With this first endowment the Christians and the Unitarians in effect became joint sponsors and owners. Such a plan was not uncommon at a time when the educational reform zeal of the churches often outstripped their resources. Joint ownership, however, led to years of dissension during which contending factions talked past one another and watched suspiciously each other's motives and moves. The dissension diverted men and funds elsewhere. Hale, serving for almost thirty-five years (1865–99) as a leader among the Unitarian trustees, found his great hopes for the college "realized only in a small degree during his life." [15]

To this unhappily managed college, with its student body of 250 to 500

11. Mann, *op. cit.*, p. 433; Emerson quoted in Straker, *The Unseen Harvest,* p. 9.
12. Earnest, *op. cit.*, p. 57.
13. Mann, *op. cit.*, p. 382.
14. Straker, *The Unseen Harvest, passim.*
15. Straker, *Horace Mann and Others,* p. 84.

in Mann's years, 150 in 1875, and 100 at the turn of the century, many leaders came and went. The president after Mann, Thomas Hill, was able to write in 1860:[16]

All goes smoothly, except finances. . . . I have moved a great many trees, dug around others, trimmed, smoothed and graveled walks and roads, planted quantities of shrubs and vines, etc., and altogether made the appearance of things more respectable.

But the faculty had to give back part of their salaries, and the president received no income for months at a time. He departed after three years, leaving a legacy of "ivy, trumpet vine, and woodbine." [17] His successor remained four years—and so it went. Between its opening and 1920, a span of sixty-seven years, the college had ten presidents, seven acting presidents, and one period of four years (1902–6) during which the dean performed the duties of president. The two men who served longer than six years, one for sixteen (Daniel A. Long, 1883–99) and the other for eleven (Simeon D. Fess, 1906–17) were doctors of divinity. In addition to having a period of bankruptcy in the late eighteen-fifties, the college was dormant during the Civil War and then later closed for a year in 1881–82.

During these long, lean decades, the output of students was very small. A large graduating class of twenty-eight in 1860 was not to be exceeded until sixty-five years later, in 1925. In thirty-four of the fifty years between 1860 and 1910 graduating classes had five or fewer students. In five of those years (1865, 1880, 1881, 1882, 1898) there were no graduates at all; on three occasions (1863, 1864, 1883) there was just one; and in two years (1876, 1879) there were only two graduates. Only four years (1862, 1888, 1908, 1909) brought "large" graduating classes of ten to fifteen.[18] There could not be many graduates because the number of students at the college level was typically small. In 1900, for example, the majority of the students were in preparatory classes beneath the college level or were in special programs in music and elocution.[19]

The health of the college varied from poor to bad during the period up to 1910—and then took a turn for the worse. Morbid curiosity is required to review the affairs of the college between 1910 and 1920. In 1910 the budget was down to ten thousand dollars, and the scale of operation entailed buying sixteen new books for the library and granting twenty-two bachelor's degrees to graduating students. The staff numbered thirteen, with the president paid $1,000 a year (Mann's salary a half century earlier was pegged at $3,000); the highest ranking professor was paid $800, and only another seven persons received over $150. At the trustees' annual

16. *Ibid.*, p. 62.
17. *Ibid.*, p. 63.
18. *Alumni Directory of Antioch College, 1857–1960* (Yellow Springs, Ohio, Antioch College, no date).
19. *Catalogue of Antioch College, 1900–1901.*

meeting, the president complained that "finances do not materialize," and "the salaries paid are insufficient to support the necessary teaching force." [20] The board also had to face a long-standing overdraft.

In the following year enrollment declined from 169 to 126, and the budget fell to nine thousand dollars. By 1913 the number of graduating students (which had peaked at twenty-two in 1910) had fallen to ten and varied between ten and sixteen during the next five years. In 1915 and 1916 the budget went down to $7,800. In 1917 the president, who had been serving "part of the time at no pay" and was also in Washington part of the time as a congressman from Ohio, resigned. At this point, the Board of Trustees decided they would "not guarantee any amount to the faculty beyond the income from the funds and the students." During 1918 the college struggled along under an acting president. By then all semblance of momentum had been lost, and it was clear that short of drastic action the college would finally go under. As described in a later semiofficial analysis of the college, it was "moribund after an honorable but exhausting half century's struggle with finances. . . ." [21]

That the trustees were inclined by 1919 to hand over the institution to anyone on short notice and even on flimsy grounds was indicated by a special meeting in February of that year called to consider turning Antioch into a national YMCA college. The trustees had been approached by a few men connected with the YMCA who purportedly spoke for a movement to establish a national Y college and knew how to obtain the necessary resources. At the meeting when the proposal was first put on the table, the trustees offered to resign to allow for replacements who would represent the Y. Two trustees did so on the spot, with the understanding that more would soon follow suit. The trustees in their haste approved the YMCA plan in principle and elected the spokesman for the Y group as president of the college. Alas, the proposal presented to the board did not "have the proper authoritative backing" in the YMCA, and at a second special meeting three months later the new president unhappily admitted that, although acting in good faith, he was not prepared to raise the necessary endowment. The whole deal fell through. The board rescinded all previous action and took back the presidency. An observer straying into Yellow Springs at the time might well have considered the Y the more fortunate of the two parties.

Life goes on, however, even after one has taken back a college he has given away, and as it turned out the new world was but days away. A month later, at the 1919 annual meeting of the Antioch board, Arthur E. Morgan, of Dayton, Ohio, took a vacant seat. A candidate of the Uni-

20. Source of all material reported here is Trustees Minutes, 1910–20, Antioch College.
21. Algo D. Henderson and Dorothy Hall, *Antioch College: Its Design for Liberal Education* (New York, Harper & Row, Publishers, 1946), p. 1.

tarians, Morgan was placed on the board to help protect the Unitarian interest in the Antioch endowment, a role that Charles W. Eliot, Unitarian and president emeritus of Harvard University, thought him eminently capable of filling. The new trustee soon found his appointment a fortunate one. He had long formulated educational designs in his mind and for a number of years had searched in more than a casual way for a college or school in which to practice them. Upon visiting the Antioch campus, he was impressed with its several remaining virtues—the legacy of the ideals of Mann, the physical plant (although the buildings were in disrepair), and the adjacent extended wildlife area. The new trustee also became aware that his fellow board members had no plans for the college and were painfully conscious of imminent demise. The old regime had lost its vigor and its purpose. If it could not control collapse, it certainly could not control the new spirit entering the scene. The college was available for the asking, and Morgan assumed command.

## The Ends of Transformation

Moving with force and dispatch, Morgan arranged a series of special board meetings, and on the first of these occasions (six weeks after he was made a member of the board!) he presented a "Plan of Practical Industrial Education." The board immediately endorsed the proposal and authorized Morgan to "proceed to carry out the plan for Antioch College along the lines proposed." [22] At this point, he became *de facto* head of the college.

When Morgan came to Antioch at the age of forty-two, he had behind him a twenty-year career as a nationally renowned water control engineer, including an appointment as chief engineer of the Ohio Miami Conservancy District, organized after the disastrous Dayton flood of 1913. This substantial work, later defined by Morgan as a detour in purpose, was guided by a rare blend of idealism and pragmatism. He wanted to plan for major social reconstruction, an interest that together with his engineering competence led, after Antioch, to appointment as a director of the Tennessee Valley Authority. Morgan was no mere engineer, and later no mere New Dealer. His commitments to engineering and to social planning were fathered by his image of a more perfect world. He moved from engineering to social engineering in pursuit of utopia, and his utopianism was a critical element in the revision of the college.

THE UTOPIAN URGE

Because college presidents, by role and habit, make grand pronouncements about great purposes, it is often difficult to discern the difference

22. Quoted from a later account, "The Antioch Program," November 4, 1931, Antiochiana, Antioch College.

between serious design and normal commencement rhetoric. How is the man of unusual vision and force distinguished? We can look for evidence in consistency of purpose over a long period of time. We can find indications in persistent action; the man who believes his own words works long and hard to fulfill them. We can also see suggestions of this force and vision in disappointment. The gap between the ideas of the utopian leader and the acts that follow is predictably large, for followers exhibit the weaknesses of mortals, compromise the vision, and hence fail the leader.

The consistency in ideals, the persistence in action, and the disappointment are strikingly clear in the case of Morgan. A confessed idealist, Morgan sustained his commitment to great purposes over decades. His self-education—three years of high school and no formal training in engineering—was a product of years of varied work experience and philosophical rumination. This education culminated in his view that natural experience was the great educator and that formal instruction filled in the gaps left by experience. Work, education, and the rest of life should have close ties if men are to develop good character. Upon visiting a university in 1908, Morgan commented in his diary that "introspection has reached a great development there," and more's the pity because "there is a spirit about it that misses the meaning of life." [23] He believed that the small community offered the best possibilities for living, working, and learning together, and this view guided his actions for a lifetime. As the philosophy was worked out, so was the dedication: One should attempt great work, and necessary to great work was a disciplined, ascetic code of behavior.

As his engineering career progressed, Morgan turned increasingly to a close study of educational philosophies and practices. Before World War I he bought land in western Massachusetts as a possible site for a new school. He moved into an active role among the progressive education experimenters and pioneers of the day. "Long bemused by Pestalozzi's *Leonard and Gertrude*," [24] he took the lead in establishing the Moraine Park School in Dayton, Ohio, in 1916. It became a noted experimental school of the time. His growing place in the educational idealism and reform of the era was further reflected in his serving as the first president of the Progressive Education Association, organized by a small coterie of private-school educators and laymen in 1919, only a few months before he joined the Antioch board. But these private-school progressives were a tame group for Morgan. While they searched for the modest changes that would broaden and invigorate the traditional studies of the school, Morgan wanted to establish a "different genus" and was constructing in his mind models that would break radically with the past.

23. Reported in Louis Adamic, *My America* (New York, Harper & Row, Publishers, 1938), p. 599.
24. Lawrence A. Cremin, *The Transformation of the School* (New York, Alfred A. Knopf, Inc., 1962), p. 278.

These models had their parentage, in part, in general utopian thought. Morgan's deep interest in utopian thinkers spanned much of his adult life. His close studies of the work of Edward Bellamy began before his time at Antioch and led later to the writing of two books.[25] Morgan analyzed the genesis of Bellamy's utopian concepts and attempted to deduce the optimal conditions of isolation and contact for the establishment of a different genus in society. He studied similarly Thomas More and other classic utopians. His *Nowhere Was Somewhere* (1946)[26] reflected a consuming belief that visions of utopia usually were backed up by reality and were useful guides to the reshaping of present structures. Subtitled "How History Makes Utopias and How Utopias Make History," this book attempted to demonstrate that More's *Utopia* was less a product of fanciful imaginaiton than an account of an actual country and its social system—Peru at the time of the Incan empire. In short, the utopian, to Morgan's thinking, was not necessarily the impossible or the impractical. Rather, he felt, "utopias are as essential to human societies as plans are essential for building bridges"; a leader needs not only "great power of action" but also "a correspondingly great pattern of action"; "the work of the utopian is to discover or to create better patterns, and to present them so effectively that they will win the acceptance of men"; "the social engineer is imperative," and "utopias are among the chief sources of suggestion for the social engineer"; "most utopias of any value are the work of intelligent and imaginative men who have been active participants or disciplined observers of affairs." [27]

These beliefs, expressed later, were but a continuation of the utopian bent of Morgan's thinking about Antioch as he developed plans in the nineteen-twenties. It was a utopian thinker, not an administrator, who in those early years said of his college: "We dream of a college such as never has existed. We are not satisfied just to meet conventional situations in conventional ways"; "the man who sows the seed may never see the harvest, but . . . it is he who makes destiny." Antioch should be "a lever to move the world." [28] And it was a utopian thinker who, ten years later, in 1931, steeped in disappointment but still fighting for his dream, asked the faculty whether it was not yet possible for Antioch to be "a great adventure in standing for a radically different pattern of life"; if it only could be, then the college would be "a most significant factor in our civilization." He still wanted "to create a radically new environment which would be favor-

25. *Edward Bellamy, A Biography* (New York, Columbia University Press, 1944); and *The Philosophy of Edward Bellamy* (New York, King's Crown Press, 1945).
26. *Nowhere was Somewhere* (Chapel Hill, N.C., The University of North Carolina Press, 1946).
27. *Ibid.*, pp. 3, 4, 5, 155–56, 156.
28. *A Compendium of Antioch Notes* (Yellow Springs, Ohio, Kahoe and Company, 1930), pp. 24–25, 226.

able to the birth of great events." If others replied that this bore hard on men, he countered, in the grand manner, that "the great event must not lightly lose the chance to be born"; and "ideas have a right to be born, even at great inconvenience to persons." [29] Antioch was in need of great expectations and intense commitment.

## THE ANTIOCH AIMS

The "great pattern" presented for Antioch in the early nineteen-twenties was unique then and would still be today. It conceived of a span of general education greatly exceeding that encompassed by the traditional liberal arts or that envisioned by the general educationists who have mounted one effort after another, in the years since World War I, in a losing campaign to save American higher education from specialism. Morgan's aim was to mold individuals who would become imaginative proprietors in the small community, there to offer economic and political leadership in the evolution toward a more perfect society. This pattern of life after college called for a "well-proportioned education" to mold the "entire personality of the student." Such terms as balance and symmetry became part of the Antioch creed; there was to be "education in life as well as books"; and it was essential for the student to develop "life aims and purposes."

This was general education with a vengeance, deliberately extending the efforts of the educator beyond the classroom because books were not enough. Prominent among the "aims of the New Antioch" in a 1920 statement of plans was "the securing of a more rounded development through alternation of study and experience," with the experience taking the form of work in industry.[30] The division of time between school and industry would allow—and this was a second aim—"self-support for the college student." It also offered the possibility, a third aim, of "self-support for the college." Why could not the college supplement its income from tuition with income from the earnings of small industries directed by the college, industries that would preferably be located on campus? Employment off campus, if needed, could be found in five hundred industries that, according to the president's own census, were located within a radius of thirty miles. If the college could combine work experiences with "cultural education" and "vocational courses," *and* also build "physical fitness," *and* cause "the development of a spirit of moral enthusiasm and of social service," then it might turn out the whole man, the dedicated man, the man properly educated for utopia. This isolated educational test tube called Antioch

29. "On the Future of Antioch," an address by Arthur E. Morgan, June 18, 1931. Antiochiana, Antioch College.
30. Arthur E. Morgan, *The Plan for the New Antioch,* December, 1920, Antiochiana, Antioch College.

would attempt no less than to bring all of life's activities together within the campus.[31] Antioch would be the community.

## The Means of Transformation

Through the winter of 1919–20, while still serving in his initial role of trustee, Morgan searched for a new president, new faculty members, new trustees, and money. In the spring of 1920 the old board of trustees approved a number of planks in the Morgan platform. The college was to remain coeducational, expand to five hundred students, and elevate itself greatly in quality. It would adopt a cooperative work program, the student dividing his time between work and study for six years. The trustees appointed a reorganization committee, with Morgan as chairman; two months later, in July, 1920, Morgan was elected president of the college. Unsuccessful in finding a man to his liking who was willing to undertake the work, Morgan had decided to do it himself.

At his disposal the new president had a corporate entity named Antioch College, some buildings, the historic association of the campus with the name and ideals of Horace Mann—and not much more. To accomplish his aims he needed purpose and a host of means for realizing purpose—specifically, trustees, a faculty, a student body, money, and a public reputation—most features that a college starting from scratch would need. He even needed accreditation. He had purpose in his own visions and designs and a special curriculum already approved in principle, but he would have to extract all the means from an environment unwilling to provide the needs of a moribund college. His success in gaining the needed resources, essentially accomplished within a few years, marks his early days at Antioch as an imposing case of transforming institutional leadership.

PERSONNEL

*Trustees.* Among the assets Morgan had were contacts developed during his engineering career with important figures around the country—ties that happened to include the friendship of a great president (then president emeritus) of Harvard, Charles W. Eliot. Drawing on these relationships, Morgan worked vigorously and rapidly to change the composition of the board of trustees. The procedure was simplicity itself: Line up a new man of national renown and then persuade one of the old-time trustees that this imposing figure was too valuable a man to let get away. Morgan encountered little opposition in doing what presidents are rarely given to do—to persuade a number of incumbent trustees that they lack the resources or capacity to help and therefore should resign for the good of the college. As organizational changes go, the changeover was a blitz.

31. Arthur E. Morgan, "Advancement of Latent Human Powers," *School and Society,* Vol. 15 (January, 1922), pp. 80–87.

Three weeks before Morgan became president, when he had assumed the responsibility as first among the trustees, three members of the board resigned and four Morgan-selected men were added. One new member was Charles F. Kettering, a Dayton industrialist who had associated himself with Morgan in the Moraine Park School adventure in 1916 and was shortly to become the most important financial supporter of the college. During the meeting at which Morgan was elected president, three more trustees resigned and were replaced. Two months later, in October, 1920, six men resigned and were replaced. Thus, within three months, twelve of nineteen trustees resigned, leaving only one third of the previous board on the scene.[32]

The old board of 1919–20 was made up almost entirely of men from Ohio (seventeen out of nineteen), largely from the area around the college. Their average age was over sixty;[33] four were ministers. Morgan's new board of twenty, including the president, contained thirteen men from Ohio, four from New York, two from Massachusetts, and one from Michigan. Ministers were no more. The new trustees were successful industrialists and other men of prominence with an interest in education. Five of the new group were Harvard men.[34] One, Edwin F. Gay, had even been dean of the Harvard Graduate School of Business Administration and had perhaps fallen only slightly in becoming president of the *New York Evening Post.* Another Harvard graduate among the new trustees was Ellery Sedgwick, editor of the *Atlantic Monthly.* Among the other important additions were a New York City banker; a New York lawyer from the firm of McAdoo, Cotton, and Franklin; another New Yorker from the investment house of Lee, Higginson, and Co.; and the chief engineer of Ford Industries. Kettering, already mentioned, was at the time vice-president and chief engineer of General Motors Corporation.

Thus, the new board had names, resources, and business acumen and, in its social composition, had turned to the outside. The shift away from local people continued during the twenties; by 1930 about half the board came from states other than Ohio. When one considers that even the most national of colleges generally maintains a cluster of trustees from nearby to staff and to attend frequent meetings of an executive committee of the board, the change at Antioch in the twenties clearly represented a nationalizing of membership. On a college board the functions of busy men from distant places are many: to lend their personal reputations (and offer their personal fortunes!) as coin for college building; to introduce the college and its officials into circles that count; to bring to the finance and management of the college the point of view of large organizations; to balance the

32. Trustees Minutes, 1920, Antioch College.
33. Interview with Arthur E. Morgan, February 2, 1960.
34. *Catalogue of Antioch College, 1921–1922;* and Charles W. Eliot, "Antioch College," *School and Society,* Vol. 18 (July, 1923), pp. 35–41.

localism often reflected in trustees drawn from nearby. But no matter from whence they came, the Antioch trustees constituted a board selected by and devoted to Morgan. Little or no evidence was to appear of serious differences in point of view between the board and the president.

*Faculty.* The transformation of the full-time staff was equally extensive and thorough. The faculty in 1919–20 consisted of thirteen teachers—nine professors, two instructors, and two assistants. One of the professors was doubling as acting president, and the rest of the staff consisted of a librarian and a dean of women. Two in this staff had Ph.D.'s, while three-quarters had only a bachelor's degree. When Morgan's program went into effect two years later (1921–22), the staff had grown to twenty-five faculty members, the president, two librarians, and a dean of women. Only five of the thirteen teachers from the earlier group had been retained, along with the first librarian and the dean of women, while twenty new faculty had been brought to the college. Thus, in Morgan's first year of full administration, "his" faculty outnumbered the old by four to one. Twenty more newcomers came the following year, swelling the staff to forty-three "officers of instruction" and six "officers of administration." Now the old faculty was reduced to four.[35] Thus within three years the faculty of the first Antioch, in effect, no longer existed. Only one professor was to survive the first decade of the new regime.

Many a college president, new to the job and seeking to reform a college, has stumbled over his inability to change the blood of the faculty; Morgan had no such problem. *His* problem in building a faculty was to find men who would suit him and would come. Very early, in the winter of 1920–21, Morgan noted that "we have met with discouragement" in the search for faculty.[36] The nub of the problem lay in finding those whose personal qualities fit Morgan's utopian hopes and in the strain between these qualities and the normal criteria of academic competence. Idealizing the man of vigor who had learned by experience, Morgan hoped to leaven if not complete the faculty with men who had had practical experience. Such men would be especially useful for the work program, perhaps even necessary for its success. The ideal man was one who, forceful in personality, broad in interest, matured by practical experience and reflection, would also commit himself totally to the adventure of working out a new education and a new philosophy of life at Antioch. Morgan quickly found such men to be in short supply. Men in industry who met his personal conception were usually too successful and beyond his means. One who came to teach accounting at the high salary of five thousand dollars shortly returned to industry at double the salary.[37]

35. *Catalogue of Antioch College, 1919–1920; Catalogue of Antioch College, 1921–1922; Catalogue of Antioch College, 1922–1923.*
36. *The Plan for the New Antioch.*
37. Interview with Arthur E. Morgan, February 26, 1960.

In addition, the established criteria of academic acceptability were not to be ignored, even though it was an open matter how much weight would be assigned them. Certainly some men with sound scholarly abilities would be necessary for classroom quality. The academic credentials of the faculty would have to be ample if the college were to achieve a favorable reputation, particularly since the work program brought the label of "vocational school" to many minds. Morgan was early aware of this distinctive problem of reputation, a problem that was indeed to remain with the college for decades. As a result, the concept of the ideal faculty man had to be adjusted toward the academic, toward a combination of two sets of values. Eliot, a good friend of Antioch, tried his hand at a definition in 1923, when in a speech in Boston he spoke of the appropriate faculty for the college as being men who possessed "not only sound scholarship and unusual teaching ability but well-balanced personality and the capacity for leadership through personal contact and acquaintance with the students, outside of, as well as in, the classroom." [38] Morgan, in the retrospect of several decades, put it more succinctly: "I tried to get intelligent, scholarly people with capacity for freedom from conventional patterns." [39] Later (in the early thirties), disappointed in the unwillingness of the faculty to follow him into the wilderness, Morgan stated that faculty selection had been a critical step—that he should have played down scholarship even more than he did and gone for broke on the personal qualities that fit in with his ideals and aspirations.

Despite the leader's later disappointment, the faculty brought to the campus were for the most part young and vigorous, devoted to the president's ideals, and possessed of the character appropriate for around-the-clock interaction with students. The president hunted hard for this kind of man and took his chances: Ondess L. Inman, professor of biology at the college from 1921 until his death in 1942, was brought from a teaching fellow position at Harvard, still fresh from the Ph.D., and made full professor. Others hired in the early years (1921–25) who were to stay and epitomize the Antioch traditions of general education and deep involvement with students included Clyde Stewart Adams in chemistry; John G. Frayne in physics; Allyn C. Swinnerton in geology; Lincoln R. Gibbs in English; William M. Leiserson in economics; Manmatha Nath Chatterjee in social science; J. D. Dawson in mathematics, later to become an institution as director of the work-study program and dean of students, serving for more than four decades until 1967; and Algo Henderson in business administration, later to become academic dean and then president. Among those for whom Morgan had high hopes but who did not stay was Hendrik Van Loon, the historian, who hard at work finishing his broad study of mankind remained for only a year as professor of social science

38. *Loc. cit.*, p. 36.
39. Morgan interview, February 26, 1960.

before going on to greener pastures. Between 1925 and 1930 still other key figures were added: W. Boyd Alexander (1929), who began as a personnel director and then served for almost three decades as dean of administration, dean of faculty, and vice-president under four presidents, until his retirement in 1963; Basil H. Pillard (1928), discussed below; Henry Federighi (1929) in biology; and Gwilym D. Owen (1929) in physics. Nearly all these senior or important professors were personally picked by the president, and most had personal beliefs and styles appropriate for the transformation of the college. That they were in a short time to disappoint the leader does not change the fact that, after Morgan, they become the principal carriers of the patterns formed in the first decade. Quite noticeably, the faculty had not all been bred to the manor of scholarship. Half of the faculty in 1929–30 had only the bachelor's degree as the highest credential, and less than a third could claim the doctorate. (In contrast, about a half of the Swarthmore faculty at the time had Ph.D.'s.) Scholars were in the faculty, but the search for men of engaging personality, vigor, and commitment had compromised scholarly criteria more than halfway. From the first few years of the transformation the Antioch staff developed a preference for the well-rounded man over the more professionally competent but narrower subject matter specialist.

Typifying the Morgan point of view was Pillard, who between 1928 and the mid-fifties influenced many generations of students. Pillard's highest academic calling card when he came to the college was a bachelor's degree from Yale. His experience consisted of one year in schoolteaching and eight years in business, including work as a copywriter and an account executive in an advertising agency. This background would not normally place a man on a liberal arts college faculty, to put it mildly, but it was no barrier at Antioch. Pillard came to teach business administration, then later moved to English literature and served as dean of students while continuing to teach. It mattered little where he was located on campus or whether he was in or out of the classroom. He was a great teacher in that he led students to examine their values. A discussion of *Death of a Salesman* was a springboard to a philosophical dialogue. The students would forget the play—and probably did not learn much about its structure and style—but they grappled long and hard with questions of basic values. Pillard was so effective in his teaching that he elicited the admiration of faculty members whose whole approach was to the contrary; e.g., the Young Turks of the fifties who were critical of the college for not sufficiently emphasizing classroom teaching of specialized subject matter.

STUDENTS

Morgan, well aware that for the implementation of his designs the kind of student obtained was no worse than second in importance, if that, to the composition of the faculty, worked hard at attracting and selecting students. At the time, colleges commonly used high school certificates and entrance examinations as admission criteria. To these items, Morgan added high school grades, intelligence tests, letters of recommendation, and even student autobiographies. He placed much weight on assessment through personal interview, a task that he assigned himself in the first years in order to select and reject on grounds of apparent vigor, maturity, and sense of values.

We have no direct indication of the many qualities of the students thereby obtained other than information, discussed below, which showed high intelligence and high academic achievement. But the change in numbers of students alone was significant, and the change in the locales of recruitment was remarkable. In 1919–20, the college had forty-five students, of whom four were graduating seniors. All but one was from Ohio, with thirty-five from the towns of Yellow Springs, Zenia, and Springfield, within ten miles of the college. The city of Dayton, a mere twenty miles away, was represented by one student. In the following year, immediately before transformation, there were thirty-nine students, of whom five were graduating seniors. Then the change! In the first year of the new order (1921–22), the student body numbered 203, five times greater than before, and the entering freshman class totaled 131, nine times greater than previously. Eighty-one students, or 40 per. cent, were from outside Ohio, with fifteen from New York. Of the 122 from within the state, fifty-three were from Dayton. Within the freshman class alone, sixty-nine were from Ohio and sixty-two from elsewhere. Thus, in the first year of the transforming effort, the student body was increased markedly in size, parents in the nearest large city were persuaded to send their sons and daughters, and a sizable number of students were recruited from outside the state and from as far away as New York City.

The following year the student body again expanded rapidly. Enrollment boomed from 203 to 393, with a whopping freshman class of 254. The majority were now from out of state, bulking 60 per cent in the whole student body and two-thirds among the freshmen. Thus, within two years, the college moved decisively away from a home town student body. Accomplished in the early twenties, this turn to the outside and to a broad base of recruitment and support jumped the college ahead of most leading colleges in this respect. Even such a later pacesetter as Swarthmore was only then beginning its turn to broad recruitment; Reed was still primarily a school for Portland; and the Ivy League universities and Little Ivy colleges of the East Coast had not yet learned to send their recruiters far and wide, as they were later to do, but were still relating contentedly to the upper-class population of neighboring cities and countryside.

The student body continued to grow during the twenties but at a more moderate rate, reaching a plateau of about 650 in the early thirties. By then the turn to the outside had progressed to the point where fewer than one student out of five was from Ohio, let alone from the local towns. The students came from more than forty states: a third from New York, Pennsylvania, and New Jersey; a fourth from the North Central states other than Ohio; 10 per cent from New England; 7 per cent from the South; and 5 per cent from the Far West.

Thus, the sweeping changes in trustees and faculty were paralleled by broad changes in the student body. Numbers were increased from below a viable threshold to a generous size that meant much income from tuition. The recruitment base was changed from a small sector in southwestern Ohio to the national scene, ensuring heterogeneity in student values. Henceforth, big city, cosmopolitan orientations would contend with the points of view induced by rural and small town backgrounds. The Antioch of the thirties, forties, and fifties contained relatively sophisticated students. Thus actions of the early twenties constitute a striking case of changing a student body through changing the emphasis in recruitment.

MONEY

Shortly before assuming the presidency, Morgan was authorized by himself and the board to raise half a million dollars. A sum this large would have been sweet music at many small colleges of the time, and with the pitiful financial state of Antioch, it would have resulted in a gigantic increase in available funds. This much money was not forthcoming however, and paying for the expansion of faculty and students was to remain unfinished business throughout the transforming years. But the early effort, even when short of the goal, did raise the level of expenditure considerably. Morgan's efforts were such that if the college were to have gone to the sheriff—and bankruptcy was a possibility during the twenties and thirties—it would have gone in the grand manner. The college borrowed $300,000 from its new benefactor, Kettering, and the president took on the raising of annual gift monies as a personal responsibility. He financed the college year by year on the strength of what he could personally bring back from his travels, an effort that cost him much in time and energy and in the opportunity to be on campus to take a full hand in the shaping of faculty and students. By 1925–26 gifts for operating expenses alone were totaling over $100,000 a year, a far cry from the meager budgets of $10,000 and less before 1920. Between 1921 and 1934 the college raised over $2,300,000 from gifts—$1,500,000 for general purposes and $800,000 earmarked for plant and land. By the end of the first decade (1929–30) the college had a budget of $430,000 (Table 1–1)—forty times greater than the budget of the nineteen-tens. Free gifts and grants from private sources, including foundations, amounted to nearly 50 per cent of the budget; income from endowment was meager, bordering on 2 per cent.

These figures reflect the fact that President Morgan did not commit himself strongly to the building of endowment but rather chose to rely on tuition, annual gifts, and whatever income the college-controlled small industries would produce. However, the industry plan, for which the president had had high hopes, did not develop well, and income was not forthcoming from this source. Later, in the early thirties, the depression shrank the annual gifts to half of what they had been. Tuition then became the largest source of income, and from that point on, with little endowment, heavy reliance on tuition income became a permanent feature of the Antioch plan. Although many liberal arts colleges cover less than half their expenses from tuition fees, Antioch finances three-quarters or more of its expenses from tuition. This situation results from having a work-study program that permits two sets of students to use the campus facilities normal to one—essentially, two students in every bed. To glance at a budget in the early forties (1942–43): 73 per cent of an over-all expenditure of $386,000 was covered by tuition, only 3 per cent by endowment, and 7 per cent by miscellaneous sources.[40] Thus 83 per cent of costs were covered by "assured income," and 17 per cent (sixty-six thousand dollars) had to be gained from gifts—a much lower reliance on gifts than had been evident twenty years before.

TABLE 1–1. Annual Income, 1929–30, Antioch College

| Source Of Income | Amount | Percentage |
|---|---|---|
| Gifts and grants | $209,302 | 48.6 |
| Student fees | 196,223 | 45.6 |
| Endowment | 9,921 | 2.3 |
| Miscellaneous rentals | 8,236 | 1.9 |
| Halls and bookstore | 6,982 | 1.6 |
| Total | $430,664 | 100.0 |

Source: "The Antioch Program, 1933–34. A Report on the Affairs of Antioch College," p. 8. Antiochana, Antioch College.

In short, Morgan financed the new Antioch through the twenties largely by gifts and partly by borrowing. He did not develop an endowment base, and when first the campus industry plan failed and then the depression dried up private gifts, the college came to base its finances largely on tuition. Interestingly, in the critical decade of the twenties the foundations were of little help. Abraham Flexner and his colleagues on the General Education Board backed Reed and Swarthmore but judged Antioch to be an unpromising place, another Ohio college whose demise would improve the educational landscape. Never one to dodge an honest opinion, Flexner said as much to Morgan and the faculty and to others outside the college. The backing of Kettering and a few other individuals (Samuel S. Fels,

40. An Antioch College Prospectus, 1942. Antiochiana, Antioch College.

Hugh T. Birch, Allen C. Balch) who put their faith in Morgan, plus the built-in subsidy of the cooperative plan, carried the college through the lean years. After 1930 the major national foundations became more helpful, but between 1920 and 1942 their contributions fell considerably below those of the individual benefactors of the college. The General Education Board gave $140,000, and the Carnegie Corporation $116,000, while the Ketterings, through the Charles F. Kettering Foundation, gave $861,000, and the Fels family, through the Samuel S. Fels Fund, gave $580,000.[41]

IMAGE

Academic men often do not do very well in public relations—to do well is even suspect—and seekers after utopia are notoriously blind to public feeling as they zealously pursue one goal to the exclusion of others. Because the new Antioch was both academic and idealistic, it stood in double jeopardy of having at best indifferent and at worst hostile relations with the public. Morgan cared little for the opinions of others, but he had a sharp sense of the importance of outside attention and widespread public support. He worked willingly and hard at projecting an image of the college he wanted Antioch to be. Trustees and faculty could be recruited through personal persuasion, by promises best made in conversation, but a steady flow of new money and especially of new and able students could not be assured this way. One had to broadcast and to spread the word to a large audience out of which a few applicants appropriate to the college would offer themselves. One had to convey a story of difference and to claim distinction. In this effort, the president had phenomenal success.

In 1921 five national magazines offered information about Morgan and Antioch. *School and Society* and *World's Work* spoke of Antioch as offering a new type of college education.[42] Liberal journals began what was to be a long love affair with the college: *The New Republic* stated that the Antioch plan would produce a well-rounded, liberal, rational student, and *The Nation* perceived that the plan would "restore things to their natural basis." [43] The scientific community also spoke out: The *Scientific American* discussed "the happy medium of the classically, technically, and practically trained student." [44] The following year (1922) Morgan placed articles of his own in *School and Society* and in the *Atlantic Monthly; The New Republic* printed a second piece; Ida M. Tarbell came through in

41. *An Antioch College Prospectus.*
42. "New Type of College Education," *School and Society*, Vol. 13 (February, 1921), p. 259; "Arthur E. Morgan's New Type of College," *World's Work*, Vol. 41 (February, 1921), pp. 405–9.
43. "Antioch Plan," *The New Republic*, Vol. XXVII No. 346 (July, 1921), pp. 205–6; "Antioch Idea," *The Nation*, Vol. 113 (September, 1921), p. 263.
44. "The Self Supporting College," *Scientific American*, Vol. 125A (December, 1921), p. 130.

*Collier's* with a laudatory account of "Morgan of Antioch." [45] Not to be outdone, Bruce Barton wrote in the *American Mercury,* circulation two million, on the "courage to dive off the dock," a theme he applied to both Morgan's own career and the ideal Antioch student.[46] And so it went through the years of the Morgan regime: e.g., "Education by Book and Life" (*Literary Digest,* 1923); "The Answer of Antioch" (*Outlook,* 1926); "Notes on an Educational Pilgrimage to Antioch" (*School and Society,* 1929).[47]

Meanwhile, *The New York Times* offered a helping hand in news accounts and editorials. In 1925, for example, the *Times* reported two speeches by Morgan and devoted two accounts to the pronouncements of the Reverend C. F. Potter, who, feeling that Antioch was no less than the most important educational development in the world, was indeed ready to dive off the dock.[48] Desiring to preach "the gospel of Antioch in place of the tiresome gospels of the church," the Reverend Mr. Potter resigned as pastor of the West Side Unitarian Church in New York City to take a position with the college. This incident moved the *Times* to editorialize on the new secular religion and the ardor of its converts. The pinnacle of praise was yet to come, however; in a pamphlet entitled "College Prolongs Infancy," published in 1932 and reported in the press, Horace M. Kallen put Antioch in a class by itself as an experimental, progressive college. Kallen maintained that academic reforms such as those then under way at Wisconsin, Harvard, and Chicago were but futile juggling of the same pieces; only the Antioch idea of combining education with life struck at the root of the problem.[49] After such heady praise it was almost a comedown to receive from *Newsweek* a few years later the inevitable accolade —that this college was "the West's little Harvard." [50]

These magazine and newspaper accounts, aided and often instigated by Morgan, were but one prong of a many-sided effort to lodge the name and conception of Antioch in the minds of the educated public. Morgan took to the lecture platform, speaking throughout the country and particularly in the East, as well as in the Ohio region. With his connections and reputation from his engineering days, the speeches were often favorably located and well reported. Few college presidents could link arms with President

45. Morgan, "Advancement of Latent Human Powers," *loc. cit.;* "What Is College For?" *Atlantic Monthly,* Vol. 129, No. 5 (May, 1922), pp. 642–50; "Antioch Idea at Work," *The New Republic,* Vol. XXX, No. 390 (May, 1922), pp. 372–75; "Morgan of Antioch," *Collier's,* Vol. 69 (June, 1922), pp. 7–8.

46. "Courage to Dive off the Dock," *American Mercury,* Vol. 94 (August, 1922), pp. 24–25.

47. *Literary Digest,* Vol. 79 (November, 1923), pp. 28–29; *Outlook,* Vol. 142 (February, 1926), pp. 211–13; *School and Society,* Vol. 29 (April, 1929), pp. 449–58.

48. *The New York Times,* February 22 and May 14; and May 4 and May 14, 1925, respectively.

49. *Ibid.,* November 13, 1932.

50. *Newsweek,* Vol. 6 (November, 1935), p. 39.

Emeritus Eliot of Harvard in praise of their own small colleges, but Morgan at the Hotel Somerset in Boston on a spring night in 1923 shared the podium with his old friend. Eliot, the leading spokesman on education in the country over four decades, lauded the man and the college: The "whole experiment at Antioch College is original in a high degree." [51] Morgan had "invented" a very original board of trustees; he had put together a fascinating work-study program; he was in the process of attempting to invent "a new kind of faculty," seeking those with well-balanced personalities, leadership abilities outside the classroom, sound scholarship, unusual teaching ability; he was engaging in an "intensively interesting experiment on the means of sifting candidates for admission. . . ." And it certainly bore mentioning to the patrician audience that five of the new Antioch trustees were Harvard men. For a small college in the southwest corner of Ohio, this was high praise from a very high source, in a setting where extravagant comments about another college were hardly commonplace.

Another prong in the effort to construct an image and to win support was the organizing of Friends of Antioch in different cities. Eliot became president of the Friends of Antioch in America, and the New York chapter of the Friends, in a brochure prepared in 1925 ("'Budgeting for Life': The Antioch Idea"), quoted Eliot as saying that the college was "the most interesting educational project now being attempted in the United States." The New York group, including Franklin D. Roosevelt (then in private law practice), met with Morgan to raise money for the "annual deficit of $100,000 and plan a $5,000,000 endowment, and funds for a new dormitory, science building, auditorium and gymnasium." [52] Such large intentions were beyond fulfillment—the endowment was not raised—but for Morgan and the college these supporting groups served as if they were prestigious alumni. Their work helped spread the Antioch word among influential citizens through personal contact and among educated men generally through the accounts of the mass media.

The magazine articles, the news accounts, the speeches, the group meetings, all were impressive, but all were fragile in the irregularity of their occurrence, and the president sought a regular, dependable medium for his message. This forum was *Antioch Notes*, a small publication initiated in 1923, subsidized by the college, and put out biweekly for eight months of the year. Each issue of the *Notes* offered a discussion by Morgan on any of a wide range of topics—science, ethics, religion, government, international relations, and education[53]—and usually a few additional pages of information about the college. Morgan ensured wide distribution of his *Notes* by building a circulation list of twenty thousand that extended from

51. *Loc. cit.*, p. 35.
52. The New York *Herald Tribune*, April 19, 1925.
53. *A Compendium of Antioch Notes*.

high school principals to the Supreme Court justices. Supreme Court Justice Louis Brandeis was reported to have considered the *Notes* "an American version of the Spectator Papers," and purportedly, Franklin D. Roosevelt read them throughout the late twenties and early thirties.[54] This publication had many features to recommend it over the average college catalogue and typical fund-raising brochure: It discussed ideas, and it had great value not only in making known the college but also in giving salience to the differences claimed by the man and the institution.

With all this, the college won national attention and repute within a short time. The steady and often eye-catching publicity was important in transforming the student body from hometown to national, helping to shift the center of recruitment within a few years from the Yellow Springs environs to the Middle Atlantic states and the North Central region as a whole.

## Success and Failure

### MARKS OF STUDENT QUALITY

Unlike the university, which is judged largely by its research, graduate training, and professional schools, the liberal arts college becomes known through the caliber of its undergraduate students. Evidence of success in the transformation of Antioch in the twenties must first be sought on the grounds commonly used, the quality of entering students and of graduates. Although incomplete, the historical record adequately indicates that the effort of the twenties moved Antioch far from its previous parochialism, lifting it rapidly to the forefront of American colleges. Among the more than five hundred liberal arts colleges of 1920, Antioch surely ranked in the bottom quarter, and the company that one keeps down there is appalling. Within a decade, however, the college was perched comfortably in the top twenty-five to fifty, and a case could be made—and it was by the college—that it placed in the first ten.

On student ability Morgan was able to report to his board in December, 1921, that the first class of new students placed "well above the average college freshman" on Thurstone intelligence tests—in fact, only four colleges using the test showed higher scores.[55] By the end of the decade, such statements about student quality were firmly grounded. In 1930, when the Carnegie Foundation for the Advancement of Teaching tested students at thirty-two liberal arts colleges in Pennsylvania, Antioch requested that its students also be allowed to take the battery of tests. The college scored highest in "intelligence" and next to highest on "general

54. Adamic, *op. cit.*, p. 604.
55. Drawn from a trustees report, in Maury Waters, *Arthur Morgan's First Years at Antioch College.* Unpublished paper, Antiochiana, Antioch College, 1951.

culture."⁵⁶ In 1932 on a battery of intelligence and achievement tests administered nationally by the American Council on Education (A.C.E.), Antioch freshmen ranked second in average score for the entire battery among students of 205 colleges and universities. Antioch sophomores, on tests given at 138 colleges in thirty-eight states, tied for highest on intelligence and in general science, and ranked eighth on the total general score of test battery.⁵⁷ In the following year (1933), when the A.C.E. tests for sophomores were administered at 134 colleges in forty states, Antioch ranked in the top 10 per cent of the colleges on eight out of twelve rankings provided by the tests, placing from third to nineteenth across the tests.⁵⁸ In 1934 intelligence scores were made public—a rare event—for the 235 colleges with students taking the Education Psychological Examination of the A.C.E. The median scores for the colleges ranged from 97.0 for a Pennsylvania state college to 273.8 for Haverford. Antioch placed eleventh with an average of 224.5, below such high scorers as Chicago, Middlebury, Rochester, and Trinity, and above such known institutions as Bowdoin, Brooklyn, Carlton, Clark, Dartmouth, Lehigh, Michigan, Tufts, and Vanderbilt. The Antioch ability level was similar to that of Oberlin and Reed.⁵⁹

Such scores and rankings left little doubt that student quality had been achieved. This quality was a product of rigorous screening, publicity, and growing reputation. The college had a reasonably strong number of applicants by the end of the decade, about two for every student admitted (411 to 232 in 1929; 507 to 193 in 1931; 425 to 187 in 1933).⁶⁰ By that time a good reputation was stimulating applications from bright students and was causing others to veer away. If the applicants had been a normal assortment of college students, a one-out-of-two selection would hardly have produced the ability levels evidenced in the test scores.

The graduates of the college during these transforming years had somewhat varied choices of career. About a third went to work in business, as Morgan had hoped his students would do (Table 1–2). Almost another third were teaching at some level or were at the time in graduate school. The remaining one-third were scattered in social work, scientific and engineering jobs, and others. Notably, a trend toward graduate study was under way. The portion of the senior class entering graduate school from 1925 to 1930 varied between 20 and 30 per cent, comparing favorably on this score with the proportion in all but a few colleges in the country. In

56. "The Antioch Program, 1933–34. A Report on the Affairs of Antioch College," pp. 27–28. Antiochiana, Antioch College.
57. *Ibid.*, p. 25, pp. 27–28.
58. *Ibid.*, pp. 27–28.
59. Ruth Strang, *Educational Guidance* (New York, The Macmillan Company, 1947), App. D.
60. "The Antioch Program, 1933–34," p. 18.

the future Antioch was going to produce not businessmen for the small town but scholars, schoolteachers, social workers, and civil servants. Its business graduates, too, would more likely be found in the publishing houses of the big cities than in the granaries of rural America.

TABLE 1-2. *Occupations of Antioch Graduates, 1921–33*

| Occupation | Number* | Percentage |
|---|---|---|
| Business | 161 | 36 |
| Education | 90 | 20 |
| Graduate study | 48 | 11 |
| Social work | 26 | 6 |
| Science | 25 | 6 |
| Engineering | 22 | 5 |
| All other employment | 35 | 8 |
| (Law) | (7) | (2) |
| (Medicine) | (3) | (1) |
| Married (housewife) | 38 | 8 |
| Total | 445 | 100 |

*Those with a known occupation; another seventy-five graduates identified in this census were deceased, unemployed, or of unknown occupation.
Source: "The Antioch Program, 1933–34. A Report on the Affairs of Antioch College," p. 29a. Antiochiana, Antioch College.

THE RELATIVITY OF SUCCESS

Graded against normal academic standards, Antioch by the early thirties was clearly a successful liberal arts college. It had a distinctive program, good students, and good faculty. It had come from obscurity to national recognition and was especially esteemed by liberals and progressives of the day. However, the college could be disliked on various grounds. It could be called a boastful infant. Its teaching methods could be seen as an unfortunate intrusion of progressivism into higher education. Its work program could be defined by academicians as an instance of vulgar vocationalism rather than as a new tool of liberal learning. But distractors could hardly say that the college was not a successful venture. Work program or not, the college was beating all but a handful of the "pure" liberal arts colleges at their own game—the intellectual life of classroom and book. Whatever the value of occupational work in a liberal education, the style, climate, and student and faculty mix contributed to a better than average education. At the maximum something was going on at Antioch that was occurring nowhere else in American higher education, and by 1930 it was cause for pride at Antioch, pride about the role and status of the college in the nation as a whole.

It is one thing, however, to judge the success of a college against earthly peers, all of whom have made their compromises, and quite another to throw its practices up against ideals. Ideals generate harsh judgment, and the more utopian they are the more likely they are to judge that performance has failed the promise. So it was with Morgan. In the bright light of the aims that had sustained his personal drive, the college was badly blemished, even a failure. That certain programs did not work out as planned was part of the trouble but a minor part. In his view, the critical defects were largely in commitment.

Among the program failures was the plan to have students work in small plants located on or near the campus, often in industries controlled by the college and producing income for it. This plan faded rapidly. The college involved itself in a bronze foundry, a printing establishment, even a firm manufacturing an "Antioch Shoe," but none of these small industries remained on campus, and those that survived in Yellow Springs became a major source neither of student employment [61] nor of income for the college. Industries like foundries, printing firms, and shoe companies were not likely to hold the interest of the faculty and students permanently. The president's early census of five hundred nearby industries failed to reckon with the greater attractiveness of working and living in more distant places. The staff and the students themselves found cooperative jobs for students less in small plants on the edges of the campus and increasingly in large corporations and public agencies in Cleveland, Chicago, and New York, as well as in Dayton. The dispersion of co-op employers that took place in the twelve years Morgan was active head of the college is shown in Table 1–3. In the first year all but 1 of 113 employers were located in Ohio; five years later 30 per cent of the employers were in ten other states; by 1930 the proportion outside Ohio was one-half; and in 1933 over two-thirds were located in twenty-one states outside Ohio. By the end of Morgan's tenure the firms participating in the work program were geographically distant and entirely separate from the college in purpose and operation.

Along with this change in the work plan, the calendar of work-study alternation also changed. In 1920 Morgan hoped to provide very close integration by alternating the student between work and study at two-week intervals. When his plan went into effect the following year, the alternation was extended to five-week periods. By 1930 the college was using ten- as well as five-week blocs, and still later it introduced eight- and twelve-week intervals, with the student having, in one year, eight weeks on campus and eight weeks off, followed by twelve weeks on and twelve weeks off. Under these various schedules, the alternating sets of students became known as the "A" and "B" Divisions, with members of the one division somewhat set apart from the members of the other.

What the work program finally became, then, was not what President Morgan originally had in mind. The tight fusing of study, work, and "life"

61. Henderson and Hall, *op. cit.*, p. 6.

essential to his conception of a new social genus was possible only if the geographic boundaries of a small town could be thrown around the students or if the students could be encapsulated in some other way in a total institution designed and controlled by the college. The movement to distant cities tore open the boundaries of the community and made tight integration impossible. The prospects of training the young for leadership in small enterprises then dimmed, as the students tasted the fruits of the large agencies and corporations and contemplated through the eyes of the academic professors the delights of graduate school and its higher training. Antioch was to be no ancient Peru or anything like it.

TABLE 1-3. *Geographical Location of Work-Plan Employers, 1921–33, Antioch College*

| Year | Number of Employers | Number in Ohio | Number in Other States | Percentage in Other States | Number of Other States |
|------|------|------|------|------|------|
| 1921–22 | 113 | 112 | 1 | 1 | 1 |
| 1922–23 | 129 | 121 | 8 | 6 | 6 |
| 1923–24 | 152 | 131 | 21 | 14 | 8 |
| 1924–25 | 136 | 109 | 27 | 20 | 12 |
| 1925–26 | 154 | 107 | 47 | 30 | 11 |
| 1926–27 | 198 | 140 | 58 | 29 | 10 |
| 1927–28 | 205 | 121 | 84 | 41 | 12 |
| 1928–29 | 185 | 104 | 81 | 44 | 13 |
| 1929–30 | 190 | 103 | 87 | 46 | 13 |
| 1930–31 | 236 | 102 | 134 | 57 | 15 |
| 1931–32 | 175 | 68 | 107 | 61 | 13 |
| 1932–33 | 182 | 58 | 124 | 68 | 21 |

Source: "The Antioch Program, 1933–34. A Report on the Affairs of Antioch College," p. 3. Antiochiana, Antioch College.

Still, these undesired emerging elements of the new Antioch could be faced down. The president had an open mind about the alternation of work and study and was willing to modify the calendar. The dispersal of students to far-off places was a handicap in inculcating a sense of community, but this and other obstacles could be overcome if only there were commitment and discipline. At this point, the president thought, the followers were failing. The faculty and students were not willing to commit themselves wholeheartedly to working out a new plan of life and education; they were not willing to break sharply with the past and with the ways of others; they were not willing to shed their hedonism for hard work and plain living, for the ascetic, disciplined life necessary to fulfill the plan. By the early thirties the president's disappointment was deep. His feelings, expressed on many occasions, public and private, were summed up well in an address given at the college in 1931. The address is worth quoting at length as evidence of Morgan's strong vision, intense personal drive, and feeling that the institution had failed.[62]

The president began with praise: "We have made significant progress in educational methods"; "Antioch to a considerable extent deserves the reputation it has won as a pioneer in education" (p. 8). But then he moved quickly to the point:

Yet, when I compare Antioch as it is with what I believe to be my reasonable expectations for such an institution, and what were certainly my hopes for Antioch, I feel a very keen and deep-seated disappointment. I am disappointed by the infrequent occurrence of great expectations. I am disappointed in that commonsense judgement of our faithful, experienced people that really we have done very well, that all human changes come by slow degrees, and that we must not expect too much. I am disappointed that we do not break through the current ways of life with greater creative discontent.

What I am primarily disappointed in is this—that, taking our institution as a whole, we too largely accept as a whole the mental and emotional pattern of the day, and that we are bent chiefly on improving and refining it in detail. (p. 9)

The president then reiterated his vision:

Today the greatest defect in our education is the deficiency in emphasis upon ethical and spiritual purpose, and upon personal and social responsibility. . . . Except as we correct that dominant defect our Antioch aim of well-proportioned education will be largely an empty phrase. (p. 10)

And he asked again for commitment:

Had we but a larger portion of great leadership, great expectation, and singleness of purpose, Antioch could be a most significant factor in our civilization. It cannot be that except as it is dominated by great expectations in both faculty and upperclass students. It cannot be that while security and standard social status are controlling motives. (p. 16)

The president made no concessions to the niceties of academic diplomacy but criticized the spirit of compromise in the faculty:

Repeatedly I have heard in our conferences a sonorous academic phrase, "inevitability of gradualness." That is a perfect phrase to originate in academic halls where heroic action would be bad form. I am told not to be impatient, that all things come slowly. (p. 18)

The question is not whether we have moved too fast, but whether we have not moved so slowly that the great prospect is lost. (p. 18)

The quality of great adventure which to my mind is Antioch's reason for being, and without which our aim for full personal development cannot be achieved, does not have a clear right of way. To too great an extent there is a craving for a secure and quiet niche where one may live his life without danger of disturbance. I observe a growing tendency in the student body and elsewhere

62. "On the Future of Antioch," an address by Arthur E. Morgan, June 18, 1931. Antiochiana, Antioch College.

to establish a round of trivial events in accordance with the prevailing social pattern. Being at home in the world as it is is seen as a major social aim. (p. 20)

I feel that lack of a dominant and controlling purpose to create a radically new environment which would be favorable to the birth of great events. (p. 20)

And finally, the president maintained that the gap between ideals and action was so wide that his personal credibility and integrity were at stake, perhaps necessitating his departure:

I have had certain hopes and purposes for Antioch and I have talked of these in trying to raise money. For short periods I can present my hopes as in process of fulfillment, but unless such statements become more and more nearly true in fact, they become closer and closer to hypocrisy. In the long run the facts and the story must not conflict. Either the facts must conform to my statements, or I must tell a different story, or I must become silent. (pp. 21–22)

In the reconciliation of goals with the means of achievement and with the possibilities offered by the environment, men make critical choices. Some faculty and students at Antioch felt that Morgan was not adaptable enough, that he erred on the side of sticking to goals vague in formulation and too sweeping in intention and scope. But President Morgan after 1930 clearly felt just the opposite, that he should have stuck to his designs even more vigorously than he did, shaped the means, pushed back the environment, and taken the big chance. If he had the opportunity to do it over again, he told the faculty, he would have selected them more carefully to avoid those who "came here to teach my subject," those who were not interested in Antioch as a "revolution," as a "way of life." His greatest sense of guilt, therefore, was not in being too utopian "but in being too practical in presenting a picture of Antioch to prospective faculty members that was in focus with their habitual range of vision." [63] Later, in a general assessment of why utopias fail, Morgan was strongly conscious of the need to select men carefully, then to judge them closely through a probationary period, and finally to eliminate those out of harmony with the spirit and aims of the project, if one were to avoid "dilution" of a utopian venture.[64] Also, if he were to do it over again, he would have worked on a much smaller scale, one that would have allowed him more day-to-day contact with students. With the size of the college, fund-raising had taken most of his time and had kept him away from the campus. He believed he should have begun "with a half-dozen or a dozen students and increased that number gradually, but perhaps never beyond a few score, and try to work out with them a way of life, a way of developing character." [65]

63. "On Being Practical," memo to Antioch faculty, January 8, 1932. Antiochiana, Antioch College.
64. *Nowhere Was Somewhere*, p. 167.
65. Quoted in Adamic, *op. cit.*, p. 604.

Thus, in the view of its transforming president, Antioch had, under his leadership, survived, prospered, and won a reputation it deserved, but the college had adjusted too much, scaling down its ends until they meshed comfortably with the ordinary motives of the day. As "merely" another successful liberal arts college it was the dilution of a dream. However diluted, the dream had been instrumental in the rapid and thorough alteration of the college. Behind the energy and resources that so many poured into the college was Morgan's personal dynamism, an intense and unrelenting drive that was, in turn, generated and guided by utopian designs and great expectations. The big change at Antioch had been induced by a vision.

# Chapter 2. Embodiment

SIGNIFICANT change in the character of Antioch College did not stop with the departure of Arthur Morgan. Patterns begun in his era became more prominent, and some central elements of the modern Antioch developed largely in the thirties. In the main, however, the first decade stands as a period of transformation, and the thirties, under a new president, as the time when the transformation became firmly embodied in the structure and operation of the college. This settling down produced an era of exciting challenge, with the college confronted by a host of pressures and problems. As far as the participants knew, the experiment was still under way, its outcomes not yet decided. Those responsible also had to face painful decisions on financing the college during the depression. Then, too, the sense of personal stake in the college was being widely extended as governance passed, to an unusual degree, into the hands of the faculty and students. Meanwhile, the major economic and political issues of the thirties were pulling the developing social consciousness of students and faculty to external social reform, which expanded the reputation of the college as a center of liberal intellectualism and direct political action. Finally, in a quiet background, a gentle ethos was developing that would make Antioch a home for liberal Quakers and Unitarians. By World War II the work of these middle years—the second decade—had produced a relatively fixed mosaic of programs and organizational devices, tangible elements located within a campus ethos that, while intangible, was indeed palpable to those who stepped on campus. The elements and the ethos also had received a definite public face, a crystallized reputation that explained to various outsiders what the college was and what it stood for.

By the early forties Antioch had an unusual educational program built around work, classroom, and campus participation; an unusual authority structure in which influence was exerted through three campus governments; an ethos in which morality and intellectuality sometimes cooperated and sometimes conflicted; a distinctive reputation, eliciting hearty praise or damnation from those who thought they knew it well; an experiment paid off, literally in the settling of debts and symbolically in the gaining of a high place among colleges. The sum was a distinctive character well institutionalized.

## Program: Study and Work

CAMPUS STUDY

The purpose of a college should be partially revealed in the curriculum; i.e., in course offerings, majors, and requirements for graduation. These normal and routine matters tell us something about how a college spends its resources, particularly the time and energy of teachers and students. If a college purportedly devoted to pure liberal arts is otherwise in practice, direct evidence is usually found in (a) the presence of many vocational fields (nursing, business, engineering), (b) heavy enrollment in these fields, with a minority of students in the liberal disciplines, and (c) a set of courses and course requirements that reveal a service posture for the English and history departments. Conversely, a liberal arts college devoted almost purely to the liberal arts reveals the fact in a curriculum circumscribed by the traditional liberal arts fields. In this latter case, of course, investigation past the formalisms of the catalogue is still needed to identify a living devotion from a dead one

Morgan's unusual plan, if viable, was bound to find distinctive expression in the regular classroom-centered curriculum since the plan defined general education in wide terms, contained no taboos about "vocationalism," and indeed in spirit was close to hostile to the existing liberal arts pattern. "Perhaps the earliest of the progressive experiments in the colleges" [1] (later ones included Black Mountain, Sarah Lawrence, Bennington, Goddard, Bard), Antioch gave an interpretation of general education sufficiently revisionist to cut a swath through the structure and content of the college curriculm.

That the Antioch classroom would not be tightly traditional was

1. Frederick Rudolph, *The American College and University* (New York, Alfred A. Knopf, Inc., 1962), pp. 474–77.

signified by Morgan's early faculty appointments. Among twenty new appointees in 1921–22, only eight were in the liberal arts. Two were in personnel administration (to administer the work program), and ten others were in civil engineering, industrial health and research, accounting, architecture, education, and household economics. He made appointments of a similar character during the rest of the twenties to provide a combination of liberal and vocational courses and to give students "specific training in health and hygiene, in handling a personal budget, in scientific method, and in pursuing life aims. . . ." [2] Courses were organized not only in physical education, which is common enough, but also in personal finance, home management, college aims, and life aims. Too, the appointments in the liberal arts included men such as Professor Basil H. Pillard, previously discussed, who turned their courses into arenas of discussion and paid little heed to lines of specialization.

The scope and emphasis of general education at Antioch soon became reflected in a core program binding on all students. One assumption often made about "experimental" or "progressive" colleges is that they are open and permissive in their curriculum—that students wander around doing as they please. But who knows better what is good for others than a reformer? Reform colleges, like reform governments, may often be more structured and more rigid than their traditional counterparts. The second Antioch from the start had an imposing array of requirements that the faculty never ceased revising and usually elaborating. The general education core that had developed by 1930 is shown in Table 2–1. Especially heavy in the first three years, the G.E. requirements appeared in every year of the student's program. There was, to begin, the common spread of courses: in the natural sciences (physics, chemistry, biology, geology) and mathematics; in the social sciences (economics, integrated courses combining history, government, and sociology) and psychology; and in the humanities (English and philosophy). There were also unusual courses, ones not found at Reed or Swarthmore: "Finance 101–102," in the first year, in which the student was required "to make out a budget for his income and expenses, and to endeavor to govern his expenditures by it throughout the year"; "Education 101: College Aims," also for the entering student, to introduce him to the aims and standards of the college; "Industrial Administration 102: Industrial Civilization and Its Problems," also in the first year, "designed to introduce the freshman student to the industrial world into which he may be sent as a worker under the Antioch cooperative program"; "Aesthetics 111–112," in the fifth year, "designed to provide a comprehensive view of the activities of man as they are motivated by his sense of beauty," with course work that varied from learning about the

2. Algo D. Henderson and Dorothy Hall, *Antioch College: Its Design for Liberal Education* (New York, Harper & Row, Publishers, 1946), p. 4.

TABLE 2–1. *Required Courses, Antioch College,*
1930–31

General Required Courses for the A.B. Degree. Students are advised to take courses in the years indicated, but may, by petition, either anticipate or postpone required courses if necessary to work out a satisfactory program in a field of concentration.

**First Year**

| First Semester | Second Semester |
|---|---|
| English 101 | English 102 |
| Mathematics 101 | Mathematics 102 |
| °Chemistry 101 | Chemistry 102 |
| Finance 101 | Finance 102 |
| Education 101 | Industrial Administration 102 |
| Physical Education 101 | Physical Education 102 |

**Second Year**

| | |
|---|---|
| English 151 | English 152 |
| °Physics 101 | Physics 102 |
| Biology 101 | Biology 102 |
| Physical Education 103 | Physical Education 104 |

**Third Year**

| | |
|---|---|
| Social Science 111 | Social Science 112 |
| Geology 101 | Geology 102 |
| or Economics 101 | or Economics 102 |
| Psychology 101 | Psychology 102 |
| Physical Education 105 | Physical Education 106 |

**Fourth Year**

| | |
|---|---|
| Social Science 211 | Social Science 212 |
| Economics 101 | Economics 102 |
| or Geology 101 | or Geology 102 |
| Physical Education 107 | Physical Education 108 |

**Fifth Year**

| | |
|---|---|
| Social Science 231 | Social Science 232 |
| Aesthetics 111 | Aesthetics 112 |

**Sixth Year**

| | |
|---|---|
| Philosophy 251 | Philosophy 252 |
| Comprehensive Examination | Comprehensive Examination |

°May be waived by examination.

Source: Catalogue of Antioch College, 1930–1931; Antioch College Bulletin, Vol. XXVI, No. 8 (1930–31), p. 67.

philosophical aspects of aesthetics to viewing architecture and land scaping in neighboring cities.[3]

This core curriculum reflected "the theory that there are certain skills, and a general body of knowledge—in science, art, literature, social

3. *Catalogue of Antioch College, 1930–1931; Antioch College Bulletin*, Vol. XXVI, No. 8 (1930–31), pp. 79, 90, 81, 73.

studies, and philosophy—properly common to educated men and women." [4]
At Antioch the particular progressive education twist to this old doctrine
mixed traditional, subject-oriented approaches with much learning by
doing and much self-conscious formulation of personal aims. The required
aesthetics course, for example, whose name had shifted by the mid-thirties
from "applied aesthetics" to "creative aesthetics," blended the history of
art, formal aesthetics, and practical experience. The student moved
through four categories of an ethnography of art—primitive, Greek,
gothic, and oriental. To take the first:

> During the first part of the year the student, who may be considered in a
> "primitive" artistic state himself, studies primitive art (including that of the
> American Indian) in the light of the historical conditions and ideas which
> produced it; he seeks to discover the aesthetic canons which govern it; and
> finally he attempts, in the laboratory, himself to create works of art in the primi-
> tive vein.

Following a basic tenet of progressive education, the students thus began
with materials in keeping with their own stage of development. If anything was to be avoided, it was sterile art history: "The course throughout
eschews 'preciosity' and attempts to be practical and concrete." The final
object? "Not exact and intensive knowledge of facts and dates in art so
much as a new attitude towards it." [5]

Notable in the formulation of the early required courses at Antioch was
a disregard for the negative sentiments elicited in the faculties of leading
liberal arts colleges by symbols and practices that smacked of vulgar
vocationalism and practicality. Courses required of all with such titles as
"education" and "industrial administration" were bad enough. The one in
aesthetics was "obviously" a mishmash, in which hand work would
compete with "serious study," and no self-respecting art historian or
student of aesthetics would touch it. And a course in personal finance, in
the name of liberal arts? "Indeed!" And, indeed, alteration of the required
core through the years eliminated or renamed and weakened these
courses. By the end of the thirties, personal finance and industrial administration were gone. Education 101, College Aims, had become an orientation course that covered study habits, personal finance, adjustment to
college, and educational plans. This course evolved toward a marginal
status—finally, one unit—in the program of the student. The aesthetics
course remained. Thus, by the time the general education requirements
had found their lasting format, they had pulled back toward a normal
spread of courses plus some work in the arts. The performing arts had
become an important part of the curriculum, in contrast to the extracurricular status they occupy in most colleges of comparable standing.

4. *Antioch Notes*, Vol. 14, No. 8 (April, 1937), no page numbers.
5. *Ibid.*, No. 9 (April, 1937), no page numbers.

Whatever the evolution of particular course titles and contents, the concept of general education courses was firmly fixed, and students continued to give much of their time to them. And when life aims lost out as a distinctive subject in a special course, it was still confronted in the courses of the great teachers, in comprehensive examinations, and in self-reflective papers required of all students first as freshmen and then again as seniors. The final general education hurdles were no light matter. Seniors had to write comprehensive examinations in the required course program and in the field of concentration. And the senior paper, introduced in the early forties, produced enough free-floating anxiety across the senior class to warrant, in the hours after its due date, an Antioch tradition of a spontaneous parade and an equally spontaneous beer bust.

Thus, in the rounding off and firm institutionalization of the general education part, the classroom program became more regularly respectable in its labels and compartments than it had been previously, but the distinctive concerns of the Morgan era, modestly attenuated, continued to come through to the student.

WORK AND THE ALTERNATING CYCLE

Along with the other components of the curriculum, the cycle of study and work was well established when Morgan left the college, and it was to remain central in the minds of insiders and outsiders. For many, it was *the* unique feature. It deeply affected students' lives. At a minimum, it had the students packing and running for the bus every five or eight or ten or twelve weeks—whatever the current periods of work and study—to get off campus to the job in the city or to leave the job to return to the campus. A work position also had to be negotiated some weeks in advance with a campus counselor, or the risk had to be taken that one could find a suitable job on one's own after arriving in a distant city. Living quarters had to be found on short notice: It was not uncommon to leave campus on a Friday to report to a position the following Monday, an apartment being passed from one student to another might or might not be available. The jobs themselves varied from exceedingly routine, from which students learned above all how dull work could be, to very exciting—e.g., a cooperative position in the office of a United States senator quickly gave the student information not possessed by his professors on the workings of government. In the middle thirties about a third of the jobs were clerical and sales positions in business; about a fourth, as background for engineers and scientists, were in factories and laboratories; another fifth were in hospitals, social welfare agencies, and schools; and the remainder were scattered in many other fields.[6] Whatever their specific nature, the jobs

6. "A Continuing Heritage, Report of the President," *Antioch College Bulletin*, Vol. XXXIV, No. 1. (September, 1937), p. 19. (A special report by President Algo Henderson. Antioch did not have a regular series of annual presidential reports.)

were defined by the college as part of an Antioch education, with special credits thereby earned, and the work program as a whole remained conceptually a part of the Antioch philosophy of turning out the well-rounded, liberally educated man.

Ironically, however, the work program was never fully able to take care of itself; although institutionalized, its tracks were not well greased. A deviant pattern not well accepted by liberal arts professors, the concept of a work program had an insecure place in the general academic world. Its weakness in this larger setting made it potentially weak inside the college and increased the possibility of its sliding toward the margin of campus thought and practice. Much work was needed in the twenties and thirties to stabilize the program near the center of the curriculum, making it an element that would be more than tolerated at the periphery. By conscious design and emergent connections, this potentially precarious program became anchored in three basic organizational components: personnel, finance, and heritage and self-image.

*Personnel Structure.*   The preference for the "well-rounded man," even the "virile practical man," that Morgan had partly built into the faculty in his recruiting was a crucial though subtle element in the undergirding of the work program. This practical and generalist outlook helped to abate the scholarly specialism normal to academia, the focus on discipline and classroom that would smother an educational program residing outside the disciplines and the classrooms. Where a more traditional faculty would have, at best, suffered the job scheme, the Antioch faculty gave it substantial support. Some who supported it strongly had had experience in industry; others from the more normal academic careers had been intrigued by it and had committed themselves to it as part of the general scheme. The men recruited early became the senior faculty almost overnight, and for many of these senior figures the work program became an unquestioned commitment. They might debate its form and worry about its integration with the classroom, but they did not question its existence, its place at Antioch. The program played no part in Morgan's dialogue with the faculty in the early thirties, and the faculty did not take the opportunity upon his departure to challenge it. In short, the base of support of this deviant program lay partly in the recruitment and assimilation of faculty; at the time, to commit oneself to the college was to commit oneself to the work-study plan.

A case in point was Manmatha Nath Chatterjee. One of the several most influential teachers on the campus from the time he joined the college in 1922 until his retirement in 1953, revered by many generations of students, Professor Chatterjee had, to say the least, unusual academic credentials. Certainly he did not have the papers and scholarly style required on many another campus. Brahmin Indian by birth, engineer by training, philosopher by inclination, Chatterjee was appointed professor of social science.

In the breadth of his philosophical quest and in the forthfulness of his personality, he was close to ideal for the Morgan plan. Generalist to the extreme, he was poles apart from the empirical specialist in social science. He did not report the research literature to expound on correlations of independent and dependent variables. His concerns were global: man and society, laws of living, wealth and welfare, behavior in democracy, race and civilization, education for our time.[7] Through persistent Socratic questioning, he challenged students to think about the very core of their values. In this effort all experience was grist for the mill. For a professional scholar the world of work would be extraneous; for Chatterjee, work might have something to say to the young. He had neither professional reason nor trained inclination to oppose the idea that work was education. For him, therefore, the legitimacy of the work program was not in question, and so it went for others—Basil H. Pillard, W. Boyd Alexander, Clyde Stewart Adams, Henry Federighi, Otto Mathiasen, Allyn C. Swinnerton—who for years in the college were walking expressions of Morgan's values.

The work program naturally found its greatest day-to-day support in the persons held responsible for its administration. Morgan early ( 1921–22 ) appointed a director and an associate director of personnel administration to run the program. By 1924–25, the total staff of forty-six included four "officers of personnel administration." The establishment of these positions marked the beginning of a separate Personnel Division, or Extramural School, which after World War II was enlarged to eight and then to ten positions. This division found jobs for the students and students for the jobs. It maintained contact with the students when they were on the job and evaluated with them, upon their return to campus, the value of the job experience. Although located on campus, the division was off-campus oriented much of the time—to the possibility of a new job in Detroit; to the satisfaction of employers with their young workers; to the problems of students coping with work, living arrangements, and people hundreds of miles away from campus protection. Thus, the division had no responsibility for the classroom but was directly responsible for the off-campus segment of the cycle of work and study.

Once the Personnel Division was launched, its continuation in one form or another was never in doubt. It could be reorganized and renamed, as it was, even scattered to the point of attaching its personnel to teaching departments, but something like it would have to exist as long as there was a work program. The tasks involved were time-consuming and called for full attention: The necessary trips to distant cities could hardly be reconciled with the weekly schedule of the teaching professor. The work pro-

7. Manmatha Nath Chatterjee, *Out of Confusion* (Yellow Springs, Ohio, The Antioch Press, 1954).

gram, then, had to spawn its own men, personnel counselors. With their emergence the problems of the co-op plan became the problems of P.D. (Personnel Division). To alter the program was to modify this specific division, these specific positions, and these particular individuals. As the work program became institutionalized, P.D. became an Antioch institution, one known by students and remembered by alumni as a distinctive element within the college. Here was a core of full-time devotees, a group of people whose interest it was to develop and protect the program. They became the guardians of work-study policies.

Not surprisingly, the men and women who staffed this division came to have an anomalous position in the life of the college. Differences in daily work set them apart somewhat from their teaching fellows. Differential assessments normally made by professors of those who do and do not teach on a campus tended persistently to undercut esteem. For the professors at Antioch it did not necessarily follow from their general commitment to the work program that the specific activities of the counselors were as important as their own teaching. Many in the faculty continued to see their own work as central and other work as peripheral, pushing the personnel counselors toward second-class citizenship—somewhat similar to the status of counselors or student affairs' workers on other campuses. Thus, although the continued existence of the division was not in doubt, the place and status of its personnel within the college were less secure. Not as well prepared academically as the teaching faculty, defined often as "placement" or "guidance" personnel rather than as academic men, tied to an activity that had to be explained, justified, and carried out against expectations of what is appropriate for a liberal education, the men of the Personnel Division became the point of stress, organizationally, in the incorporation of this unusual scheme in the college. Potentially an Achilles heel of the whole college, the division had to receive special support and attention because it was critical for the character of the whole. This support was well established in the twenties in the person of Morgan himself and then, in the thirties, in the sentiments of the next president and of an overwhelming part of the faculty. The general faculty proved a base of support in the critical years of firm institutionalization. Then, once well established, the division became the interest-group embodiment of the concept of work and study. Not until twenty years later, in the fifties, did support falter and the division be seriously challenged.

*Finance.*   Among the unpleasant facts of life for those who work in colleges and universities is the role of money in deciding the fate of programs. Young academics commonly hope, even expect, that the cash nexus applies only in other kinds of organizations (in a college, principles determine affairs), but all come to know better: Faculties learn about the balance sheet, reluctantly and often bitterly; presidents and deans develop an acute financial sense; and budget officers and provosts have as a way of life the guarding of scarce financial resources. The contributions of a program to the balance sheet are important, often decisive.

Our earlier review of the place of tuition in the financing of the college suggested that in the budget the work program had a never-failing friend. When two students alternate in the use of the same space and facilities, the economies are considerable. The significance of this financial benefit was not lost on trustees, administrators, and faculty, and at times it was crucial. When gifts fell off sharply in the early depression years, the college began to rely largely on student tuition, supplemented by the faculty subsidy of a cut in salary. The suppression of expenditure on faculty could not go on indefinitely, especially at the subsistence level sustained at the low point of the depression. Low faculty salaries constituted negative finance, but tuition income was the positive factor, the great plus of the college. All students paid full tuition whether they were off or on campus in a given term, at a level similar to other leading private colleges. Father's checkbook, in effect, did not know the difference, and the payments of the off-campus students became a natural subsidy. Thus the work program became the equivalent of a major endowment fund, dependably providing income in addition to normal returns from tuition. The importance of the work-study cycle in this regard from the thirties can hardly be overestimated. The dependence of the college on the program, fixed in the thirties, became a rock against which any thoughts of abolition of the work program would be dashed. All who cared about the general health of the institution had to view the program with tender, loving eyes.

*Heritage and Self-Image.* In comprehending an organization, analysts and practical men alike are prone to get caught up in the intricacies of structure, personnel, and budget, passing over the nebulous realm of tradition and general institutional self-concept. But the forming of tradition and a global self-image is part of the institutionalization of character in an organization and nowhere more so than in colleges. These "cultural" factors become forces in their own right, throwing up fences between the right and the wrong and providing signposts that direct men onto one trail and not another.

At Antioch the transformation of the twenties imparted a self-image in which the work program was an integrated element. In the heritage bestowed by that decade President Morgan was the central symbol, and almost to the degree that the new Antioch was Morgan, it was also the work program. The work-study cycle was at the core of the organization. To lay it aside or even to alter it sharply would be to deny the validity of the transformation—even, in the thirties, to cut down one's progeny in the full bloom of early manhood. Many in the Antioch faculty adopted the vocabulary of "symmetry," "balance," and "the whole man"—terms which referred to the work-study approach. The general educational ideal that still endured in 1960 included a legacy from the twenties that experience is the great teacher and that study must be integrated with such forms of experience as work.

Success also helps institutionalize a program. The Antioch work program did not become a national success in the sense of wide imitation by other colleges, but at the college itself and even elsewhere the program became defined as an intrinsic part of the rapid climb to prominence. Test data showing significant change in students or the high-quality "output" of graduates were interpreted in this light. To be sure, the entering students were bright and well motivated, and therefore good recruitment was part of the answer; but since the work program was viewed as *the* innovation of the college, the advocates and defenders of the college maintained that it had to be playing an important role and deserved much of the credit. The success of Antioch then became the success of the program. Few could quarrel effectively with a new formula that was showing striking results. For supporters work-study was part of the alchemy of the change from rags to riches.

The work program at Antioch is a revealing case of how a precarious academic effort can be given organizational protection.[8] Precariousness was reduced by building a core of full-time personnel; giving the core divisional autonomy; recruiting sympathetic personnel around the core group; making the program a contributor to, rather than a drain upon, the financial health of the organization; defining the program as a essential part of the over-all character; and giving it credit for the success of the whole.

## Authority

A defining characteristic of the modern Antioch is that much authority resides in the hands of faculty and students. This dispersion of authority from the administration is expressed in the governmental forms of the campus. Side by side are two, or three, meaningful governments, depending on how one wishes to sort them. One is the regular line of administrative positions and jurisdictions: president, deans, business affairs, admissions, and departments. A second is a faculty government fused closely with the administration ordinarily but also possessing some separatist tendencies, especially as the college grew in size and increased in complexity. A third is a "community government," largely student run, that has significant jurisdiction, influence, and tradition. This structure of dual and triple authorities developed largely in the thirties and was institutionalized by the end of the decade. In this organization the authority of the

8. On precarious values in organizations, see Philip Selznick, *Leadership in Administration* (New York, Harper & Row, Publishers, 1957), pp. 119–33; Burton R. Clark, "Organizational Adaptation and Precarious Values," *American Sociological Review*, Vol. 21, No. 3 (June, 1956), pp. 327–36.

great leader—the charismatic figure—became "routinized" not in bureaucracy but in webs of collegial control.[9]

FACULTY GOVERNMENT

In 1926 President Morgan created a group of faculty members that became known as the Administrative Council. The group was initially a kitchen cabinet: appointed by the president, advisory to him, and informal in procedure. In 1930 the council was written into the charter of the college. It was to consist of three faculty members elected by the faculty and three appointed by the president, with the president and dean as ex officio members. The council was given power to elect some members of the Board of Trustees, but its chief stated purpose was to advise the president. Thus Ad Cil, as the body became known, was given definite legal standing but only advisory powers in day-to-day administration.

As long as he was on the scene Morgan was in charge, no matter what the forms. Authority was largely personal authority. In the context of his overwhelming presence the council operated as a group of senior faculty members who kept abreast of internal problems and had advice ready for the leader upon his return to campus from extended trips. As often happens with kitchen cabinets, members of the council not only gave advice but also, for the president, constituted a certain entree to the faculty, with the council members (hopefully) persuading the rest of the faculty of the importance of what the president wanted to do.

As Morgan withdrew from active leadership, administrative authority evolved rapidly toward a collegial form. The dean of the college, Algo Henderson, was made acting president in 1933 and president in 1936. The new head had joined the faculty in 1925 as associate professor of accounting and became business manager and professor of business administration in 1928. His appointment as dean in 1931 gave him a particularly important role in the president's advisory group and made him the senior educational officer on campus during Morgan's extended absences. Henderson was an insider who had neither the desire nor the temperament for imitating Morgan's paternalism. Intending to practice as well as to believe in democratic government, he wanted a unified administration and faculty and chose to define himself primarily as leader of the faculty. The new president's desire and temperament fit the developing context. The able and often vigorous faculty recruited in the twenties had now taken hold, and the collegial web was fast forming around the presidential chair. As Morgan began to realize in the early thirties, the college was no longer a one-man enterprise. The faculty was inclined to exert more influence than

9. On routinization of charisma, see *Max Weber: The Theory of Social and Economic Organization,* trans. by A.M. Henderson and Talcott Parsons (New York, Oxford University Press, Inc., 1947), pp. 358–86; Reinhard Bendix, *Max Weber: An Intellectual Portrait* (Garden City, N.Y., Doubleday & Company, Inc., 1960), pp. 301–29.

it had before, as exhibited in a willingness to argue with Morgan, and devices for faculty participation in government were emerging, spurred by the long absences of the president. Any successor to Morgan would have to work in a more co-operative and circumscribed fashion than he did.

Under these conditions and with the new president's inclination toward collegiality, the Administrative Council gradually, during the thirties, extended and intensified its responsibility. It served in effect as the peak committee of the faculty and in turn of the administration, blending the two: It appointed the committees that at other colleges were normally appointed by faculty and administrative bodies; it participated in the formation of the budget and approved the budget submitted to the trustees; it made the important personnel decisions—hiring, firing, and tenure. Meeting once a week, it kept close watch on the administrative domain. It was the center of policy formation and close to the administrative implementation of policy.

The fundamental change in the thirties in the position and strength of this body was reflected in 1940 in a revision of the college charter. Under this revision, five faculty members and three students became the voting membership of the council, with the president and dean as ex officio members. No longer was the president to appoint any of the voting members: Three faculty members were elected by the faculty alone, and two of the faculty and the three students were elected by the entire campus. Any further changes in the size, membership, and method of election to the council were to be determined by the faculty. The charter no longer spoke of having the council advise the president but of a sharing of authority between the two. By that time and from then on the council was "the focal point for the formation of current policy in the College." [10] Legally only an advisory group, the council became, in fact, the most important of the governmental centers of the college:[11]

All major matters of College policy—such as the current building program— come to it for review and decision, or originate there. It passes on all questions of personnel. It counsels with the president concerning College finances and passes on the budget. It appoints faculty policy-making and administrative committees to handle admissions, student counseling, curriculum, and examinations, as well as to establish the policies of the cooperative plan. Committees on dining rooms, housing, campus planning, and the library also come under its jurisdiction. . . . And, finally, the Council is the court of final appeal on campus matters which cannot be dealt with satisfactorily elsewhere, subject of course to action by the trustees. It has charter power to adopt by-laws not inconsistent with actions of the trustees.

The council and its committees became the structural embodiment of one of the foremost characteristics of the college—strong faculty authority.

10. Henderson and Hall, *op. cit.*, p. 206.
11. *Ibid.*, pp. 206–7.

So it was by 1940—and still was two decades later. The Administrative Council permanently reduced the power of presidents to alter the college and came to be a primary source of protection for the values of the transforming era. Power found its locus in a governmental device developed and manned mainly by true believers. From the thirties Ad Cil was a body not seriously questioned or tampered with. No one in the forties and fifties attempted to take this device away from the faculty and from those in the administration who believed in it as much as did the senior faculty. The kitchen cabinet to a considerable degree became the operational heart of the college.

COMMUNITY GOVERNMENT

Outsiders have some difficulty comprehending the vaunted Antioch community government. Aware of the superficiality and sham of much student government on American campuses, some observers assume that since student government is trivial elsewhere, it must be trivial at Antioch. A second approach, common among administrators and faculty at many another college, is to see only the dangers of extending authority to students and to recoil from the nightmare thus created. A third and favorable point of view leans on the notion that this "most significant experiment," this "laboratory of democracy," is the greatest development since Rousseau. However, community government, although original, has not throughout its brief history been trivial, nightmarish, or a model of democracy. It came closest to realizing its ideals in the thirties, when the conception was new, the campus was small, and the students, often with the support of faculty and administration, were working their way to influence.

This instrument of involvement and governance developed gradually, coming on strong after the departure of Morgan. In its formation in 1926 it was an expression of the ideal of a campus as a united, small community. Morgan, as ideologue, thought it a good idea that students participate in the governing of the campus. If students learn by doing, they ought to learn democracy by participating in campus forms of it. But Morgan, as participant, was temperamentally unsuited for such a system. A towering patrician, sure in judgment, he had a dominating presence. But then he was not on campus much of the time, and a student-dominated structure, like faculty government on campus, evolved in part as a form for governance when charismatic authority was lifted. When the leader was permanently gone, these emerging forms found resonance in his successor, Henderson, who was committed to the ideals of democratic participation and was temperamentally suited to the persistent and often exasperating work necessary to embody them in campus practices and traditions. During Henderson's tenure, community government moved from a minor place in the philosophy, imagery, and administration of the campus to being *the* expression of the social consciousness of the college, a hallmark of Antioch.

The broad dimensions of community government as they emerged were relatively simple. For jurisdiction it would take up where the classroom and regular educational policy left off. For constituency it would treat the campus as one; hence students, faculty, administration, and even wives were part of it. For machinery it would establish a Community Council to which faculty and administrators as well as students, nominated on different bases, would be elected in a campus-wide vote. What could be simpler in conception—and more difficult to operate? The genius of the college in the thirties was that it made this unusual device operate in fruitful tension with the more normal machinery of the faculty and the administration. Because student participation was not imposed from the top, it did not have the fragility of a hothouse plant. The ideals and sentiments of the administration and faculty provided leeway and some impulse, and the students took it from there. The dynamic of the Community Council was that it held out to bright and active students the hope of liberation from the customary system of deans, arbitrary rules, and administrative enforcement. For the students the promise was great: They would join the adults in making the rules of the campus. They would have not a traditional student government but rather one that penetrated the sacred domains of faculty and administration.

The accepted powers of this government expanded throughout the duration of Henderson's presidency. The faculty were to control some things, particularly educational policy, through the Administrative Council, and the students were to control other things, to be worked out, through their dominance in the community government. The Community Council started with no inherent powers, but as the students expanded its boundaries, the flow of influence was ever toward it. The liquor laws of the campus had been in the hands of the administration: "Antioch students do not drink." In 1931 the council persuaded the dean to agree that "except in unusual cases, all liquor problems are to be handled by the Community Council in the future." [12] When Morgan expressed his deep disappointment in the failure of the college to measure up to his ideals, the Council decided that it, as well as the faculty, could and ought to initiate committee reports and discussion.[13] In the delicate matter of requiring faculty members to pay a fee in support of the Community Council the council debated whether it should merely recommend this action to the Administrative Council but then decided to go ahead on its own authority.[14]

12. Minutes of the Community Council, October 26, 1931, Antioch College.
13. *Ibid.*, November 18, 1931.
14. *Ibid.*, October 12, 1932.

In other areas, the Community Council became interested in racial discrimination in Yellow Springs. By 1933 it was challenging the authority of the administration to dismiss students for antisocial conduct, "the attitude of the Council being that it had not been sufficiently consulted. . . ." [15] Under increasing student pressure the smoking rules for girls evolved during these years from permission to smoke in one corner of the campus to provision of a smoking room to "do as you please." Dormitory rules, in general, came increasingly under a developing honor code, so that a girl could sign herself in on her own as she returned to her room. By 1934 the president was giving oral, confidential reports to the council on the pending college budget[16]—an action that could leave most college presidents only flabbergasted. By 1935 student rating of faculty was under way, a practice that was to wax strong at the college and more than once provoke an outburst of resentment in the faculty.

Faculty representation on the council during these years included some of the most prestigious men on campus, e.g., Bishop Paul Jones (see p. 59) and the economist William Leiserson. That they took the student-dominated council seriously helped greatly to make it a meaningful organization for the students. The principle became fairly rapidly established in those depression years that Antioch students should have as much authority as they could handle, but what they could handle was unclear. The student body was quick to form a tradition that all areas of decision were potentially open and were to be decided by trial and error. And why not? The student members of the Administrative Council and its committees were already privy to the most fundamental deliberations of the administration and faculty. The student majority on the Community Council found an increasingly wide scope of issues and policies in their hands, areas of authority that had been won by previous classes and that, the students assumed, were not to be given back. The faculty might continue to control the classroom, but out-of-classroom behavior was to be controlled largely by the students themselves. Community Council would stand alongside the Administrative Council in a bicameral relationship, with Ad Cil handling long-range issues and personnel matters and Com Cil having dominion over most day-to-day matters on the campus.

## Campus Ethos

Much has already been said about the controlling ideas that emerged on the Antioch campus in the twenties and thirties. The philosophy of symmetrical education undergirded the work program and community participation, defining a general education for which the classroom was not enough. The philosophy of campus democracy became a direct prop for

15. *Ibid.*, March 27, 1933.
16. *Ibid.*, December 10, 1934.

the community government, encouraging the administration to relinquish authority, pushing the faculty toward involvement in the time-consuming chores necessary for the continuation of an active and responsible community government, and giving the students the theoretical tools for claiming and then protecting their authority. But other fundamental points of view were developing at the college, general modes of thought and action not subsumed under the philosophies and ideas already discussed. One mode we shall call the Quaker spirit, the other militant intellectualism.

THE QUAKER CORE

The most intangible component of the ethos of the new Antioch can be likened to Quakerism or, in more hybrid terminology, liberal Unitarian Quakerism—an ethical thrust initiated by Morgan's own religious views. A deeply religious man wandering on the frontier of Unitarianism, Morgan wanted initially for the college to be a place where "the liberal values of Unitarianism would undergird the life of the community." As the early years passed, however, Morgan found the temper of his New England coreligionists neither quite to his liking nor in close fit with the college. If the Unitarians were only more aggressive, if they would only build a fire under themselves and "get in touch with average human beings," he felt, this change, together with their respect for ideas and for individual freedom, would have rendered Unitarianism an appropriate religious base for the college. But, as Morgan saw it, he and the college were developing a practical, realistic, and forward-looking liberalism that diverged from the prosperous, intellectual, and self-contented liberalism of the Unitarians. The critical difference lay in "emotional commitment"; a religion for Antioch would have to do as well as think, commit the whole self and not merely the mind. In search of a blend of emotional commitment and intellectual freedom, Morgan moved, at first informally and later formally, away from the parlor of the Unitarians and into the home of the Quakers.

Morgan's own morality—whether considered Unitarian, Quaker, or both—was the chief ingredient in the conscience of the campus when he was president, and before he was done he had brought to the campus men of similar religious spirit. The influence of these men in the thirties helped institutionalize a broadly humanitarian outlook as the ethical backdrop against which much of the drama of the next two decades was played. This backdrop sometimes guided the play, but at other times it set the stage for behavior of a contrary nature. Foremost among those who reflected and shaped this religious spirit in the thirties was an action-minded theologian, Bishop Jones.[17]

17. This account draws heavily upon a fine historical paper done by an Antioch student. Felice Gordon, *Paul Jones and Antioch*. Unpublished paper, Antiochiana, Antioch College, no date.

In the early days of the transformation, the college did not have a pastor and did not offer specific courses in religion. Religious discussion groups met on Sunday mornings, and various outsiders conducted Sunday evening vespers. When the Reverend Charles F. Potter came in 1925, he acted as the unofficial pastor and taught a course in comparative religion. But his stay was short, only two years, for the president came to feel that his pastor was not sufficiently profound. The position then remained unfilled until 1930, when Morgan engaged Bishop Jones. Charged with conducting vesper services and teaching a few religion courses, Bishop Jones became the Department of Philosophy as well as the pastor. He and the president were coinstructors in a life aims course from 1930 until Morgan left in 1933, and his courses made up the bulk of the philosophy department offerings until near the end of the thirties. The bishop remained at the college until his death in 1941, hence his tenure spanned the thirties. In the minds of many at the time and in the words of President Henderson, Bishop Jones "came about as near to epitomizing Antioch as anyone." To know something about the bishop is to learn about the developing ethical climate of the college.

Bishop Jones was no stranger to controversy and newspaper headlines when he came to Antioch. A bishop of the Episcopal Church and at the same time an avowed pacifist and socialist, he lost a church post in Utah because of his views during World War I. In the reaction that followed, he became a nationally-discussed case of persecution of pacifists. Following this incident he became, in 1919, executive secretary of the Fellowship of Reconciliation, formed a few years earlier to bring about peace from the "Christian pacifist point of view." He served a decade in this post, busying himself with pacifist writings. After then serving for a year as acting bishop in Cincinnati, he was offered and accepted the Antioch position. Thus, he was at the time a liberal theologian well known for intense engagement in practical affairs.

Antioch was already no longer a place for a formal religionist. Morgan and the faculty were hardly orthodox, and the catalogues of the college spoke of religion at Antioch in the vocabularies of humanism and science —"discovering the meaning of life," "self-mastery," "integrity of personal conduct and social relations," "the way to truth lies through sincere, open-minded inquiry, and not through unquestioning acceptance of dogma or creed." [18] The students thought along a similar line. In a poll in 1932 the majority classified their "religious" beliefs as humanism, agnosticism, and theism, rather than as Protestantism, Catholicism, and Judaism. For this developing climate Bishop Jones was the right man. Very tolerant of the views of others, he had himself come to a general humanistic outlook. A high church man in name only, he was close to the spirit of the Quakers,

18. *Catalogue of Antioch College, 1929–1930. Antioch College Bulletin*, Vol. XXV, No. 8 (1929–30), pp. 12–15.

and the group that formed around him at the college was essentially Quaker.

Up to 1931 the catalogue of Antioch College pointed out that "as to religious customs, on Sunday evenings vesper services are held at which addresses are given by visiting ministers or laymen." [19] From that year and through the rest of the thirties, the catalogue took note that the Sunday evening vespers were under the direction of Bishop Jones, and Sunday morning worship was conducted in Rockford (a small building) "after the manner of the Friends." Beginning in 1934–35 the catalogue spoke of the Rockford Circle as "the center for student religious activities on the campus." This group of faculty and students, formed in 1933 with Jones as sponsor and adviser, helped plan vesper programs, sponsored speakers who lectured before the entire student body at assemblies, and acted as a social service group for Yellow Springs. The vespers, conducted by Jones, apparently had more appeal and influence than his courses, offering a warm, informal setting in which to talk about values and aims. Jones also encouraged students to re-examine their basic values by organizing and sustaining annual Life's Meaning Conferences, which brought a number of speakers to campus.

If the bishop's nonformal religiosity fit and further developed the dominant religious mood of the college, so did his socialist and pacifist convictions fit and further other developing moods and temperaments. In a straw vote in 1932 on preference for presidential candidates, half the faculty were for Norman Thomas, the Socialist candidate, with the other half splitting evenly between Franklin D. Roosevelt and Herbert Hoover.[20] Thomas was the forerunner among the students also, receiving most of his strength from the older (as compared to the newer) students. Bishop Jones, along with a son of Morgan, organized a Thomas for President club and worked with the Yellow Springs Socialist Party. To the good people of southwestern Ohio, somewhat southern in political persuasion, a Socialist in politics was about as welcome as a rattlesnake in the back yard, and the noise made by the local citizens about these radicals in their midst could be heard for miles. Lest there be any doubt of where he stood, shortly before his death Jones ran under the Socialist label for governor of Ohio in 1940.

As a strong peace movement developed on the Antioch campus in the late thirties, Bishop Jones also became *its* personification, a position which his leadership in the taking of the Oxford peace pledge in 1938 symbolized. With his beliefs and activism, the bishop was a participant in campus government, serving willingly on the Community Council; he worked closely with students in their fight against racial discrimination in Yellow

19. *Catalogue of Antioch College, 1930–1931. Antioch College Bulletin,* Vol. XXVI, No. 8 (1930–31), p. 15.
20. Gordon, *op. cit.,* p. 40.

Springs, which was centered particularly on the theater at that time, and he helped diligently in organizing a campus teachers' union—a tie with the working man—which waxed strong for a few years. A congenial person, respected and well liked by both faculty and students, this man of religion did not attempt to force his views on others but quietly took his stand on these many lines of social action and walked the campus as a model of fusion of principle and action. Like Morgan, he had certain conservative views about personal behavior that put him out of step with liberal students—one should avoid excess and immorality, he thought, particularly the use of alcohol since it prevents good work habits. When such views dropped from the lips of others, they earned the label of prudishness, but in the context of Bishop Jones's tolerance and uncensoring permissiveness, such views were differently perceived and defined. Perhaps better than any other Antiochian, Bishop Jones combined in a way attractive to students and professors the largely implicit morality of modern liberal Quakerism with liberal social and political action. A "very practical, down-to-earth saint," he helped establish an ethos. After him a few persons in the faculty and among the students always significantly embodied this Quaker mode of thought and action.

The number of Quakers or Unitarians in the faculty and student body was never close to a majority, but as in other colleges, the counting of heads is a poor way to understand the religious climate. Just as relatively small numbers of political activists come to define the politics of a campus, so do small numbers of religious or ethical activists often define a major share of the ethical outlook. There is a stratification of influence, somewhat similar to that in politics, among those who participate extensively, those who participate less but attend to the issues, and those who are apathetic about it all. Thus, in the thirties Morgan, then Bishop Jones and the Rockford Circle—relatively small numbers of faculty and administration—set the philosophical tone of the student assemblies, decided the nature of the on-campus religious services, and gave some students a spiritual home in which they might find and nourish an ethical commitment. The religious activists were visible and integrated, and even when they did not set the terms of discussion on religion and ethics, they were an interest group whose views had to be considered. Since they were also in positions of influence in the administration and faculty, their judgments and their very style of discussion and debate counted more than the average.

This Quaker spirit became intertwined with and acted as a support for many of those features of the Morgan philosophy that became part of the long-lasting Antioch ideals. Co-operation and community, self-development and self-help, simple living, tolerance, and academic freedom all found resonance in this liberal campus religion.

MILITANT INTELLECTUALISM

Although the more religious features of the college in the thirties and afterward were closely linked to the ideals of the transformation, a non-religious mode of thought and action that was chiefly an emergent phenomenon developed on campus. Apparently neither the true believers nor the detractors of the twenties anticipated this second major element. Also difficult to characterize—it will be referred to here as a militant intellectualism—it produced a duality in the Antioch culture that has long perplexed observers.

This intellectualism took its cues neither from the principles of Morgan nor from the outlook of the liberal religions but from the avant-garde politics and culture of the metropolitan centers. Its exemplaries were not saintly. They were aggressive, fast talking, self-assured in worldly insight, and in the case of students sophisticated beyond their years. Their concern was usually political, but the variation over time, as among avant-garde intellectuals generally, has been considerable, with the depression years and the late forties a time of intense concern and the middle and late fifties a time of some coolness and detachment, a time for alienation, a time to turn to self, art, and identity. But whatever the level of involvement at Antioch in a given period, the interest, compared to that in other colleges, has been high since the depression. In 1958 Antioch students (freshmen and seniors) were higher in political commitment than those on such politically conscious campuses as Reed, Swarthmore, and the University of California, Berkeley.[21] As reported above, by 1932 the students learned strongly toward the left in politics. They were active with Bishop Jones in the Socialist Party. In the late thirties they became active in the peace movement; and they also became militant in fighting racial discrimination in nearby communities, a line of action that developed into deep town-gown conflict.

Antioch was, thus, a politically engaged campus, not as far as geography would indicate from City College of New York (CCNY), probably the most politically active college of the time. Antioch had then, as now, what other colleges have—some students whose first commitment is the politics (or the arts) of the larger society. The difference is that Antioch had more of them, never a majority but enough to shape a climate. The tiny clusters of student political activists who have existed on many campuses as a residual category, almost an underground, have been for some time at Antioch a larger, more visible, and more central part of the campus.

For this liberalism to develop at a residential college in Ohio is quite a different phenomenon from its occurrence in a municipal college. The

21. Unpublished study of student development, Center for the Study of Higher Education, University of California, Berkeley.

liberalism of the city college can be largely a result of opening doors to the brighter sons and daughters of the working class and of aspiring minorities and, in the process, willy-nilly opening the campus to reformist sentiments and the politics of the underdog. On the private preserve, however, college authorities, if so inclined, can eliminate the first condition of a liberal intellectuality by being agents for its containment. Morgan's experimentalism and commitment to academic freedom provided much latitude at Antioch. More important in the long run was that the developing Unitarian Quakerism gave different viewpoints a sympathetic hearing. Where a conservative religious point of view would have built fences to enclose "legitimate" intellectual and political terrain, the Quaker ethos offered an opening to the left, intellectually and politically. The liberal Quakers of Yellow Springs were not naysayers; they did not spell out prohibitions. Their inclination to moralize became increasingly covert, a subtle and latent moral thrust that others often came to sense but did not need to obey, indeed could readily ignore.

Probably the most important structural element in the growth of an intellectual and political cosmopolitanism at the college was a social base in the upper middle class of the big cities. This base was created in the process of attempting to acquire a bright and willing student body. Here, President Morgan got more than he bargained for. He selected students carefully for brains, motivation, and moral commitment; but the moral component, always the most difficult to judge, did not come through in the form he desired. Bright and well motivated, the students were not about to jump off the dock of modern life. A puritanical self-discipline in the name of a utopian experiment was not for them. Increasingly the students came from the most intellectually and politically aware but socially permissive families—those of urban professional men and of newly sophisticated urban businessmen. Such students were experimental and activist in a modern sense. They had few, if any, of what were fast becoming the old-fashioned, rural virtues. The tone they helped institutionalize was one of sharp questioning and debate on campus and of militant political thrusts into the surrounding society. Since the issues raised bore hard on the character of the college after World War II, we shall return to this topic at length in the following chapter.

If the quiet, almost rural moralists of the campus were on many matters at cross purposes with the militant intellectuals and activists, they still usually exchanged respect and found issues on which they could agree. Among their agreements was a de-emphasis of glamorous sports and normal college social activities. Morgan had held physical vigor high among his ideals, but for him and his Unitarian and Quaker colleagues this belief never suggested the fielding of strong varsity teams. For those who lived simply, walking, camping, and bicycling were appropriate. On this definition the militants of the campus could agree. So, too, for social activities: The moralists preferred them plain and simple; the militants, as self-defined nonconformists, were against all the trappings of the Joe College life. In general, with the requirements of the major subject, the many-tiered requirements of the general education program, the off-campus living of the work periods, the moral thrust of Morganism toward simple, even ascetic, living, and the growing nonconforming orientation of the militant students, the athletic and social events of most other colleges were simply ignored. The characters of Reed and especially of Swarthmore, as we later see, were explicitly defined and were operationally managed against dominant ideals of college sports and social life. At Antioch these student activities were never an important issue, being more implicitly than explicitly excluded. For those with some athletic inclination who strayed into Antioch—perhaps with an eye on an engineering major or the work program—the best the student culture had to offer was informal leadership in hiking and camping or a place in the all-student volunteer fire department.

## Image and Social Base

The attention paid Antioch by outsiders in the thirties did not slacken but, as in the twenties, existed at an unusually high level. Magazine articles, newspaper accounts, and editorials continued to suggest excitement, with the label "experimental college" now a fixture. The main shift in the tenor of public attention was toward acknowledgment of the fact that Antioch had proved a success. In the twenties it had been an eye-catching new scheme; now the scheme was established and validated. Congratulations on success were particularly provoked by three events: Morgan's appointment to the T.V.A. in 1933, while he still remained nominally the president of the college; a fifteenth anniversary testimonial dinner for the college in 1935; and the celebration of a Horace Mann Centennial in 1936.

On the occasion of Morgan's appointment by Roosevelt to be "the boss of Muscle Shoals," *The American Magazine* spoke of Morgan's "Antioch success," a success so tangible that it could be seen in a walk about the school. His students were successful, poised, advanced, and intent on all work.[22] *The New York Times*, taking due note, expressed its pleasure that Morgan not only would retain the presidency of the college but also would continue to write *Antioch Notes;* his philosophical commentary, offered without vagueness or technical terms, had a "unique place." The final point: The college "once Mann's" was "truly now Morgan's".[23]

During 1935 and 1936 public praise came from many quarters. According to *Newsweek*, Morgan had revitalized the college and created successful

22. Webb Waldron, "The Boss of Muscle Shoals," *The American Magazine,* Vol. 116 (August, 1933), pp. 68–69.
23. *The New York Times,* June 15, 1933.

students.[24] The *Saturday Review of Literature* claimed that the students were alert, the school plant was dignified, the faculty were capable, the ideas on sports and religion were sensible and restrained, and—miracle of miracles—the catalogue was realistic in its claims.[25] *Scribner's* wrote that the students were of the highest caliber, there was much independent study, the school government had become community government, and the job opportunities for graduates were great; Morgan has realized Mann's goal of development of the whole individual; the college was very successful, had earned a secure place in American education, was one of the boldest experimental colleges in the country, and had a right to be proud of itself on the fifteenth birthday of its refounding.[26]

*The New York Times* wrote about the college for three days running in the winter of 1935, on the occasion of a dinner in New York City honoring "Antioch's Fifteenth Year," with Morgan as guest of honor. A news account the day before carried Morgan's summary of the aims and results of this experiment. An editorial on the day of the dinner spoke of a tribute richly earned, for the "experiment has been carried out with daring and wisdom, and often with gratifying results." Here was a man and a college taking seriously "the Emersonian ideal of the 'whole personality.'" And, on the third day, back in the news column, came a report that at the dinner the night before messages of congratulation and praise from Mrs. Franklin D. Roosevelt and others had been read.[27]

The Horace Mann Conference in 1936, held at the college, commemorated the centennial of Mann's entry into education. A statue of Mann was dedicated, and speeches were made by John Dewey, Karl T. Compton (Massachusetts Institute of Technology), George F. Zook (American Council on Education), and others. This two-day occasion was further evidence of the success of the college, as well as a recognition of Mann's contributions, and was given publicity in educational journals (e.g., *School and Society*, September 26 and October 24, 1936) as well as in the attentive *New York Times* (October 11, 1936). The matter even put Antioch in movie houses through a *March of Time* pickup of scenes from the celebration.[28]

In addition to the wide reporting and general praise centered on these three events, there was much comment on specific features of the college. The year 1930 saw highly favorable accounts of the charter change that strengthened faculty influence. Henceforth, Antioch was to be something

24. "Antioch—West's Little Harvard Honors Its Study-Earn Pioneer," *Newsweek,* Vol. 6 (November 1935), p. 39.
25. C. Morley, "Notes on Ohio," *Saturday Review of Literature,* Vol. 13 (December, 1935), pp. 11–12.
26. C. A. Hallatz, "The Antioch Experiment," *Scribner's,* Vol. 100 (November, 1936), pp. 56-59.
27. *The New York Times,* November 17, 18, 19, 1935.
28. *Antioch Notes,* Vol. 14, No. 2 (November, 1936).

of a model for beleaguered faculties; here was a place that had instituted
"faculty control" *(The Nation),* a place where the faculty "runs the college"
*(School and Society).*[29] That decade found commentary on such
assorted items as a "professor of work," "cultural mathematics," an essay
contest, a barter plan for coping with the depression, research conducted
by Fels Institute at the college on smoking and on the heart action of
unborn babies, an art appreciation course, Life's Meaning Conferences,
and recreational training.[30] Many of these items were widely publicized
because they were brought to the attention of newspapers and writers by
*Antioch Notes.*

The name of the college began to be used in a way reserved for the
names of only unusual places. We do not ordinarily think of saying "St.
Olaf tackles the depression" or impute such power to the University of
Missouri; but it would not be strange to the ear of Harvard men to hear
that their alma mater was now going to do something about a national
economic recession. So, too, at Antioch. In 1932 a caption in *The New
Republic* (over a letter from Morgan) had it that "Antioch tackles the
depression."[31] Especially within the college, but also outside, the sense of
a unique self had formed and was being inflated by pride in accomplishments. The college was loaded with an aura that could hardly be missed
by the educated, informed man. The glowing editorials in *The New York
Times* alone would have warmed the breakfast coffee of the professional
man wondering whether there were anything new and good in American
higher education—a place where his son might go. We have no consumer
research for the period on what the word was among the commuters on
the 8:04 or among college-going seniors in the better high schools, but
compared to other colleges Antioch was very visible, and public awareness
would have to be correspondingly high. In the large cities and in the East
in general, this awareness was favorably disposed to the college. Little or
no negative information was around, and the liberal intellectualism and
reformist politics of the college found much resonance in sophisticated
circles.

Meanwhile, back home in Ohio, things were not rosy in the image
department, for the negative perception of the second Antioch was also

29. J. F. Kirkpatrick, "The Antioch Faculty Trust," *The Nation,* Vol. 131 (October, 1930), pp. 441–43; and H. B. English, "Faculty Participation in the Government of Antioch College," *School and Society,* Vol. 32 (October, 1930), pp. 495–96.

30. Sources, respectively: "A Professor of Work," *World Tomorrow,* Vol. 14 (January, 1931), p. 4; J. D. Dawson, "Cultural Mathematics at Antioch," *School and Society,*
Vol. 133 (January, 1931), pp. 141–44; *The New York Times,* September 1, 1932; G.R.
Leighton, "They Call It Barter," *Harpers Magazine,* Vol. 167 (August, 1933), pp. 315–
19; *The New York Times,* February 8, 1935; *The New York Times,* February 17, 1935;
*The New York Times,* February 7, 1937; "Recreational Training at a College," *Recreation,* Vol. 32 (September, 1938), p. 355.

31. "Antioch Tackles the Depression," *The New Republic,* Vol. LXXII No. 925
(August, 1932), p. 48.

becoming institutionalized. Morgan did fairly well at getting a bad name under way, although the faculty and the students saw the job through. In the twenties, displeased with the rates of the Dayton Power and Light Company, Morgan built his own electric plant and then not only supplied the college but also sold power to the town of Yellow Springs at reduced rates. This "socialistic" action got him a fight with the private utilities and also, in wider circles, the first significant identification of the college as politically dangerous. Then, Leiserson was brought to the faculty as professor of economics in 1925. He was an experienced hand in labor and welfare economics, having served on an industrial commission in Wisconsin, in labor administration in the United States Department of Labor, and on arbitration boards of the clothing industry. His courses at the college included labor relations, labor management, labor organizations, labor legislation, public utilities, business combinations and competition, and programs for economic reorganization. The courses in banking and business economics he left for the other man in the department. No shrinking scholar, Leiserson boldly and vigorously advocated unemployment insurance in Ohio. This pre-New Deal advocacy brought sharp cries of socialism, and the college came under heavy pressure, from one donor specifically, to fire the professor. The faculty supported Leiserson, and he stayed until 1933, when he became executive secretary of the National Labor Board; but the affair cost the college in financial support from the outraged donor and in reputation in Ohio.

The drift in local public relations became quite discernible in the thirties. The campus throbbed with political activism centered around the New Deal: Bishop Jones and his friends dramatized for the whole state the campus esteem for the Socialist Party; some faculty and some students made no bones about being to the left of the socialists; and the campus was not immune to the Popular Frontism then sweeping the American Left. As indicated earlier, pacifism was popular, and students were beginning their decades of picketing, marching, and otherwise demonstrating for racial integration in nearby communities. In New York City, Antioch would have been judged liberal by most of the circles that count. In southwestern Ohio, it was judged radical by the circles that count as well as by ordinary folk. The perception and sentiment that the college was dangerously leftist became the critical element of its local reputation. This image, based largely on the economic and political issues of the thirties, was to persist, affecting fund-raising and student recruitment. After World War II the Ohio segment of the student body fell below 10 per cent, a fact officials at the college considered undesirable. This change occurred not only because Antioch had attracted national prestige but also because it had negative attraction for students in its area. For a liberal liberal arts college in a conservative area, the result was perhaps close to being inevitable.

In short, by the end of the thirties Antioch was defined as a progressive college. In the liberal view the college was great—experimental, serious, intellectual—the way colleges should be. The conservative view, held most strongly near the college, was that Antioch was dangerous to youth and society.

## Financial Resources

Inspirational, transforming leaders often let finances take the hindmost. Antioch leaped ahead in the twenties because Morgan took the big chance including a plunge into debt. His style of financing—tuition and annual gifts—was hand to mouth, providing no steady and stabilizing endowment. As mentioned earlier, the president borrowed over $300,000 between 1920 and 1924 from Charles Kettering, his main benefactor, and then made little headway on retiring this loan. Altogether during the twenties and early thirties the college borrowed over $720,000; by 1942 it had paid back only $330,000, leaving at that late date obligations approaching $400,000. Interest and amortization charges on this debt amounted to a fancy $28,000 a year; and $125,000 of the total debt was a bank debt renewable every six months, and hence it could be called during a crisis. Clearly, the "mortgage" was no small matter. It was, among other things, "a serious reflection upon the college for accreditation purposes." Accreditation came from the North Central Association of Colleges and Secondary Schools, and North Central took note that Antioch ranked among the top 9 per cent of its members in educational expenditures per student, in the top 14 per cent in stable income per student, but among the bottom 6 per cent in amount of debt per student.[32] In short, the college kept up its expenditures by keeping up its debts, and the experimental decade was still not paid for in 1942. During World War II Antioch raised over a quarter million dollars, essentially to retire debts incurred in the early twenties. A ceremony held in 1943 to burn the mortgage was a pleasure long overdue.

If Antioch was living high in quality of programs, it was in part because the faculty provided their own subsidy to help carry the college through the depression. When the annual gifts fell off in the early thirties and the college was left with tuition as its only major source of income, the administration and faculty faced the critical problem of whether to discharge staff members. The decision was humane: No one was to go; all would stay and divide the reduced rations. For 1932–33 "the faculty did not receive their usual salaries, but did get compensation adequate for ordinary living needs. By agreement, the faculty waived all future claim to the remaining amounts due on salaries." [33] From this point the faculty drew

32. *An Antioch College Prospectus,* 1942. Antiochiana, Antioch College.
33. *Antioch Notes,* Vol. 11, No. 1 (September, 1933), no page numbers.

allowances in lieu of salaries, and take-home money was computed on the basis of such factors as number of children in the family. Everyone still had a job and an income that sagged to 68 per cent of the regular schedule in 1933–34, averaged 76 per cent in 1934–35, and was up to 85 per cent in 1935–36.[34] The drawing allowance device was used through the middle and late thirties and remained a principle even after World War II, by which time pay had been re-established at stated salary levels. The drawing allowance reflected an intense sense of community. In effect many in the faculty were taking shoes from their own families in order to retain junior faculty, to keep intact the college program, and to block the accumulation of debt. Here the devotion and responsibility cultivated by faculty participation in government was of inestimable value. Men then junior in the faculty would never forget this decision, freely recalling it more than twenty years later in reflecting on the thirties. Of such measures is devotion made.

The decade of transformation was, thus, eventually paid for, but the carrying of the debt in the second decade and the virtual absence of endowment cost the college in financial health and the faculty in the normal material rewards of work. Here, commitment had to serve in lieu of money, with men taking psychic rather than material rewards. Many suffered; but if they were to do it again, they would probably do it the same way. The faculty contributed part of their standard of living, while the president labored long and hard to eliminate "the budgetary inflations of more prosperous days" and to reduce the debt.[35]

## Conclusion

By 1940 the character of the second Antioch was relatively fixed, and this character had distinction. Among the pieces forming the institutional mosaic were some held in common with all other leading liberal arts colleges: bright students, able and teaching-oriented faculty, and a certain sophistication and liberality in intellectual tone. Among the elements were several held in common with only a few other colleges: strong faculty authority; political activism and a commensurate reputation; and intellectual activism, including a campus-based "Little Mag" and avant-garde performing arts. And then there were unique elements of great prominence: the full-scale work program and the community government involvement of students. All in all, this character was unusually elaborate for a small college, and this elaborateness in its integration produced an intense organization, a system of effort and involvement that could not be taken lightly by those who set foot in the college.

34. *Ibid.*, Vol. 12, No. 1 (September, 1934); Vol. 13, No. 3 (October, 1935); Vol. 14, No. 4 (December, 1936); no page numbers.
35. *Ibid.*, Vol. 14, No. 4 (December, 1936), no page numbers.

# *Chapter 3.* Adjustment

WORLD WAR II was a watershed for many American colleges. Up to that time American higher education, although generous in admissions by European standards, was still for a small minority. Enrollments in relation to the eighteen to twenty-one age group had increased steadily from 4 per cent in 1900 to 8 per cent in 1920, 12 per cent in 1930, and 16 per cent in 1940, or 4 per cent a decade. After the war and beginning with the G.I. Bill, the federal legislation that subsidized the education of veterans, the country moved rapidly into mass higher education. The proportion in college almost doubled in a few years (from the 16 per cent of 1940 to 30 per cent in 1950) and by 1960 had climbed to 37 per cent.[1] Such expansion was bound to change the whole climate in which colleges operated, for it affected the distribution of students, the size of campuses and state systems, the expectations of the average student, and the competitive position of different colleges.

The war years also ruptured the continuity of the campus. Normal student bodies were not available to carry on the ancient rituals, and the substitute students obtained by colleges participating in military educational programs—the Army Specialized Training Program and the Navy V-12 Program—hardly entered into the culture of the campus. Thus, the war

1. U. S. Bureau of the Census, *Historical Statistics of the United States, Colonial Times to 1957* (Washington, D. C., 1960), pp. 210–11; and U. S. Department of Health, Education, and Welfare, *Higher Education,* Vol. XVII (January, 1961), p. 17.

weakened the hold of traditional thought and practice, rendering colleges of fixed character somewhat more vulnerable than they would otherwise have been to the fast-changing demands of the postwar period.

Antioch was among those colleges for whom the two decades following 1945 had of necessity to be a time of adaptive evolution. Certain lines of development begun in the twenties and thirties, e.g., nonconformity and political action by students, had not been played out but rather were to come into their full significance in this later period, requiring attention and adjustment on the part of those most devoted to the institution. Changing demands of students and faculty tested the appropriateness of the developed character of the college in a society of growing expertise. The times dictated an interest in specialization within the faculty and the student body, an interest antithetical to much of what the college stood for. The problems of adaptation in this successful college show in sharp relief the strains on liberal education in an age of specialization and the conflict in values obtaining when a college becomes truly liberal in regulation of student behavior and in politics.

## The Shift Toward Professionalism

Higher education became an increasingly serious matter in the late forties and the fifties. The older veteran, who dominated the campuses in the late forties, took a no-nonsense approach to education. The war had delayed his educational and occupational progress, and now was the time to catch up. Then, no sooner had the serious veteran begun to wane as a campus force than the growing international tension turned many thoughts toward the college-educated as national manpower. A new vocabulary in governmental, business, and academic circles—"investment in education," "the knowledge industry," and "the production of scientists and engineers"—was evidence of this change.

The temper of a technological society is hardly kind to the leisurely contemplation of history and literature. Favoring the extended multiversity, the new tone placed the general education offered by the small campus in doubt. Students in the small as well as in the large colleges increasingly had to look upon their undergraduate years as a training ground for graduate or professional school. Around 1930, 25 to 30 per cent of Antioch graduates went on to further education;[2] in 1958 over half of the entering freshmen were already anticipating graduate or professional school, and four and five years later over 80 per cent of this class, as seniors, planned to continue.[3] Some of these students, knowing they would specialize later,

2. "The Antioch Program, 1933–34. A Report on the Affairs of Antioch College," p. 29. Antiochiana, Antioch College.

3. Unpublished study of student development, Center for the Study of Higher Education, University of California, Berkeley.

felt free to partake of a broad education; and many had selected Antioch in order to participate gladly in the work program and community government. But a growing band among those anticipating graduate school felt a necessity to concentrate on classroom work and the major to the exclusion of the other components of the Antioch scheme. The move toward specialized academic interest by future chemists, psychologists, and English professors became a current threatening to undercut Antioch ideals by eroding the work program and community government.

The student apprentice-specialist saw a growing number of appropriate models among the adults on campus as the faculty also swung toward narrow interests. The national trend toward academic specialization had long troubled the college. As seen earlier, Arthur Morgan's main dilemma in recruitment centered on the contradiction between his preference for generalists and the importance of specialists in gaining academic stature for the college. Despite his feeling that he compromised his preferences too much, he had left the college in the hands of people thoroughly committed to a multisided approach to education. These professors and administrators were not seriously challenged until the late fifties, by which time the young men in the faculty had become noticeably more specialized than their elders. The Ph.D. degree had been held by only 30 per cent of the faculty in 1930, with one-half having proceeded no further than a bachelor's degree. The proportion holding the higher, more specialized degree increased to 40 per cent by 1940, was still at that level in 1950, and then jumped during the fifties to 60 per cent.[4]

The young specialists were not so attached as their elders to all that Antioch had become. About a dozen faculty members, nearly all of them new to the faculty in the fifties, formed an identification around criticism of the commitment to an array of programs and activities outside the classroom. Scholarship, they felt, should be the focus, the first and perhaps even the only business: The work program and community government were extraneous to the character of a first-rate liberal arts college. One effective spokesman for these Young Turks publicly defined their conceptions and criticisms of the college as follows:[5]

Almost gone is the day when a faculty member lived with an easy conscience and no publications, content in knowing that his catholic interests, his teaching, his campus and socially-conscious activities, or his part in the college's planning were sufficient cause for his rise through the faculty ranks.

The new faculty member is now likely to have but one aim, perhaps to emulate the scholar-specialist under whom he recently studied at the university.

4. Figures computed from faculty listings in catalogues of the college for 1930, 1940, 1950, and 1960.
5. Robert Maurer, "The Specialist and Liberal Education," *Antioch Notes*, Vol. 37, No. 4 ( January, 1960 ), no page numbers.

The teacher may feel justified in cutting himself off . . . from all interests outside his staked-out province of scholarship.

[The newer teachers] are men of another time and another place, and social idealism and scholarship are two different things.

This argument struck hard at the ideals of the majority of the faculty, senior men from the twenties and thirties and others who had joined and remained with the college because of its special nature. The counterattack, in private and public, was vigorous. One senior professor long active in campus and community affairs put it this way:[6]

It is not entirely clear in all this whether the presence of students, in any great numbers, would actually sabotage the work of the college.

The college in which community government evolved as an integral and vital part of the educational program differed in fundamental ways from one to which the preceding dicta would apply. It was conceived, not as a kind of British Museum on the Little Miami, as valuable a cultural contribution as that might have been, but as an educational institution. It was one in which necessary administration was not limited to the provision of faculty studies, a library and research facilities, and a bursar. Most quaintly of all, there were students, whose development was the primary responsibility of the faculty, and actually the college's reason for being.

There may be some who feel that they are of another time and another place. Actually, let's face it. We are here, and in the insistent present. And this is why it might be best if we got straightened out on what we are committed to doing.

A young faculty member, committed to the developed character of the college, had no doubt about whose time and place this was:[7]

The administration must recruit faculty members who are in sympathy with the aims of the college's student program. On the other side, it is entirely up to the teacher who finds himself in the ambiguous position of a specialist uninterested in the virtues of a liberal arts program to resolve his conflict by seeking more congenial pastures elsewhere.

The faculty, in short, was not about to give up its holistic approach. Despite the thrusts of the often respected younger scholars, the commitment to traditional character was still firmly in place. Yet the young men had a point: Times were changing and perhaps a self-defined experimental college ought not sit still on the forms of bygone days. As President James P. Dixon (1959– ) explained to the Board of Trustees in 1962, the expansion of knowledge in the modern period was the fundamental cause of the "tendency to retreat from the holistic notion to a definition of the college as a workshop for the scholar." If the work program and community gov-

6. John C. Sparks, "Discussion of Community Government—Faculty Meeting, 29 September, 1960," mimeo. Antioch College.
7. David Carney, "The Specialist and Teaching," *Antioch Notes*, Vol. 38, No. 4 (January, 1961), no page numbers.

ernment were to remain vigorous, the college would probably need, on the one side, to guard its recruitment, but would also need, on the other side, to rethink the forms of its holistic approach and probably to revamp them to fit the demands of the scholarly teacher and the apprentice-expert student.

The scheme of alternating periods of study and work had been revised through the years to accommodate individual students, and freshmen and seniors, according to plan, were on campus more often than off. As a result there were usually a hundred to two hundred more students on than off campus, and the college was not gaining full advantage of the additional time, space, and resources made possible by the work plan. In 1961, after several years of debate on principles and consideration of alternative operating plans, the college modified the work program in such a way as to recommit itself to off-campus educational experience. It redefined the alternating period as part of the college character by initiation of a full two-college plan. A scheme worked out for the normal student involved a four-quarter, full-year schedule for five years. At any given time the number of enrolled and tuition-paying students off campus would equal or exceed the number on campus. With space for eight hundred, the college expanded to an enrollment of sixteen hundred. The new, full two-college plan made student tuition an even larger part of the financial foundation: it covered 80 to 90 per cent of operating costs, and thus, any future major decrease in student time off campus would have direct, heavy financial repercussions. The decision of 1961 made it clear to all that the practice of off-campus education would be around for a long time. It was an effective, practical way to recommit the college fully to the work-study program.

At the same time the program was made more flexible and more acceptable to the internal critics. A concept from earlier days, that of an extramural program, was reactivated. Each student would, indeed, spend every other period out of the classroom, but he need not be on a job. The extramural experience could be foreign study—a new Antioch Abroad Program. It could be independent study, attendance at another college or university, or anything else that might occur to a student or faculty member that would warrant definition and credit as a reasonably systematic and effective educational experience. Thus, those students who felt, with the Young Turks, that eight, nine, or ten periods of work were too many (redundant became the critical word) could have only four or five such sessions, especially if they were bound for graduate school, and in place of work, they could use study abroad and other plans for several extramural sessions. Thus, while recommitting itself to the work program, the college also seriously modified it by allowing alternatives.

The specialization of the post-World War II faculty and the challenge to the work program in the fifties increased the unease of the Personnel Division, the full-time staff responsible for the operation of the work scheme. Their travail included a loss of tenure when for a period begun during the presidency of Samuel Gould (1954–59), the definition of teacher and academic man swung back toward the normal professional one that excluded those whose work was located outside the classroom. The P.D. counselors, always somewhat shy of full legitimacy, moved toward the marginal position of nonfaculty. Problems of staff stability and separation increased accordingly, with the counselors pulling together in self-defense. Part of any solution to the problem of the role of the work program was the status of this group in the college.

When in the early sixties the work program was rechristened the extramural program, the Personnel Division became the Extramural Department, the counselors were given the new title of extramural associate (in specific fields, e.g., humanities), and they again became eligible for tenure. Along with this improved position, however, went an understanding that the staff of this department should increasingly have the academic background and talent, including specialization in an academic field, normally appropriate to professors and satisfactory for part-time teaching in the regular departments. The counselors were moved from the administration of the Dean of Students to that of the Dean of the Faculty. The balance struck in an adaptive change again attempted to reassert a traditional component but, at the same time, to render it capable of responding to new demands antithetical to old ways, specifically to the demands of specialized academic knowledge and performance.

For this experimental college the problem of adaptive balance in its work program was clearly one of how to combine its historic progressivism with modern professionalism. The tension between general education and specialization inherent in American college education had to be acute at Antioch because of the unusual breadth of its conception of general education and specifically because it had committed itself to major programs that were away from the direct day-to-day control of the professor. The specialist, through his own work, could not quietly erode a program that was structurally separated, was defended by a full-time staff, and had contributed strongly to college income. The legitimacy of the program had to be directly challenged and overtly deliberated; out of this deliberation came the new policy.

As it was with the work program, so it was with community government, which also resided outside the definition of college that the young specialists in the faculty in the fifties and early sixties were willing to articulate. Some on campus might want to play this game after school, they maintained, but it should be clearly understood that it was extracurricular, not on a par with the regular classroom, and that the "socially-conscious activities" of the college should not be confused with scholarship. Here, in contrast to the work program situation, faculty sentiment could directly undercut since community government could not function without the weekly, even daily, input of faculty time and energy. Specifically, faculty members had to serve on Community Council, there to sit endless hours in the late afternoon or evening, often party to dreary debate and often outvoted by students determined to make the same mistakes or to invent new ones. Those who liked this kind of activity or who were at least willing to suffer it as a duty became fewer in number. Older men grew too tired to volunteer again, and more of the younger men wanted to turn to their books or their families at the end of the day.

While loss of community is commonly bemoaned on campuses by alumni, students, and older faculties, at Antioch it had to be more than bemoaned. The ideals of campus community had been taken seriously at this college, and much hard work in the twenties and particularly in the thirties had gone into providing the normative and structural ingredients for it. With community government a core of the institutional self-definition, the gradual weakening of its operations was bound to cause agonizing reappraisal by those who cared. When enough faculty would not stand for election to the council to provide alternatives for the voters, indeed when there were not even enough to fill the faculty positions without an obvious drawing of straws to take an unwanted turn at an obnoxious duty, what then? Should community government be abandoned? By the early sixties its strongest defenders in the faculty were ready to say it had become a shell of its former self:[8]

Community government has, in my view, degenerated seriously in the postwar period until it has become almost a caricature of itself.

[There has been] a long slow crumbling through the years. [Among the reasons for this is that] there has been a drastic decline in faculty interest, and in student-faculty interaction in non-academic enterprise. . . .

If faculty members could not muster the enthusiasm necessary to sit around the tables of the council and its committees and to otherwise participate in community government, their shift in interest toward professional concerns was indeed at fault. But this shift was not the only cause of the decline in faculty interest and was not the basic cause of the travail of community government. The faculty were also put off by changes in student attitudes toward the relation of community to one's private affairs and social acts. These changes in attitude were the fundamental problems in adapting the governance of the campus to the post-World War II setting.

## The Tension Between Freedom and Responsibility

The student body at Antioch grew increasingly independent after the war, drawing apart from faculty and administration. This separation was a

8. John C. Sparks, *The Antiochian*, Vol. 34, No. 1 (January, 1963), pp. 4–5.

function partly of the growing size of the campus and the disposition of the faculty, discussed above, to pull away to other interests and partly of the rupturing of student traditions of community by the war years, followed by an assumption of great personal freedom by the veterans in the late forties. Most important, however, was the sustained push for individual freedom after the veterans' day by class after class of the liberated children of the avant-garde suburbs. The adolescent who defined democracy to mean personal freedom above everything else and who then chose to attend Antioch because of its reputation for permissiveness came to see the college as a vehicle of freedom. It was then his sworn duty to increase freedom on campus, to expand the zone of tolerance of student behavior against the forces of reaction.

The student body had always possessed a tendency to become an insistent interest group within community government since students have some genuine interests different from those of the faculty and the administration—and of the wives of the faculty and the administration. But in the twenties and thirties a well-supported ideology of consensus had readily contained student separatism. The tendency became considerably stronger after 1945 as students came to college ready to assert the rights of young adults. Students aggressive in seeking maximum autonomy tended to turn community government into a protective association, one that would ward off adult surveillance and control. The student members of the council were elected largely by students. If they were not already strong defenders of students' rights, they could be directly pressured, even recalled. With the ideology of freedom and the structure of community government as shields, the students did largely as they pleased, on and off campus. No matter how much student actions might outrage local sentiments, campus authorities had relatively little leverage on student behavior.

Outsiders, however, rarely understood the subtle distinction between community government and the campus as a whole and persisted in expecting collective control, *in loco parentis,* over the individual student. Held responsible for what students as individuals and community government as a collectivity did, the administration and faculty—and many students—found the tension between freedom and responsibility growing intolerable. To understand the peculiar quality of the Antioch problem, we have to consider it within the context of the handling of student conduct in different colleges.

OPEN FACE HEDONISM

A common task of deans of students and vice-chancellors of student activities is to overlook and if necessary to cover up student behavior that if dragged into the light will be viewed as misconduct by many persons on and off campus. Without a certain amount of looking the other way, the administrator would himself soon collapse from frustration and guilty knowledge in coping with deviant behavior and breakage of social rules. When the official cannot look the other way, discussion and disclosure of what he knows often worsen public relations. Thus, for the good of the organization, he ordinarily must not see much of what goes on, he must keep disclosure within the family, and he must have rules that present to the public an honorable posture.

Many residential colleges, for example, finding themselves *in loco parentis*, have in the past simply refused to talk intelligently about sex. In place of discussion, they have a list of prohibitions that hopefully present a discouraging face to students and a reassuring face to the public. For such colleges no one has yet shown what the impact of this administrative posture is on the students' sexual life. Since this approach defines sex as illicit and warns of harsh punishment, it at least pushes the locale of intimacy away from the administration building to the automobile parked off campus, the deeper sectors of the woods, the recesses of the fraternity house, or the ubiquitous motel just down the highway. The rule-oriented approach may depress sexual activity, but this outcome depends more on the background of the students and on their inclination to submit to or to subvert official regulation than on the rules.

The brighter the student body in modern times, the more the difficulties with strict rules. The brighter students are more sophisticated, more inclined to think and do for themselves, more able to torment the college officer with sharp thrusts of reason and ridicule. The better liberal arts colleges have increasingly relaxed their rules and taken the position that conduct, from sex to drinking, dress, and library loans, is open for discussion. Progressive colleges, in particular, take an open attitude because they are strongly committed to student initiative, expressiveness, and responsibility. By 1940 Antioch had become a model of the open attitude, its philosophy and program dictating that students be treated as adults. The work program alone, with its periods of unchaperoned living off campus, made this definition necessary. Thus, the college had little of the posture of containment. It did not present this face to students or to the outside world.

The Achilles heel of this position is that others can easily see officials as condoning, even encouraging, what happens when responsibility slides toward license. Students come to college with a variety of moral standards, and some have standards defined by others as no standards. For all but the best of men, responsibility occasionally fares badly in the presence of libidinal drives and impulse. Norms bend, blur, and break. When the moral offense occurs, the colleges with an impeccable list of thou-shalt-nots easily establish institutional innocence; they point to the warning of the rules, punish the transgressors, and promise future vigilance. In contrast, the colleges that have set foot down the road of student responsibility are caught without protection in depth provided by massive prohibition, and this posture opens the door to the public charge of encouraging lust and license.

Campuses that vigorously pursue student responsibility commonly have honor codes as a form of social control, but nearly everywhere at the schools of the bright and sophisticated, the students have eroded the old-fashioned morality of the codes, moving from control to freedom. Students have gradually redefined their codes to mean "do as you think best for yourself and do not be the judge of others"—which, with little change, can become "every man for himself." Whether in reference to dress, cleanliness, sex, alcohol, marijuana, or general deportment, the honor codes have tended to become emptied of normative proscriptions. At Reed, as we shall later see, this tendency reached an extreme. At Antioch the trend also ran strong. The honor system, which served as an aid to self-discipline for some students, has, for others, buttressed a personal philosophy of individualism and provided an ideological defense of behavior that draws disapproval and potential sanction.

The Antioch community experienced a high point of permissiveness toward student behavior in the late forties and early fifties. An attitude of tolerance had grown within the faculty and administration as the effort to expand student responsibility moved steadily ahead in the presidency of Algo Henderson (1936–48). Then came the World War II veterans—older and more mature, worldly, and, at Antioch, liberal and independent. Their time on campus happened to overlap with an adventuresome attempt to run the college on the principles of group dynamics, an effort sustained by Douglas McGregor, an authority on human relations, during the five years of his presidency (1948–54). McGregor tried to buttress community government with a decentralized town meeting scheme. The whole community met in various spots—classrooms, lounges, faculty homes—to discuss campus issues. Participation apparently reached an all-time high, and students made themselves heard clearly in the councils of the college. But the procedure was very time demanding and finally entailed too great a loss of influence and drive from the center. With small-group discussions of every issue, the diffusion of authority inherent in multigovernment became scatteration.[9] Decision-making by mass consensus, from the bottom up, moved the college further down the road marked on campus by the phrase, "You do not say 'No' to an Antioch student." For some in the administration, faculty, and student body, if anyone had become more equal than others, it was the student.

Thus, as the students pushed for maximum personal liberty, the adults of the campus gave and gave, and the problems grew. They included violation of open hall hours and use of the gym for "social purposes";

9. After his Antioch experience, McGregor concluded that a college president could not operate successfully as an advisor to his organization; rather, "the boss must boss." "On Leadership," *Antioch Notes*, Vol. 31, No. 9 (May, 1954), no page numbers.

student cheating in examinations; nonreturn of library books; theft of lab equipment; significant financial losses in the bookstore and cafeteria under self-service arrangements; increasing complaints from employers about students' lack of consideration for others on the job; and a rising tide of parental concern about "the atmosphere." The Administrative Council, confronted with this impressive catalogue of specific problems in 1952 concluded that "the honor code is deteriorating seriously":[10]

> In situation after situation, student feeling seems to be "so many people are ignoring the honor system that there's nothing we can do about it—we're outnumbered."
>
> There seems to be a general "social pressure against social pressure": the concerned individual is labeled a do-gooder, social worker, or busy-body.
>
> There is evidence of a growing feeling that what one individual does is nobody else's business; that each individual's standards are "the best for him."
>
> Many students and faculty members assume that the only justification for standards and regulations is "public relations."

Given the general cultural definitions of the time, a college can proceed only so far in the direction of student individualism, and Antioch was not about to test all the limits. The concerns of faculty and administration for some order, for an adult-influenced morality, for good public relations, and for the name of the college brought a counterattack, and the battle was joined between the adults, appearing to the students as agents of retrenchment, and the students, appearing to the adults as irresponsible hedonists. Thus, the president after McGregor, Gould, fought the battle of student conduct. Part of his mission was to reduce the quotient of beards and bare feet and to diminish the public perception, strong in Ohio and not unknown elsewhere, that the campus was a den of immorality.

As early as 1946, as well as during and after Gould's presidency, the issue that persisted and excited interest above all others on campus was open halls. Could men visit in the women's dormitories and vice versa, and if so during what hours and days? During these hours should room doors be shut or open the width of a book, a foot, or all the way? How should women dress in their dorms going to and from the shower when men are known to be around? When a couple is alone, do feet have to be on the floor? Must lights be on? What are the rights of a roommate for privacy and sleep when lovers are in session? Year after year students went around and around with one another and with the faculty and administration on the rationales and details of employing dormitory facilities for the entertainment of the other sex. The war veterans had thrown open the privileges; their younger successors in large number were determined to keep them. Faculty members found themselves going to the mat time and again, locked in such heavy debate with students on this and other issues that

10. Administrative Council Minutes, April 23, 1952. Antioch College.

Community Council became known as a bear pit. The rules were modified again and again—changing the days, extending the hours—reflecting the unwillingness of one or another major party to let go of the issue. The adults in the community could cite many incidents of license and tragedy resulting from this form of personal freedom. The students, safeguarding a precious freedom available in few other colleges, could point with telling effectiveness to the public relations concern that added vigor to the position of the administration.

President Dixon, Gould's successor and an Antioch graduate strongly sympathetic to the character of the college, had a relatively laissez faire attitude on open halls and student morality. But he also took the position early in his presidency that the college was too near the brink of moral and financial disaster for the administration to sit by. Holding that "the impression of irresponsibility created by the present open hall system interferes with recruitment of students and securing funds, and is endangering the survival of the institution," he suggested shortening the visiting hours, and he backed his suggestion with firmness:[11]

> Some kind of action will be taken. . . . If the solution does not in my judgment solve the dilemma, I'll have to seek for some other solution, because this is my responsibility. . . . We stand in danger of the present circumstances. . . . We need to make clear what are our intentions in terms of community. Individual behavior has to be regulated. . . . We tend not to be hooked on to the rest of the world.

The college was finding that student conduct and public reaction to it were points of considerable vulnerability.

POLITICAL ACTION

If sex in the dormitory was *the* problem of on-campus conduct, the problem in the highly visible off-campus locales was student political action. The tension between student freedom and responsibility is noticeable when a radical faction takes the name of the college to the civil rights picket line or to a public demonstration. When the invasion of Cuba by Cuban refugees and the American Central Intelligence Agency took place in April, 1961, the Antioch chapter of the Fair Play for Cuba Committee hit the bricks within a few hours, picketing in protest around the state capitol in Columbus, but the thirty-five protest marchers did not take the fifty-mile ride as individuals. They were not bashful in identifying themselves, and as in dozens of incidents during the previous years, mass media charged the protest to the college: "pro-Castro demonstrators from Antioch." Public comments, excited by the patriotic passion of the day, were more than usually inflamed. The reaction went so far as an attack on the

11. President Dixon's testimony before the Community Council, as reported in *Antioch College Record*, April 21, 1961.

campus by students of Ohio Northern University. President Dixon was hanged in effigy—"Traiter [sic] to Ohio"—together with Fidel Castro, and crosses were burned on campus. Serious as it was, with its implications of physical reprisal and midnight terror, this direct attack could be later dismissed as the work of a dozen boys from a fraternity house, but the outrage of the general citizenry, of the Ohio mass media, and of the men in and around the Board of Trustees could not be overlooked. The situation called for action by the college.

The obvious response, one fixed in the mores of traditional academic administration, was an apology and an explanation that the students were acting as individual citizens, not as representatives of the college; but even though sorely embarrassed by its radical fringe, the college did not make a public apology. The day following the picketing by the Castro supporters, President Dixon told a news conference that social action was part of education at Antioch and hence that the college encouraged rather than discouraged the direct involvement of students in community, national, and world affairs. This statement, with minor revision, was later widely quoted and was used in national efforts to define the principle of academic freedom for students.

The public defense was vigorous, but the private doubts remained. Should students, spurred by passion, rush off campus to demonstrate their views just as soon as they could paint their signs? This was freedom, but was it educational and responsible? A round of discussion began, prodded by the administration, about the right of the rest of the campus to be consulted before a picket line was formed. A forty-eight–hour notification —or cooling-off period—was instituted, under the elegant concept of "due process of consultation." A group contemplating action had to notify, discuss, and be advised. Students could have, indeed were encouraged to have, their social action, but they had to come back from the brink of anarchy. The president summarized the results as follows:[12]

Antioch College has sanctioned student social action as legitimate within our definition of education. We put the individual and his concerns, and then the small group and its concerns, at the center of our values. It happens also that on the issue of racial equality this has long been our institutional policy. Our experience with using the resources of the world for education in work and study has convinced us that participative action is, at least for some people, an important aspect of scholarly inquiry.

We have said that Antioch will not try to define the social truth for individuals or groups, but that when the truths they reach appear to lead to social action, their truths and the ways they are to be applied must be shared with the entire college community. This is our mandate of due process of consultation. It is intended to evaluate the proposed action of individuals against the needs of

12. James P. Dixon, "The New Evangelism," *Antioch Notes*, Vol. 41, No. 2 (October, 1963), no page numbers.

the institution as a whole, and to inform individual action with the best judgment and wisdom of community members. Thus education can take place. Otherwise, the random dictates of individual conscience would push the community toward a state of anarchy that could be dealt with only by the most authoritarian techniques.

The problem of responsible social action would not be easily solved at Antioch but rather would remain inherent in its character. The picketing of racially segregated businesses in neighboring communities, so persistently carried out over two decades that it seemed a way of life, resulted in a new high of tumult and anger when, in the spring of 1963, mass action around the barbershop of a die-hard segregationist in Yellow Springs led to the use of fire hoses and sixteen arrests—this in the most progressive community in southwest Ohio, with a Negro police chief. The college, a few weeks later, had to decide whether it would graduate a student sitting in jail charged with trespassing and inciting to riot. It did! The following spring (1964) the conflict escalated; forty Antioch students, together this time with sixty others (mainly from nearby Central State, a Negro college), disobeyed a court order prohibiting a mass demonstration and were duly arrested.

The commitment to social action as a form of education had put the college on a path that few would deliberately tread. In a new period of student sophistication and assertive political action, this commitment ensured administrative difficulties. As elsewhere, there would need to be the steady continuity of resources, organization, and teaching necessary for ordinary education. On top of that, much energy would be needed to reconcile the sharp thrusts of direct, often radical, political action. Despite the success of the college and the strength of its fixed distinctive character, this road was not an easy one for faculty or administration.

## Antioch 1960

Thus, despite the institutionalization of a certain character at Antioch in the twenties and thirties, this character was by no means entirely fixed in place after World War II but rather evolved significantly to cope with new demands from within and without. Antioch moved toward strong scholarship and professional preparation; it became larger and less cohesive than it had been before; it suffered growing strain in the governance of student affairs. But the evolution, although important to note and understand, did not bury the past. It did not, in reflecting social trends, make the college a carbon copy of other leading liberal arts colleges. The distinctive qualities of 1940 were still distinctive in 1960. The college of the early sixties was still a reflection of the ideals developed in the first two decades following the abrupt change of 1920. The concept of off-campus educational experience was as firmly established as ever. The forms of community government had weakened, but the spirit of political involvement, directed to off-campus issues, permeated the climate of the campus, which remained exceedingly liberal in educational and political practice.

Evidence of its differences exists in comparative data on student attitudes. Students at Antioch in 1960, when compared with students in other colleges at the time, were quite liberal in their politics, about as much as were those at Reed and Swarthmore, more than those at the University of California (Berkeley) and San Francisco State College, and sharply different in political persuasion from those at such religious colleges as St. Olaf, the University of Portland, and the University of the Pacific (see Appendix 3). They were very liberal on civil rights and civil liberties more so than students of most other known liberal institutions and probably as much as those at any college in the country. They had much social consciousness and were willing to commit themselves to public service and citizen participation. Many of the girls had attitudes appropriate for social work and teaching, giving the student body as a whole a noticeable nurturing quality.

The faculty had similar attitudes, being about as liberal politically as any in the country. In a survey in 1963 less than 10 per cent were identified with the Republican Party, and not one faculty member considered himself a conservative Republican (see Appendix 2). Men identified themselves as Democrats, chiefly as liberal Democrats; and as independent or Socialist, chiefly as liberal independent. They were very liberal on political issues—e.g., strongly opposing legislative investigation of the political beliefs of faculty members—and they were unusually willing to grant academic freedom to students—e.g., to let students publish what they pleased in their newspapers and journals. About one-half of the faculty were not identified with a religion and considered themselves largely indifferent (44 per cent) or opposed to religion, but about one-sixth of the faculty claimed they were deeply religious, a proportion considerably larger than that at Reed, the University of California (Berkeley), and San Francisco State College.

In sum, the dominant economic and educational trends of the postwar period pressed hard on Antioch to attenuate the elements of its character that most deviated from those of the mainstream. The problem of continuity of character was one of adjusting to the times while maintaining a culture that deviated from that of nearly all other liberal arts colleges as well as from that of the noneducational world.

Clearly by the early sixties selection and assimilation, especially of faculty, were crucial steps. If Morgan felt in the early thirties that he had failed in selection, so did the most fervent proponents of his plan three decades later. The vigorous opposition of young men in the faculty to the work program meant to many of the older figures that by lifting their eyes from the selection process for a decade or so, during the regimes of Presidents McGregor and Gould, they had endangered the Antioch distinction. The college would clearly have to be sensitive about its values in future selection to ensure sufficient support in the faculty for its traditional character. This process would not be easy since expertise in a discipline would often need to be the paramount criterion in asking one man rather than another to join the faculty. The strength and continuity of established character depended on the capacity of the college to recruit and hold men who combined support of uncommon general education programs with the specialized competence respected within a discipline and esteemed by the bright and well-prepared students the college was recruiting. In the early sixties, the college still had enough such men constituting the core of the faculty in scholarly standing and campus power so that its basic contradictions remained contained by an evolving consensus.

The Antioch reputation gave it much selection of student body, and hence it had an unusually sophisticated and liberal entering class. Also, compared to other colleges, Antioch had impact on its students, significantly accentuating the already high sophistication and liberality of the majority and converting some in the minority who were initially weak on these characteristics.[13] This impact resulted in part from an intensity of interaction stronger than that which occurs on most other campuses.

On any campus one can find some groups of students characterized by intense involvement, but nearly always that is a characterization of the part and not the whole; at the same time the involvement of other students is loose, even passive, and significant portions of the faculty may have the quietude of calm scholars. The administrations on most campuses are rule-oriented and not involved emotionally in the affairs of the students. Thus, although one or two parts of any campus may heat up, other parts remain cool, offering sanctuary to those who prefer the quiet life or find they must occasionally back away from intense involvement to maintain equilibrium.

At Antioch escape from intense involvement was difficult. In countless ways the normal pace of life could engage one's emotions and drag one in. The traditions and practices of intended community and the long-standing effort to make a community out of strangers heightened the intensity of affairs. The strong ideological commitment of faculty and students to academic freedom not only was a condition for speaking up but also provided an urge to do so. Community government, as earlier explained, was an elaborate bit of machinery for involvement. The norms of the student culture pressed students to be engaged in campus and world affairs. As a result, many were caught up.

But the intensity seemed also to contribute to dropping out. Some students found the hectic pace too much; some found the political action too

13. Unpublished study of student development Center for the Study of Higher Education, University of California, Berkeley.

radical; some were shocked socially by what went on under permissive regulations. And then some had their off-campus experiences turn into opportunities, professional or social, that pulled them away from the campus. It became common for the college to lose half of its students between entry and graduation, a rate not as high as at Reed (as we see later) but higher than that found at Swarthmore and most other highly selective colleges.

The intensity of this small campus was evident in the way that students, faculty and administrators spoke out on issues that touched the interest or caught the attention of nearly everyone on campus.

Data from field notes help illustrate the point. On a visit to the college (April, 1961) the campus was found in full debate over open halls. Community Council had invited testimony from members of the community, over a two-week period, on proposed new standards. The president, the dean of students, and a number of respected and intensely interested members of the faculty were testifying, along with students, before the council. Mimeographed copies of various proposals were being distributed at a rapid rate. This issue alone excited the campus: Students who wanted the halls open as much as possible were circulating referendum and recall petitions. In addition, the Fair Play for Cuba picketing at the state capitol was taking place, a militant bit of action on which few could be neutral, and the flaming cross attack that immediately followed shook everyone. The campus was electric with excitement, and there were few hours for sleeping.

On another visit (February, 1962), a single issue of the student newspaper contained accounts of the following happenings:[14]

(1) One assistant professor whose contract had not been renewed for the following year, instead of going away muttering quietly as professors usually do, was in open conflict, presenting her case time and again in long angry letters in the student newspaper and orally to students and faculty in office and corridor. Her pleas reached everyone on campus and touched many hearts, virtually making it necessary for everyone, whether student or faculty member or administrator, to form a judgment, one that would seem informed and reasoned in conversation with others.

(2) Community Council had voted to create a Civil Liberties Review Board to act as a judicial body in cases of alleged violation of the Civil Liberties Code (of community government). The code was a written statement of standards and regulations governing political action on and off campus. The creation of a review board was seen as an important issue since it might become a court in which those who went too far, transgressing the code, would be sentenced to punishment. To ensure against this, the council decided to give the board no power of sanctions.

14. Antioch College *Record*, February 16, 1962.

(3) An Antioch delegation of eighty-nine students had arrived at the White House to participate in picketing organized by Turn Toward Peace. Preparation for this trip had drawn much attention, with many more than those who went having to decide personally whether to make the trip. After the "Washington Action," a Dayton newspaper ran a feature story on the participation of the Antioch students, and the leaders of the delegation held evening meetings on campus to discuss the value of the demonstration.

(4) The Educational Policies Committee was considering changes in upper-year seminars and in the orientation given to students before going off on study abroad, matters of interest to nearly all students on campus.

(5) A new community manager had been appointed for the following fall, for six months; the new C.M. presented some of his ideas; and the Interim Council (sometimes known as In Cil!) explained their criteria for making this appointment.

(6) A peace walker who had made it from San Francisco to Moscow had given a talk on campus.

(7) A student visiting from Smith College idealized the campus in a letter to the editor, comparing it with her own school, "where restrictions are plentiful, where an atmosphere of artificiality often tends to prevail."

(8) The current community manager, in his column, pointed to the weakness of the honor system in preventing theft: each year about five hundred dollars worth of silverware vanished from the cafeteria.

(9) A recent graduate (or dropout) complained bitterly in a long letter to the editor that the president was trying to give the college a new image and to do so was recruiting spiritless students who made the C-Shop (Coffee Shop) a sad place in which no one sang or cried or translated thought into action.

Meanwhile, students were deep in choosing jobs for the next quarter off campus and were absorbed in midterm examinations.

Such a time was sufficiently quiet, however, that the editor of the paper chose to comment on "6th Week Limbo." Compared to some other weeks, it was indeed a modestly quiet time.

As we look back over the move to distinctive character and national prominence at Antioch, we see an organization take on the characteristics of a saga. What was later to become the legend was initiated at a time of deep crisis by a bold, determined president. Bringing new purpose to an old institution, he struck hard at every component of the campus to shape an appropriate organizational tool; and although he came to define the effort as one falling far short of the goal, others on and off the campus saw it as a successful innovation. Soon a strong Antioch group, full of belief that the college had special value, was willing to labor hard in its behalf and was accumulating the power to defend the new character that they continued to develop. A strong sense of community, emerged, along with the marked self-consciousness of a unique social institution and much pride in the accomplishments of several decades of sustained effort. The original innovating purpose had become an embracing and emotional account of what the group had done in past struggles and of why, despite its small size, it had a valuable, unique place in the educational world and in the larger society. To those who cared, there was an Antioch saga. That emotionally rich definition of the situation was supported throughout the structures of the campus—in the faculty, the curriculum, the student body, and the external constituencies. Supported so well by an integrated structure, the saga was not only a satisfying definition of the past and present but also a durable vision of what would be desirable in the future.

# PART II
*Reed*

# *Chapter 4.* Initiation

LONG BEFORE its fiftieth birthday in 1962 Reed College had become a bright star in the academic heavens, casting as strong a light as any college of its size in the land. For years its name figured in discussions of top colleges, and some placed it first in undergraduate accomplishment. Its students were known as independent and liberal as well as bright, capable of an endless fondling of ideas, even of talking others to death. Public comments ran to colorful prose: an "academic anarchy" that "produces more big brains than many big universities"; an "academic gadfly"; "a place that goes for beards, guitars, and sandals" and is "intellectually one of the nation's richest campuses." [1] Clearly a pacesetter on the West Coast, the college was also an important national model of liberal spirit and quality in the liberal arts. For a tiny campus off in the Pacific Northwest, it had amassed a superior record and reputation. Portland, Oregon, is a long way from the cities and suburbs of the Eastern Seaboard, where the money and sophistication of an established upper class have helped to fashion superior institutions. All in all, Reed rocketed to the top in an unlikely setting.

1. Richard L. Neuberger, "School for Smart Young Things," *The Saturday Evening Post*, Vol. 225 (October 1952), pp. 36–37, 95–101; Sam Castan, "Portland's Academic Gadfly," *Look*, Vol. 26, No. 7 (March, 1962), pp. 77–80; "A Thinking Reed," *Time*, Vol. 80 (December, 1962), p. 38.

To describe the Reed way to academic esteem is simple on the one hand, and complex and subtle on the other. The simple answer is that Reed started off on the academic high road with seriousness and standards and never deviated from it. The complex answer is that starting off and staying on that road are sufficiently difficult that most colleges have long managed not to do so; something uncommon must have occurred in Portland. Reed arrived on the back of dedication, presidential zeal during the initial period, and a faculty with the capacity to hang tough once the character of the institution had taken shape. Reed illuminates the functions and dysfunctions of stubbornness in a group of academic men and instructs us in the ways and means of college-building.

The Reed story is not one of radical transformation after a period of tradition. During the tenures of the first two presidents, 1911–24, the basic elements of the present Reed were established. From its origin it was an innovating institution, and despite deep stress, it managed to embody and protect its early ideals in personnel and practice, in self-conception and reputation. The early period was one of ups and downs: up on the wings of elegant purpose; down the slide of crumbling finances and inability to gain resonance in its environment. Strong in purpose but weak in support at the end of its first decade, the college had to be renewed by its second president before its purposes were to find a stable home.

## The Intent

No one party acting in splendid isolation decided the general form of the college. No church defined its nature, no public board laid down guidelines from on high, no wealthy donor was so sure of himself as to wrap up future character in the binding clauses of a legacy. The intent of the college emerged from the terms of an estate, the wishes and interpretations of local trustees, the guiding advice of a national foundation, and the rigorous specifications of the first president.

Simeon Reed was a man from Massachusetts who, as a youth before the Civil War, went west and made his fortune through river trade, real estate, and other assorted ventures befitting the times. All his wealth he bequeathed to his wife, suggesting that some part of the legacy be used for purposes of permanent value to the good people of Portland, that the family "contribute to the beauty of the city and to the intelligence, prosperity, and happiness of the inhabitants." [2] Pondering the matter after her husband's death, Amanda Reed decided that an institution of learning would certainly benefit Portland and specified in her own will, drawn up in 1895, that the estate, in excess of two million dollars, be so used. The will did not dictate a level and kind of education; it specified in this re-

2. Last will and testament of Simeon Gannett Reed. Reed College Archives.

spect only that the new school be free from sectarian influence. It decidedly leaned toward the establishment of a school for "practical knowledge," and because of the known preference of the Reeds for affairs of commerce and practice rather than of the intellect and the arts, there was a good chance that the Reed Institute would open as a vocational school. The bequest named five trustees, several of whom were intimately acquainted with the preferences of the Reeds. Critical, however, was the fact that the trustees were formally free to do what they thought best; they, not the Reeds, finally had to interpret need and feasibility.

The Pacific Northwest had many educational needs at the time, and the trustees did not think that vocational education was the foremost. After the death of Mrs. Reed in 1904, while the courts were clearing away the harassing litigation of relatives made unhappy by the will, the trustees edged toward the idea of establishing a college of arts and sciences as the first enterprise of the Reed Institute. But mindful of the Reeds' inclination toward a technical facility, the liberal arts possibility rested uneasily with them. To help in making the decision, two trustees toured the country, observing technical institutes and colleges and seeking counsel. Still in a quandary, the trustees sought the advice of the General Education Board.

The General Education Board was the first of the large general foundations for the support of education and a giant of its time. Established by John D. Rockefeller in 1902, a decade before the more general Rockefeller Foundation, the board was a vigorous national office seeking to improve the quality of American education. Among other interests, the board encouraged experimentation and supported institutions that would set the pace in a state or region. In the twenties the G.E.B. was to play a fundamental role in establishing the Swarthmore experiment in honors. The board, when consulted by the neophyte Reed trustees, had little doubt about the shape that the new venture should take. Wallace Buttrick, secretary of the board at the time, spent several weeks in Portland studying the situation and then pressed hard for the establishment of a liberal arts college:[3] "It is evident . . . that the city of Portland, the state of Oregon, and the Pacific Northwest are now well supplied with schools of trades and other technical schools." At the same time, "Oregon has not been able to develop one college of strictly collegiate rank." A strong college of arts and sciences in Portland "would furnish ideals for the state," including the state university. In his firm opinion, "the time is now ripe for concerted action for the establishment of an institution of higher learning there." Or as put a few years later by the first president: "The General Education Board declared two years ago that in all America there was no better unoccupied spot than the City of Portland, Oregon, for a College of Lib-

3. From "A Summary of the Extensive Report Presented by Secretary Buttrick to the General Education Board at the Time of the Founding of Reed College," *Reed College Self-Evaluation Report*, Vol. II (March, 1958).

eral Arts and Sciences." [4] This was strong encouragement from an imposing and respected authority, the kind of recommendation that eased the
way for a decision in favor of liberal arts over technical training. Thus
advised, the trustees decided in favor of a liberal arts college of the highest possible caliber.

In 1910, to find a president for a new college "of strictly collegiate rank"
that "would furnish ideals" for its state and region, the trustees were well
advised to seek the advice of eminent national figures, particularly Buttrick at the G.E.B. and Charles W. Eliot, president emeritus of Harvard,
whose role as the leading educational statesman of the day called for his
assisting in just such matters. Early among the names that came from
these respected quarters was that of a former student of Eliot's, William T.
Foster, then lecturing in educational administration at Columbia University, on leave from his position as professor of English and Argumentation
at Bowdoin College. Deeply unhappy about the state of American higher
education, young Foster already had reform in mind. He wanted colleges
to stop the nonsense and get down to serious work. His ideal college, he
was then writing,[5] was one:

that combats laziness, superficiality, dissipation, excessive indulgence in what we
are pleased to call college life, by making the moral and intellectual requirements, before and after entrance, an honest, sustained, and adequate challenge
to the best powers of the best American youth.

What was bothering Foster also bothered some other thoughtful educators at the time: The scholarship of the faculties of leading American
universities and colleges was admirable, they thought, but the quality of
student life had somehow gone wrong. Perhaps it was because size and
specialization had removed the professor from the student, replacing
Hopkins' log—a student on one end and the faculty member on the other
—with the large, impersonal lecture hall. Perhaps it was because the elective principle had turned the student consumer into arbiter of the curriculum, installing a rootless flexibility. Certainly, the worst of all for the
critics was that the student had learned to use the college for "extraneous"
reasons. Intercollegiate athletics, favored several decades earlier by leading educators as constructive outlets for youthful energies, had grown into
a monster that together with an elaborate social life had taken control of
the interests of students. The concern was widespread. "At Harvard certainly by 1900 everyone was aware that something disastrous had happened to Harvard College, however proud one felt about what President

4. William T. Foster, "The Frontier" (Campus Day address, June 8, 1912), *Reed
College Record*, No. 8 (December, 1912).
5. *Administration of the College Curriculum* (Boston, Houghton Mifflin Company,
1911), p. 340.

Eliot had done to make it Harvard University." [6] At Amherst, in thirty years the campus injunction had changed from "Glorify God in your body and in your spirit" to "Beat Williams." [7]

The prestige of the institution with all groups was as high as ever it has been, but it was clear to independent observers that the college was not altogether deserving of its repute. More and more students were being graduated with less and less effort.[8]

The life of the student at Yale was captured in a classic novel in which the hero as entering freshman arrives in New Haven as the complete man of the world with gloved hands, buckskin vest, and lilac silk necktie "in snug contact with the high collar whose points, painfully but in perfect style, attacked his chin." [9] Abraham Flexner, in his book *The American College*, published in 1908, had scathingly and tellingly denounced the life of play and trivial study in all colleges.[10] Somewhat earlier, Woodrow Wilson had launched his "holy war" against the side shows and frills of the Princeton campus. Although his crusade was beaten back by alumni, trustees, faculty, and students who preferred to worship false gods, Wilson, among all the critics, had highlighted the targets for educational reform.

Foster, true son of academic rigor, was as outraged and desirous of reform as Wilson. That college was a place for gentlemen was, for him, "twaddle." He defined the young gentleman contemptuously as "a youth free from the suspicion of thoroughness or definite purpose." [11] And he was quick to note the discouraging resistance to reform commonly found in long-established institutions. He maintained that several hundred colleges in the land would gladly make radical changes were it not for the pressure of their own traditions defended by an army of graduates. The possibilities of radical change, then, resided in places without nineteenth century hangovers. At a new college in the Far West he would be unencumbered with alumni, unrestrained by the heavy hand of past commitments, and therefore able to move ahead rapidly. As Foster wrote in early college publications: "Reed College purposes to take full advantage of its splendid freedom from harassing traditions." [12] When the trustees accepted Foster's condition of a strong effort to achieve the highest, he packed his starched white collars and moved to Portland.

6. Frederick Rudolph, *The American College and University* (New York, Alfred A. Knopf, Inc., 1962), p. 445.
7. Thomas Le Duc, *Piety and Intellect at Amherst College, 1865–1912* (New York, Columbia University Press, 1946), p. 128.
8. *Ibid.,* p. 135.
9. Owen Johnson, *Stover at Yale* (Collier Books; New York, The Macmillan Company, 1968 [originally published in 1912]), p. 1.
10. *The American College* (New York, Century Company, 1908).
11. *Administration of the College Curriculum*, p. 159.
12. "First Annual Catalog, 1911–1912," *Reed College Record*, No. 5 (January, 1912), p. 19

The new president had a strong sense of the practical as well as of the moral importance of a special effort. He thought a private college had to find a distinctive niche. If on the one side Reed should avoid the gentlemanly model still dominant in Boston and Philadelphia, it should on the other not seek to duplicate the ways of neighboring public colleges, for then it may as well be a branch of a state institution. "A generation ago, there were other reasons for founding private colleges, but today they can justify their existence only by doing a kind of work which at present seems impossible for state schools." [13] The college, then, should depart radically from all prevailing major practices. In fact, it would not even spell the way others did. Reed would turn its back on the anachronisms of spelling found in the English language and write in the style recommended by the Simplified Spelling Board, e.g., offises, concurd, involvs, alfabetical. Foster later spoke of his crusade for spelling reform as deliberately symbolic, "that Reed College would continue to stand staunchly—and if necessary, stand alone—for whatever was right." [14]

The unifying theme in Foster's announced platform was "to establish a college in which intellectual enthusiasm should be dominant." If the life of the student was to be one of "persistent and serious study," there had to be an "uncompromising elimination" of the activities that compete with studies—above all, of "intercollegiate games and fraternities and sororities." [15] And uncompromising was the word for the president's intentions. He was almost completely free of the desire to follow well-worn paths or to accommodate to popular views. Enunciated in a continuing stream of speeches, articles, and college publications, as we later see, his commitment to a single goal was virtually fanatical. His style of goal-setting soon caused supporters and him to define the college proudly as Utopian and caused the irritation of important outsiders to grow in leaps and bounds.

To leave the East for the untutored Northwest, there to build a college from the ground up, was to set forth on a difficult path, but Foster, like Arthur Morgan, had confidence in the power that could purportedly ensue when courage is married to insight. He wrote,[16] as Reed was entering his life, of the growing conviction that

a small college with the requisite insight and courage to become a Johns Hopkins for undergraduates, the Balliol of America, would soon take first rank among us, and find its degree the most highly prized in America. Though it were located in the forests of Aroostook County, or on the shores of Puget Sound, there would be, every autumn, a beaten path to and from its gateway.

13. "First Report of the President, 1910–1919," *Reed College Record*, No. 34 (December, 1919), p. 13.
14. "Pay the Price and Take It" (commencement address), *Reed College Bulletin*, Vol. 27, No. 1 (November, 1948), p. 5.
15. "First Report of the President," *loc. cit.*, p. 14.
16. *Administration of the College Curriculum*, p. 334.

Since he felt he had the insight and the courage, that small college would be Reed.

## The Character-Defining Years

Here was high-minded and tough intent, a definite decision for departure from common ways. Although a necessary step in the forming of later character, the statement of intent would mean nothing if not embodied in many aspects of the unbuilt college. The lofty statements, bordering on arrogance, had to be reflected in uncommon procedures that would ignore or attempt to alter the prevailing definitions of college life rather than to accommodate them. The first president had much leeway in which to reform reality in the image of the idea. His givens, his fixed elements, were few. The endowment and the trustees were at hand, not of his making; but everything else had to be assembled from the ground up, and the president could have a strong hand in the building. Free not only of inherited faculty, alumni, and traditions but also of sectarian constraints, Foster was indeed in a new and open field of college building. His requirements were primarily four: a faculty appropriate to the intent; campus practices that would distinctively embody and signify academic seriousness; an intelligent and serious student body; and a reputation that would bring support sufficient for his purposes. These were the initial primary sectors of policy and administration. In each, the critical actions taken led to defining patterns.

### FACULTY RECRUITMENT

The attraction of new faculty is not always a critical matter. For routine institutions a wide spectrum of men can often be utilized; if a man of first quality cannot be found, then one of lesser ability can be taken; if academic men are in short supply, then one can, at least for a time, fill up the ranks with nonacademics. In institutions of low academic quality, students and parents are often none the wiser. Colleges following a set path also can usually recruit for technical competence alone, not needing a particular personal value commitment in order to mold the place in a distinctive form.

At Reed the first president knew well that faculty recruitment was critical, and the later history of the institution proved it more critical than he could imagine. He, at least, knew that the decision to depart from customary form would need support in faculty values and habits and that the decision for excellence would require a high level of professional competence in the faculty. Later the faculty built by him and then rebuilt by the second president had considerable stability and continuity at the top. Few senior figures entered the faculty between the late twenties and World War II. Thus, those who came to the faculty early and remained formed a

relatively small senior staff that carried forward the values of the college
for several decades. Reed also was to become an extreme instance of faculty control, giving those who persisted unusual influence in institutional
policy.

President Foster was in a position to compete financially in recruiting
faculty, and with the openness of his new campus, he offered adventure
and innovation. During the first six years of his tenure he attracted young
men from the best places—Harvard, Chicago, Stanford, University of California. Foster himself had good credentials, being Bostonian and Ivy
League, and he was at the time a vigorous thirty-two years old. The key
men he brought to Portland were either solid New Englanders in social
and educational background or men whose early success had brought
them into the leading Eastern academic manors. His professor of mathematics, a Chicago Ph.D., was taken from Williams College. His first professor of biology was a Bostonian with a Ph.D. from Columbia who had
been teaching at Berkeley. His new man in philosophy was born in Connecticut, went to Brown and Harvard, and had taught at Wesleyan
(Connecticut) and Northwestern. The professor of economics and sociology, out of Georgia and Mercer University, had his higher training at
Columbia and had taught at Princeton. The professor of psychology and
dean of women, born in Massachusetts, had her B.A. and Ph.D. from
Radcliffe and had taught at Mt. Holyoke. The professor of education was
an Englishman with degrees from Chicago and Harvard and teaching
experience at Illinois and Washington. The professor of chemistry was
Yale, B.A. and Ph.D.; the man in Greek and Latin had a Stanford B.A. and
a Chicago Ph.D. and had taught at Chicago and Yale. Even the professor
of mechanical drawing and surveying, used principally as an administrator
in charge of campus development, had impeccable credentials: New
Hampshire, Philips Exeter, Massachusetts Institute of Technology, and
Bowdoin. Among the full professors of the first several years only the
professor of English had much local background, having taught in a high
school and a small college in the Pacific Northwest.

The recruitment from the East and from the highest academic sources
continued down through the ranks. The president's secretary came from
Mt. Holyoke. His young, active instructor in social science, who was to
help raise the hackles of Portland, was a Bostonian, Harvard B.A., and
Harvard Divinity School, who had taught in the Cambridge Latin School.
The first instructor in modern languages was from Maine and Bowdoin.
Among the several others brought in in the first several years at low rank
was Karl T. Compton, then finishing graduate work at Princeton. In short,
the faculty came not from a variety of jobs, as at Antioch, but from the
best of academic places. They were a group of Easterners, outsiders in the
Portland area, whose academic backgrounds were appropriate to the high
road that Foster had in mind.

This first faculty was also young and energetic. Foster, like Morgan, was willing to take chances by raising young men in rank. F. L. Griffin, free to shape the mathematics curriculum to his heart's content, was thirty; William Ogburn in social science was twenty-five; the campus development professor was twenty-six; and the dean of women, twenty-nine. The president's secretary, who was to help run the institution through difficult days, was twenty-six. Of the first dozen faculty hired, only one was over forty. In the early pictures, one almost needs a program to tell the faculty from the students. They were the kind of faculty who would live in the student dormitories and often outplay the students in intramural baseball. Vigor in the faculty the young college was not to lack, and vigor was to become a lasting characteristic, changing gradually over time from a combination of the intellectual and the physical to the intellectual alone.

Of the faculty that Foster recruited in his first several years, few remained through World War I and the troubles at the college shortly thereafter, but the half dozen who did had ample cause to be true believers in a Reed destiny. They were in on the origin of a college with a decided sense of being different, of being what a college ought to be in the ideals of professors, and they were an integral part, the very center, of academic development at the college. Without the side shows—the athletic director, the star athlete, the fraternal Big Man on Campus—the faculty were It. What they did in their work was by far the most important activity on campus in the official scheme of things. As authority moved toward the faculty after 1916, those who came and stubbornly stayed also became personally responsible for the survival and welfare of the college. Before Foster left in 1919, he had recruited a few more members who were to become part of a long-standing cadre: a full professor of physics, in 1915, who quickly moved to the center of affairs and was to count in policy-making until his retirement in 1948; and a young political scientist, in 1918, who was to be at the heart of policy deliberations for the next four decades.

### DISTINCTIVE PRACTICES

*Admissions.* Foster had promised, even sworn, in his declarations of intent that no students would be admitted to Reed on condition. In his published doctoral dissertation, he had heaped scorn on the prevalent practice of filling the seats in the freshman class with students who did not meet the stated minimal standards but were admitted anyway, on condition or as special students. This was a game, according to him, that even the best were playing: In 1909, 58 per cent of 607 freshmen at Harvard and 57 per cent at Yale and Columbia were substandard; at Princeton 210 out of 360 were admitted with conditions.[17] The colleges were sinners all,

17. *Ibid.*, pp. 324–25.

in Foster's eyes, throwing away their standards before the teacher even
called the roll. The special student, freshman on trial, provisional candidate for a degree, or student on probation sat in the same classes as those
who entered by the front door, confident that an institution "so devoted to
democratic ideals as to make his entrance easy will not make his continued
residence diffcult." [18] "Oh, spirit of democracy, what scrambles for numbers and fees are performed in thy name!" [19]

Reed simply would not do this, he maintained, and the college did not.
The first catalogue carried on for eighteen pages about the scholarship,
"helth" [sic] and character requirements for admission, with subsections
entitled "No Entrance Conditions Permitted" and "No Special Students
Admitted." The prospective student was told, "No students are admitted
on condition. As this is a departure from the prevailing practis [sic]
among American colleges, it needs some explanation"—and Foster went
on to describe the laxity, indolence, and weakening of standards that
would obtain if Reed followed "prevailing practis." For those who could
not read, or reading did not believe, the president personally scrutinized
all applications to ensure a clear decision between prepared and unpre-
pared in line with the stated criteria of high school accomplishment, certi-
fication by high school authorities, entrance examinations, and a personal
interview that allowed him to judge further the motivations of the student.
Here, Reed got the jump on most leading institutions by ten to fifteen
years. After World War I, at a time of greatly expanded student enrollment, some quality-seeking colleges became very selective. This new college in Portland simply opened its doors on that basis.

*Curricular Hurdles.* The president and the faculty also followed
through on the promise to make the classroom stern and challenging. Contrary to many other reformers of the time, Foster was not bothered by the
free choice of students under the flowering elective system. He did not set
about to form broad, integrated, mandated courses and imposing se-
quences of required courses, but rather attempted to surround free election with a number of safeguards. In addition to superior teaching, to be
achieved through faculty recruitment, and seriously motivated students,
achieved through student selection, hurdles could be set in the curriculum.
Long-lasting ones were worked out or germinated in the first decade. The
hurdles were those practices normal to graduate study in the United States
that were introduced in the undergraduate years. One such practice, established at the outset, was to have every student write a thesis and then
to be examined orally on it by a committee of faculty members. Another
was to have all students take comprehensive examinations, a practice that

18. *Ibid.*, p. 325.
19. *Ibid.*, p. 327.

in the early twenties was to become firmly fixed at Reed in the form of the Junior Qual (Junior Qualifying Examination). Placed at the end of the junior year, the examination was in effect an advanced admissions test since students had to pass it to enter the senior year! A qualifying comprehensive, a thesis, an examination on the thesis—these practices constitute the backbone of requirements for the master's and doctor's degrees in American universities. Sometimes one or even all of these requirements are found in undergraduate programs but usually apply only to part of the student body, the honor students. The difference here was twofold: Reed started these practices early, in the nineteen-tens and early twenties, before honors work had importantly invaded the American scene; and it applied these imposing hurdles to all its students, thus in effect defining them all as honor students and defining the college entirely as an honors college. As a result, there was never a formal opening for a gentleman's C, no room for the "pass" man. The imposing curricular hurdles were squarely in line with Foster's earlier prescription that the ideal college "shuts its doors promptly on idlers by means of a discipline from which there is no escape." [20] Against the idler, the college prepared a defense in depth.

If there had been a gentleman at Reed in search of an easy C, he would not have found it easy even to learn his grade, for another special and lasting element on which the faculty decided early was not to inform students month by month, semester by semester, about their specific numerical or letter grades; recorded grades were not passed along until graduation. This no grades practice emerged about 1915 to reduce grade awareness and competitiveness. Of little salience initially—catalogues of the time did not bother to mention it—this policy developed gradually in the self-definition of the college as a definite part of a prideful tradition. Faculty and students alike claimed it a symbol of knowledge for knowledge's sake, an indication that Reed avoided the crass concern for grades that ostensibly obtained elsewhere.

*The Extracurricular.* The president and early staff downgraded extracurricular activities from the start and forced them into a role of supporting the academic. The college refused to field any regular sports teams to play other colleges, to the dismay of the nearby citizens who wanted something to cheer. The first statement of athletic policy was blunt and hostile:[21]

No paid coaches, no seasonal coaches, no preseason coaches, no paid officials, no training tables, no traveling expenses, no grandstands; therefore, no inducement to enter the College, or to remain in college, or to neglect his studies, or to over-exert physically for the sake of winning games.

20. *Ibid.*, p. 338.
21. Quoted in Foster, "First Report of the President," *loc. cit.*, p. 25.

Under a policy of athletics for all ("for all the students and faculty, especially those who need it most"), the entire sports program was kept intramural and distinctly amateurish. The president proudly quoted high rates of participation, in lieu of intercollegiate victories:[22] For a week in 1914, "56 per cent took part in gymnastics, 44 per cent in handball, 34 per cent in football, 32 per cent in tug-of-war, 27 per cent in tennis, 18 per cent in basketball, and 15 per cent in track games." For a week in 1916, "92.8 per cent of the men students and 93.5 per cent of the women students took part in one or more of the following athletic games: tennis, tug-of-war, handball, hockey, foot-ball, squash and track games," with the heaviest participation in tennis. These practices soon gave the student body a high and mighty tradition, one that proudly identified Reed with the absence of sports.

As went sports, so went the social life. Fraternities and sororities and anything resembling them were never allowed. The Reed record is clean of secret societies, initiating and tapping ceremonies, hijinks in the fraternal lodge, and weekend migrations to other campuses. The somber catalogue, black covered and without pictures, promised new students only that social affairs were "inexpensiv [sic] and simple," that the social life was "wholesome, sensible, democratic," and that the dwelling halls and main building had "social rooms." Festivities were all-campus in form: a stunt night by a women's association, an annual Campus Day of work and play, a choral Christmas program. There was strong pressure to have social activities designed "to improve the learning atmosphere." When the students appeared to be getting out of hand, they were brought back to the mark: For example, when they went in wholeheartedly for 1913–14, the faculty reprimanded them and set limits on dancing occasions.[23] Compared to the highly developed individualism of Reed students in the fifties, the style of the first decade was positively social since the students did have campus-wide clubs and were trying different social activities. But under the watchful eye of the president and faculty and the constraints of an emerging tradition of scholarship first, their extracurricular activities were thin compared to those found at the time on other campuses where Friday to Sunday, week in and week out, belonged to the realm of wine, women, and song. Reed was, in fact as well as in theory, no place for the gentleman or for the athlete or for anyone else who would seek, through social activities alone, to be Big Man on Campus.

*Administrative and Faculty Practices.*    Faculties of liberal arts colleges normally do not think of themselves as agents of community reform, espe-

22. *Ibid.,* pp. 30–31, 29.
23. Dorothy O. Johansen, "Historical Aspects of Student Activities," *The Sallyport* (alumni journal), Vol. 25, No. 2 (Winter, 1963), pp. 9–12. I am also indebted to Professor Johansen for allowing me to draw generally on her unpublished work on the history of Reed.

cially in the sterner places. To seek to build a pure liberal arts college is to avoid not only vocationalism but also the work that public colleges and universities develop as service to the community. President Foster had in mind for Reed, however, an unusual combination of stern college and community involvement. He and his associates, while they were building Reed, would also help Portland rid itself of its vices and raise the citizenry to enlightenment.

From the outset the president spoke of Portland as the "city-wide campus." He went into the extension business, offering series of free lectures. For example, in 1913 he and eleven other speakers gave a lecture series at the Portland Hotel on Sexual Hygiene and Morals.[24] Some ninety courses altogether were given in the city during the nineteen-tens, with annual (accumulative seat) attendance increasing from 3,000 in 1911–12 to 48,000 in 1916–17.[25] The president also claimed after only three years of the existence of Reed that "members of the faculty have aided in the work of the art museum, the public library, the vice commission, health bureaus, and the home for delinquent girls"; that one faculty member had headed the Oregon Civic League, a good-government organization; that another in the faculty had chaired a committee of one hundred whose campaign helped carry the state of Oregon for prohibition.[26]

In other words, the college, in a few years, was a do-gooder, one that made no bones about its mission to improve and uplift, "to see to it that no individual in the city of Portland, Oregon, should fail to gain some benefit from Reed College." [27] Beyond the extension lectures, beyond the serving of faculty on art commissions and good-government boards, the college, in a highly visible way, probed the sores of the city: A young man in the social sciences and his students made a study of unemployed men in Portland, publishing and distributing the results to interested citizens;[28] the president organized a committee of sixty investigators who looked into the threat of motion pictures and vaudeville shows to the morals of the young and the old by covering every theater in the city and making a report to the mayor.[29] The college militant was standing guard: "The mayor, commissioner, and all the people of the city are led to understand that they are

24. "Syllabus of a Course in Sexual Hygiene and Morals," *Reed College Record*, No. 9 (January, 1913).
25. Foster "First Report of the President," *loc. cit.*, p. 39.
26. "Reed College, Portland, Oregon," in *The University and the Municipality*, U.S. Bureau of Education Bulletin No. 38 (Washington, D.C., 1915), Government Printing Office, pp. 58–61. Foster's companion writers in this volume were all presidents of municipal universities—e g New York University, Boston University, Toledo University, University of Cincinnati.
27. *Ibid.*, pp. 58–59.
28. Arthur E. Wood, "A Study of the Unemployed in Portland, Oregon," *Reed College Record*, No. 18 (December, 1914).
29. William Trufant Foster, "Vaudeville and Motion Picture Shows," *Reed College Record*, No. 16 (September, 1914).

free to call upon the college for aid of any kind at any time, and they are constantly doing so." [30] The practices of social service were a strong component of the early institutional self-image.

Foster and his faculty had several other marks of exceptional style. One, simplified spelling, was a personal quirk of the president and did not survive after he left the college at the end of the decade. As mentioned, the unusual spelling symbolized a stubborn will to be rational as one saw it, even if that meant being uncomfortably different from others. The spelling had high visibility, being present in one public document after another, and was persistently carried forward by the president from year to year despite its obviously irksome quality. To read Reed prose was to be constantly brought up short by words with missing letters ("confirmd"), the letter *c* replaced by *s* ("offises"), and *ph* by *f* ("alfabetical"). Foster's spelling was in itself a simple item, a minor institutional habit, but it annoyed local people. An administrator sensitive to the community and eager for equilibrium would never have used it. Only an intellectually secure and stubborn man, committed fully to his own view of the long run, would have been so impractical.

In the administration of the college *the* distinctive idea that was to persist and with profound effects was a high degree of faculty participation. Foster, like Morgan, believed in a faculty role in campus government and was willing after the first few years to help institute the initial forms of strong faculty influence. A major and blatant breach of academic freedom occurred at the University of Utah in 1915 in the form of the arbitrary firing of argumentative professors. Four were dropped, seventeen colleagues resigned in protest, and the newly formed American Association of University Professors sent out a professor from the East to make its first investigation of crimes against academic freedom.[31] One of the fired professors, A. A. Knowlton, moved to Reed as professor of physics. The Utah scandal stirred academic men everywhere, especially in the Rocky Mountains and West Coast states, and at Reed it coincided with and helped accelerate a move toward clear codification of campus government. Foster, at his own invitation, spent two days in Salt Lake City studying what had occurred there and concluded as one of the lessons that a college campus required a "regularly constituted means whereby the president could get the views of the faculty" and "clear, straight-forward, accepted methods for dealing with such an emergency." [32] The president and a committee of the faculty wrote a constitution for Reed College in 1915 and got it approved the following year by the Board of Trustees.

30. Foster, "Reed College, Portland, Oregon," *loc. cit.*, p. 59.

31. Walter P. Metzger, "The First Investigation," *AAUP Bulletin*, Vol. 47, No. 3 (September, 1961), pp. 206–10.

32. "Faculty Participation in College Government," *School and Society*, Vol. 3, (April, 1916), pp. 594–99, quotation on p. 599.

Much was to follow, but not immediately. As at Antioch, a strong and innovating president had planted the seeds of faculty dominance in his own time by bringing into existence the formal clauses and the informal expectations of faculty control. But, again as at Antioch, the president remained dominant through the years of his own tenure, able and inclined to exercise a commanding influence until the final days in office. Later, after the critical period of character formation, the early governmental forms and expectations went on to fulfillment. In order to understand the ways in which the character of Reed was continued and protected, we will discuss later at some length (in chapter 5) its unusual system of authority.

REPUTATION AND STUDENT RECRUITMENT

Along with vigorous faculty and distinctive campus practices, the first president needed also a general reputation for the college, to help define and fix its character, and a dependable supply of bright, serious students. These "external" features would, of course, be shaped considerably by what was occurring within the campus and would, in turn, shape the internal features: e.g., campus practices help determine reputation, which affects recruitment, which then in turn gives the student body certain capacities and inclinations that help set the tone of campus affairs.

Foster's efforts to create a reputation of academic severity were soon successful. Through his pronouncements, the observable practices of the campus, and the comments of the mass media, Reed quickly became known on the outside as an academic highbrow. The president vigorously publicized the college. From the time he assumed office, he embarked on a deliberate effort to make known—to prospective faculty, potential students, and other outsiders—that here was a college with a difference, one that would be unique on the national scene and particularly unlike its collegiate neighbors in the Pacific Northwest. The early bulletins of the college, avoiding the sleepy prose common in catalogues, asserted in no uncertain terms that Reed was tough. These publications pounded on the theme that students interested in sports or social life should stay away, that only the deadly serious need apply:[33]

Intercollegiate athletics, fraternities, sororities and most of the diversions that men are pleased to call "college life," as distinguisht [sic] from college work, have no place in Reed College. Those whose dominant interests lie outside the courses of study, should not apply for admission. Only those who want to work, and to work hard, and who are determined to gain the greatest possible benefits from their studies, are welcomd [sic]. Only those whose habits are consistent with this purpose are welcomd [sic]. Others will be disappointed, for the scholarship demands will leave little time for outside activities, other than those which are necessary for the maintenance of helth [sic].

33. "First Annual Catalog, 1911–1912," *loc. cit.*, p. 24.

The catalogues and other public statements of the college also clearly and consistently set forth the distinctive practices earlier reviewed: "Reed College will admit no conditional students and no special students"; the number of students would be rigidly limited—"nothing whatever will be sacrificed in the interests of mere numbers"; students would have to write a thesis and be orally examined on it. When the president faced the outside and attempted to enlighten parents and possible students, he depicted, to put it bluntly but accurately, a life suitable for academic puritans. Since observable emerging practices of the campus so dramatically reflected the claim of severity, there was within a few years little doubt that what he so sharply presented to the public was congruent with what was occurring in campus behavior.

Public opinion, in the face of the claims and practices, soon took a general form that was to become long lasting: praise from a distance and opposition from nearby. The president voiced his convictions and policies and cultivated a national image by writing magazine articles for *The Nation* (1909, 1915), *Science* (1912), *Harpers Magazine* (1916), *School and Society* (1916), *Education Review* (1917), and others. By 1919 he had a personal publication list of over sixty articles, most of them about Reed. Particularly supportive was *The Nation*, which helped Foster publicize the college before it even opened. This liberal journal claimed in 1910 that this new college in the West was attracting attention because it did not plan to scatter its funds among university functions but rather to use them to secure the best teachers and to emphasize teaching over research. It expressed the hope that President Foster would treat his faculty with more consideration than other colleges did, not as wheels in a big machine. These comments were reprinted in *Science* magazine.[34] The clamor for teaching and general education over research and specialization was already rising by this time in liberal and educational journals, with small colleges favored over the brutal university. For the critics, Reed had all the attributes of a model liberal arts college.

When the college went out to obtain supporting testimonies at the end of its first decade, it was able to elicit high praise: David Starr Jordan, chancellor, Stanford University—"Reed College is recognized as standing in the very front rank of colleges. . . ."; G. Stanley Hall, president, Clark University—"You have to my mind solved better more problems in college education than any institution I know of"; the chancellor of New York University—"The large-minded and penetrating views of life and education which have been put forth by the President of Reed College have served to give that institution a national reputation of a very high and enviable character"; a professor of English at the University of Texas—"The plans of Reed College and the audacious sanity behind them greatly

34. "The New College in the West," *The Nation,* Vol. 91 (August, 1910),pp. 116–17; *Science,* Vol. XXXII, No. 815 (August, 1910), pp. 208–10.

delighted me"; a professor of German at the University of Iowa—"I believe that Reed College is one of the great achievements in American Education"; a professor of zoology at the University of Illinois—"Reed College is certainly an unique experiment and one to which all of us interested in college affairs look with great interest." One of the leading philanthropists of the day and, at the time, assistant secretary of war, F. P. Keppel was quoted as saying: "Reed College has certainly attracted attention thruout the country. I would be a rash man to say that it represents the final word in collegiate education, but it certainly represents a significant and important experiment." And Eliot, president emeritus of Harvard University, was willing to help the college with a direct fund-raising pitch to the citizens of Portland:[35]

Reed College has achieved in a few years a standing in the country which is of decided advantage to the City of Portland and the State of Oregon. It has also provided educational advantages which make Portland a better place to live in. It has contributed to the formation of a sound public opinion in the City and the State on questions of serious public interest.

There was exaggeration in these statements solicited for a fund-raising brochure, but such high praise simply could not have been secured by a mediocre liberal arts college. Reed looked unusual and very good in the eyes of national liberal commentators and educated men generally in other parts of the country.

But up close it was very different. Reed was not taking part in any athletic leagues and hence was not pulling its weight in Saturday spectator sports. This nonparticipation was considered somewhat un-American in a sports-minded part of the country and was more than a little annoying to sportswriters and other molders of opinion in the local press. Claims of academic severity also had a holier-than-thou tone. Since the claims were being uttered and the supporting practices initiated by a New Englander in stiff collar who talked long and loud about how much Portland needed Reed, a dislike of eastern snobbery played a part in the attitudes formed in the first decade. When Foster and his colleagues went downtown to engage in a number of civic reform efforts, the college also picked up an image of do-goodism. Since key members of the Reed faculty took strong pacifist or radical positions in the nineteen-tens, the asceticism, the snobbery, and the do-goodism appeared to be overlaid by very unsound political philosophies. Here was an alien band versed in irritating local sentiments. Even when, sorely troubled financially after World War I, the college tried its hand at direct public relations, it stiffly lectured the city on what Reed had done for it:[36] "He who runs away without reading will

35. *The City and Its College* (Portland, Ore., Reed College, undated [circa 1919]), 64 pages.
36. *Ibid.*

miss a few timely pages that concern him—pages which have taken eight years to prepare"; "to have a college whose standards are thus recognized thruout the world is of some value to the city"; the college was "making democracy safe for Oregon" by "explaining impartially the questions at issue" before an election; "Portland will deny to the people of Portland the opportunities for college education found in other cities until it adds endowment funds, or their equivalent, to the present resources of Reed College"; "the failure of the people of Portland to subscribe this comparatively small amount is unthinkable."

The reaction by the end of the decade was close to savage. When Foster left in 1919, the local press expressed all its resentment in reviewing the reasons for his departure.

*On academic distinction and sternness:* [37]

President Foster was doomed at least to partial failure from the very start. His ideas were tainted with Pharisaism. In the first advertisement he announced "a college that is different." None of the minor imperfections of other American universities would be incorporated into Reed. This college was 99.9 per cent pure. Never Pharisaical, Portland did not take kindly to the boasted self-righteousness.

He wanted to create an intellectual aristocracy far removed from the masses.

*On uplifting Portland:* [38]

He did not know and never learned Portland. He was a stranger to the Oregon spirit, and in eight years he did not make its acquaintance.

He has no tact. [He asked Portland for support but then in effect said:] Come to me and be uplifted. To teach you and raise you up to the higher intellectual life is my special mission. Portland smiled, and declined the invitation.

*On radicalism:* [39]

[He] permitted the preaching of radicalism by some members of the faculty in a way that had a pernicious effect upon the minds of immature students.

*On pacifism:* [40]

Public concern at the president's pacifism in the early days of the war and the radical change in his attitude subsequent to his visit [to France as a Red Cross inspector] entered into consideration. . . . In the early days of conflict Dr. Foster was an avowed pacifist, it is pointed out, exercising his oratorical abilities more or less promiscuously in that direction.

*On administrative capacity:* [41]

37. Portland *Telegram,* December 23, 1919.
38. *Ibid.*
39. *Ibid.*
40. *Oregon Journal* (Portland), December 19, 1919.
41. *Ibid.*

Irked by the president's attitude as head of the college, members of the faculty have been quietly dissatisfied for some time. . . .

A scholar and brilliant thinker, Dr. Foster is held to have been impressed with his authority and to have exercised it in such a way that faculty members found cooperation difficult to secure. . . .

A member of the board said: "we took into consideration the feelings of the teaching staff and the other things that have come to our attention regarding his administrative abilities. . . ."

And with more complaints, especially on the absence of intercollegiate sports, the catalogue of local grievances against Reed was impressive in size and scope. Around the person of the president and in a setting where the property interests seemingly lacked acquaintance with the concept of a college, the college had, in its first years, alienated itself considerably from local support.

At the same time Reed had to build a student body from a local base. The movement of colleges to national clienteles was not yet under way in the nineteen-tens; Reed was geographically isolated in the Pacific Northwest, and the initial claim to a special educational role included a commitment to give that part of the country, and Portland in particular, a quality private college. From the beginning President Foster turned to local boys and girls. Since the college was to be small, at least at the beginning, he would not need many students—hence the sentiments of the majority of local people need not defeat him on this front—and he set about to hand pick entering classes, starting in 1911 with fifty freshmen, evenly divided between men and women. By the time the college had all four classes of students in 1914–15, the student body totaled about 225, and 43 were graduating. Enrollment stabilized in the 250 to 300 range after 1915, except for a dip down to 207 in 1917–18 and a surge up to 319 the following year, and continued at that level until the late twenties.

Most of the early students were from the Pacific Northwest and predominantly from Portland. In the first year, 84 per cent came from Portland, another 14 per cent from the rest of Oregon, and only 2 per cent from outside the state; in 1919–20, the proportion from the immediate city was still as high as 70 per cent, which together with another 15 per cent from the rest of Oregon, meant that only 15 per cent, or fewer than one in six, were from outside the state.[42]

The building of a local recruitment base, then, from which enough students could be drawn each year to fill a 250-student college, was not restricted by the growing negative local reputation. Increasingly, to a degree that cannot be closely determined empirically, the effect of that reputation after the first few years was to induce students to come and to keep them away. As the reputation deepened and spread, gradually becoming rooted in the thought of the countryside, students with social-

42. Foster, "First Report of the President," *loc. cit.*, p. 88.

athletic interests and students of average and less-than-average ability were bound to go elsewhere, while serious and bright types found Reed something of a magnet. The nature of the graduates by the end of the first decade suggested that even if the faculty impact were heavy, many of those walking in the doors were at least capable of intellectual development. About one-third of the early graduates went on to graduate school (33 per cent in 1915, 33 per cent in 1917, 31 per cent in 1919), a high proportion for the time. The graduates also notably entered education as a career: Over seventy out of the first two hundred graduates—the largest occupational cluster by far—became teachers, principals, or college instructors. This career emphasis was to continue, with the accent increasingly on college-level teaching. Then, too, the graduates very early won important fellowships. In 1918 a graduate won a Rhodes Scholarship for study at Oxford; in 1921 Reed had three graduates in residence at Oxford; and from that time on this small college won, on the average, a prestigious Rhodes at least every other year. (In 1936 four Reed graduates were residing concurrently at Oxford as Rhodes Scholars.)[43] Such distinguished schools as Harvard, Princeton, and Columbia also awarded fellowships to Reed graduates. In short, within a few years academics elsewhere viewed Reed graduates as bright and serious. This reputation probably could have been built only with unusual student selection and appeal within the Portland schools. In any event, Reed established a national reputation for quality while still based on local recruitment.

Reed was proving it could be done, in its style, but the price of local dependence was yet to be paid. Raising funds locally, as well as recruiting locally, could be dangerous for a college fast developing a character out of joint with its immediate social setting. Without supplies from the outside, the college was, in fact, becoming an outpost in hostile territory, living off its original stockpile of resources. If it were to fall into dire financial straits and find potential local donors too unsympathetic to come to its rescue, then life could quickly become exceedingly difficult.

VULNERABILITY AND DECLINE

*The Crumbling of the Financial Base.* The Reed endowment, although not grand, appeared adequate at the outset. By the end of the first ten years, however, it had slipped into a precarious condition. President Foster, having avoided the preparation of an annual report for many years, was compelled by a "grave emergency" to issue his first report on the state of the college. What had happened between 1910 and 1919 was a sad tale in college finance, a story of the troubles of inflation compounded by poor investment and lack of public support.

43. *Ibid.*, p. 95; and "The First Quarter Century: Retrospect and Appraisal, 1911–1936," *Reed College Bulletin,* Vol. 15, No. 4 (November, 1936), p. 17.

Buttrick of the General Education Board had noted optimistically in 1910:[44]

The value of the bequest for the Reed Institute is already in excess of $2,000,000. It consists largely of real estate in the city of Portland, the annual income of which already approaches $70,000. A large part of the property is unimproved and this is increasing in value more rapidly than the improved real estate. It is well located inside property.

This is enough to endow a college of liberal arts but of course not enough also to build it. It is expressly provided in the bequest that not more than $150,000 of the principal shall be used for buildings and equipment. To this, of course, considerable accumulated interest may be added, but it will be necessary for the trustess of the Reed Institute to secure large cooperation on the part of the citizens of Portland if they shall decide to establish a college of the arts and sciences. Portland is a wealthy city and should be able to do this.

To put up the first buildings, costing over $400,000, the trustees were able to draw on a half million dollars of interest that had accumulated in the seven years between Mrs. Reed's death and the opening of the college. Then, an annual income of over seventy thousand dollars from endowment, together with tuition, would have allowed the college to cover operating expenditures. But the endowment was kept in real estate, property that was largely unimproved and supposedly well located inside the city. This policy amounted to speculation in real estate, to gambling on a steady or enhanced value of forty pieces of property. Unfortunately, the bloom was off the vine. Real estate values fell, the unimproved property was not developed, and the college went on paying taxes on property of decreasing income yield. In 1911 and 1912 the catalogue optimistically predicted that "by the time the first class enters upon its senior year [1914], the annual income available . . . probably will be in excess of one hundred thousand dollars." [45] But beginning in 1913 the optimism was replaced by the brute facts of taxes paid and income lost:[46]

The value of the present endowment is variously estimated. Much of the property is real estate which is not now income-bearing. It is the policy of the Trustees to improve this property without unnecessary delay. The holdings of Reed College in the City of Portland were taxed in 1913 at a valuation of about one and one-half million dollars.

The same paragraph, with only the year changed, appeared in the catalogues of 1914, 1915, 1916, 1917, and 1918. The 1919 emergency resulted

44. "A Summary of the Extensive Report Presented by Secretary Buttrick to the General Education Board at the Time of the Founding of Reed College," *loc. cit.*, Appendix, p. 7.
45. "First Annual Catalog, 1911–12" and "Second Annual Catalog," *Reed College Record*, No. 5, January, 1912 and No. 10, March, 1913.
46. "Third Annual Catalog, 1913–14." *Reed College Record*, No. 14, March 1914.

in part from "the double difficulty of increast [sic] taxes and decreast [sic] income" [47] from the original endowment.

Buttrick's early flattery of Portland as a wealthy city also proved of no avail. There was certainly enough money in the area to support a small Reed, but as the relations of the college with the city worsened, down went the possibility of major donors' subscribing to the Reed cause. The city did not rush to the aid of the college, and its influential citizens, for the most part, were not about to help as long as Foster was around to inflict upon them "his prejudices, his crotchets, his quirks and his fads." [48] On top of all this came the inflation of World War I, and away went the purchasing power of those individuals and institutions, private colleges included, that were on fixed income:[49]

The salary of a professor at Reed College four years ago was $3000. That salary today is worth no more than $1,717 was worth at that time. To pay a professor in purchasing power as much as he was paid four years ago would require a salary of about $5500. Similar difficulties are met in nearly every other item of the budget.

In brief, finances moved from being good to being barely adequate shortly after the campus opened and continued to move downward during and immediately after World War I, so that by the end of the first decade Reed was in perilous shape. Endowment was inadequate, and no more seemed forthcoming; the college was paying taxes on useless property; and inflation had made the whole question of finance a nightmare.

*The Exodus of Faculty.* These worsening financial troubles, together with the enlistment of some of the young faculty in the military and the strain between some members of the faculty and the president, brought the college near the brink of rupture. Most of the faculty recruited by Foster in the early years stayed only a short time and were gone. Five departed in 1915, including the bright young man in physics, Compton, who could not get sufficient facilities for research; four were lost the following year, including a professor of English; 1917 saw the departure of professors in sociology (Ogburn) and psychology (Elizabeth H. Rowland), both having served since 1912 and the latter having doubled as dean of women; five left in 1918, including Robert Leigh in government, who later became the first president of Bennington College; and seven in 1919. The outflow of twenty-three in the five years 1915–19 approximated the size of the faculty. Some losses were unavoidable because of the pull of the war effort, but many had to be charged to the push of campus conditions. Men were not being paid adequately or were overworking or could not get appropriate facilities, and the president's stubbornness,

47. Foster, "First Report of the President," *loc. cit.,* p. 53.
48. Portland *Telegram,* December 23, 1919.
49. Foster, "First Report of the President," *loc. cit.,* p. 53.

excellent for initial direction and vigor, grated on the nerves of those who, as they invested themselves and gained in experience, wanted a more cooperative and collegial enterprise. Under this first president, the paying of faculty in the coin of control had not been allowed to proceed to the point where it would substitute for salary. The worsening of the financial condition hurt badly, and the troubles could not help but be laid in part on the doorstep of the president.

By 1917 Reed was unable to replace its losses in staff: "The drastic decline in endowment income . . . wrought havoc in certain departments. Vacancies occurring in the social sciences and in history and philosophy were not adequately filled." There was a "large and increasing use of undergraduate assistants," paid "their tuition ($100) to assist the instructors." The range of the curriculum and the quality of instruction differed greatly in practice from what was depicted in the catalogue.[50]

Matters got so bad that in 1919 the college began to dabble in intercollegiate sports. A move so decidedly contrary to the principles of the president was evidence of his diminishing personal influence:[51]

Dr. Foster's personal direction of the destinies of the college began to lapse some months ago, and, it is said, with the entrance of Reed College into intercollegiate sport, a definite departure from Foster's policies, the beginning of the end of his personal direction arrived.

Reed had for eight years declined, under Dr. Foster, to enter into intercollegiate athletics. This year, however, that policy was cast aside by the trustees. . . .

The change in policy was an effort to elicit loyalty through collegiate spirit and especially to make amends to the city of Portland. A senior professor hailed the change as "the best thing that ever happened at Reed"[52] since it brought a new spirit and new contacts, and the local press noted with satisfaction that "after nine years of athletic isolation, Reed College will make its debut in intercollegiate athletics" on the "gridiron against Pacific U."[53]

But the turn to the outside was only a temporary aberration. The Foster principle would not die; it had already become a stubborn tradition. The venture into spectator sports was abandoned just two years later at the request of the students themselves. The enthusiastic professor had left in the meantime, taking his interest in sports as well as his biological expertise to a university, and the faculty members who hung on were still committed to the initial ideals. Whatever the financing and the position of

50. Charles McKinley, *Report on Reed College Presented in Behalf of the Educational Policies Committee* (Portland, Ore., Reed College, 1934).
51. *Oregon Journal* (Portland), December 19, 1919.
52. *The Reed College Alumnus* (June, 1920), p. 8.
53. *Oregon Journal* (Portland), November 9, 1919.

the college in the hearts of local citizens, it was not going to sully itself with a side show.

Caught in a crisis of crumbling finances, loss of faculty, strain with the staff and the community, and deep personal travail, Foster submitted his resignation in the fall of 1919. He was not asked to reconsider. He left Reed at the age of forty and returned to the East, where he became director of a small foundation for economic research. His later contact with the college was minimal: he returned principally on ceremonial occasions, most notably in 1948 to receive an honorary degree and to speak at commencement on "Pay the Price and Take It."

Upon his leaving, the administration of the college passed to an expanded group of trustees and regents and to an interim committee of faculty members. This occasion was the first of several when the faculty would in one form or another serve as the administration. The job of the faculty committee was to stagger through administratively for a year or two and to help find a presidential successor. In 1919 the committee consisted of two professors and the former president's secretary. That all three members of the committee had, within a year, joined those who were leaving the leaky ship indicates the degree of instability at Reed in this period. The committee was reconstituted the second year with three other professors—and not many more were left. The staff that continued into 1920–21 numbered eight faculty members and a librarian[54]—all there was by way of knowledgeable hands to serve in receivership.

But this remnant was enough, for the troubles hit bottom that year. Classes were taught, and before the next fall a president had been found. Reed was to persist, and those who looked back a few years later said, in glowing college rhetoric: "A faithful nucleus of devoted professors preserved the fine Reed tradition in the midst of trying vicissitudes. . . ."[55] The vicissitudes had taken a promising college to the very edge of failure, and the whole business could well have been lost right there.

RENEWAL OF COMMITMENT

The second president, Richard F. Scholz, then a professor at the University of Washington, was to rank with Foster in setting the character of Reed. There was much damage to be repaired, and repair it he did in a three-year burst of institution-building before his death in 1924 at the age of forty-three. Scholz brought his own men to the faculty, altered the curriculum, and modified the organizational structure. He changed Reed, however, only to make it more of what it had set out to be—a significant model of academic seriousness and toughness. He harnessed the new

54. Portland *Oregonian*, August 22, 1920.
55. "The Reed College Alumnus," *Reed College Bulletin*, Vol. 2, No. 3 (May, 1923), p. 8. (The *Reed College Record* ended in 1921; the *Reed College Bulletin*, newly numbered, began in 1921–22.)

means to the stern ideals and practices that had become in the first decade what Reed stood for.

*The New Faculty.* The first problem in 1921 was to reconstitute the faculty, a task that any knowing successor in the presidential chair would happily anticipate. New faculty are by all odds the most important means by which a president marshals affairs along the trail of his wishes, especially if the new men are brought in at senior ranks. Thus, Scholz' great problem of weakened faculty was his great opportunity. To compose a faculty of men personally selected would be the key to whatever changes in curriculum and organization seemed necessary.

Within three years, Scholz added six full professors, five of whom were to make Reed their permanent home, and about a dozen men in the lower ranks of assistant professor and instructor. His new senior men included R. F. Arragon in history, Barry Cerf and Victor L. O. Chittick in literature, and Edward O. Sisson (who had been at the college earlier) in philosophy; all played central roles for years thereafter. As the new men came in, over a dozen of the existing staff, mostly junior men appointed in 1919 and 1920 to fill the classrooms, were let go. The faculty grew only slightly in size but became measurably stronger. The pattern of hiring and firing had one other notable characteristic: It concentrated academic strength and faculty power in the humanities. The new professors in history, literature, and philosophy were the muscle the president needed to install the program he had in mind.

*The New Program.* In many specific practices, as well as in general ideals, all was continuity at Reed. Scholz accepted his predecessor's central idea: that Reed should have the academic quality of the best of the eastern schools without the distractions they had institutionalized. Thus, the college continued to recruit bright, serious students; kept out the extracurricular side shows; and looked to its reputation of academic severity. But for the second president, the curriculum of the first decade was not a proper vehicle for quality. It was too loose, too much a reflection of the elective system, with only one or two unimportant general course requirements. Historian and Rhodes Scholar, an admirer of Oxford, Scholz wanted close relations of teachers and students centered on common intellectual pursuits:[56]

We must humanize the present system by reducing the formal mechanism of administration and substituting for the confusion of students' programs and the lack of sequence in unrelated courses an inter-related, co-ordinated and elastic course of study with humanistic orientation. We must encourage personal contacts and relationships based on a common intellectual experience and a common intellectual interest, not only between faculty and students but between members of allied departments.

56. "Inaugural Address" (June 9, 1921), *Reed College Bulletin*, Vol. 1, No. 2 (January, 1922), pp. 7–8.

In 1921, after months of planning, the president and the faculty instituted broad courses in history and world literature, to run on parallel time lines, supplemented by work in the social and natural sciences. At about this time St. John's and Columbia were attempting to build programs around the study of great books and the basic ideas of Western civilization; Alexander Meiklejohn was experimenting at Amherst with his version of general education; and Frank Aydelotte, another Rhodes Scholar who had been approached about the Reed presidency but had deflected the offer to Scholz, was entering into his program of reform at Swarthmore. It was also, it should be noted, ten years before Robert Hutchins initiated reform at Chicago. The humanities program at Reed, modified in detail many times through the years (usually toward greater integration), became the heart of the freshman year and an important part of the life of the sophomore. The Reed student found himself for the first two years largely in the hands of humanities professors. No matter how much a bright loner had buried himself in the chemistry laboratory of his high school, when he came to Reed his first year was dominated by the lectures of the humanities professors and especially by small discussion sessions around a table with an instructor, usually a senior figure, and a small group of students. The student soon had to know his Plato and demonstrate that he did through sharp verbal performance. The urge to verbalize later became virtually a universal characteristic of Reed graduates. The basic required courses in the humanities thus became another component that would touch all who entered the college and from which there was no escape. A sizable component of the faculty also became closely identified with this program, and henceforth, for many within and outside the college, the program became *the* expression of Reed ideals. These broad courses, added to the demanding junior and senior requirements retained from the Foster years, helped develop an intense curriculum consciousness in the faculty and student body that served well the original ideals of single-minded academic seriousness.

*The New Structure.*   To integrate the faculty across related disciplines, President Scholz replaced departmental organization with larger divisions. Instruction was offered in four divisions: literature and language; history and social science; mathematics and natural sciences; philosophy, psychology, and education. The divisions assumed responsibility for general courses; e.g., the Division of Language and Literature was responsible for the broad freshman and sophomore courses in literature. Without departments, the divisions had also to govern the specialized work of the students:[57]

57. "Catalog of Reed College, 1923–1924," *Reed College Bulletin,* Vol. 2, No. 3 (May, 1923), p. 26.

Toward the end of the Sophomore year, students confer with the professors of the Division in which they propose to work during their last two years, and plan a course of study. The college is interested only in seeing that the student's time is wisely and fully occupied. So far as the Junior and Senior years are concerned, it leaves to the discretion of the student and his instructors the allotment of time to the various studies, and the type of instruction.

This structure had amazing persistence: Forty years later, in the early sixties, there were still the same four divisions. Institutionalized as the units of administration of instruction, the divisions kept down the tendency to departmentalize, and while linking faculty in clusters for the general courses, they also took full charge of the student as he turned specialist. Thus, for instruction, the students might belong to the college as a whole for the first two years, but they were specifically in the hands of a division for upper-class work. Deeply involved in the early courses and in charge of the later ones, the divisions became strong means of integration within discipline-linked blocs of the staff. They became an organizational foundation for the curricular style given Reed by Scholz and his followers.

*Financial Resources.* How were these changes provided for in a college so destitute? The college doubled tuition within three years, through three increases, moving from one hundred to two hundred dollars per year, and brought this source of income up from thirty to sixty thousand dollars. The endowment investments, better managed and at last more productive, by 1924 were bringing in another twenty thousand dollars (up from thirty-eight to fifty-eight thousand dollars). The General Education Board, still interested in Reed, also threw in emergency funds, a three-year grant of twenty-five thousand dollars per year for operating expenses, to be matched by contributions secured from local citizens. For a permanent, stable base, the G.E.B. offered in 1923 to provide one-third of an endowment increase of $400,000 if the college could raise the other two-thirds.[58] The foundation device of requiring matching funds in a ratio of 2 to 1 from other sources forced the college to go to downtown Portland. A fund-raising campaign, carried out largely after President Scholz' death, raised the endowment by a half million dollars, from approximately $1,200,000 to $1,700,000, increasing income from this source in the late twenties by another $30,000.

These increases were an improvement, but they were barely adequate. The budget in the early thirties was only about $165,000 for 400 students, compared with a budget of $425,000 at Antioch for 650 alternating students and $785,000 at Swarthmore for 500 students.[59] The faculty was increasingly stretched thin, and their overwork became an important form of subsidy for the college. Student-teacher ratios of about 10 to 1 that had

58. McKinley, *loc. cit.*; and "The First Quarter Century," *loc. cit.*, p. 9.
59. *American Universities and Colleges*, 2nd ed. (Washington, D.C., American Council on Education, 1932), 667, 303, 737, respectively.

obtained up through 1923 began to slip toward 14 to 1 in the late twenties and 17 to 1 in the early thirties. Low-paid student help, reluctantly used by Foster in the nineteen-tens, reappeared in the form of graduate assistants—about five a year in the late twenties and ten in the early thirties.[60] In short, enough money was found to keep going, even to retain a small group of able, tough-minded scholars, but no one was going to get rich on what he made at Reed. And if he did, he would be too tired to spend it. The life of the college had brightened visibly from the darkness of financial sickness, but it retained a gray cast.

*Other Changes.*   Needless to say, the special irritant of Simplified Spelling was removed from the emerging character of Reed. After 1920 unusual spelling was reserved for the papers of students, clearly where it belonged in the eyes of faculty and local citizens. More important, the effort to educate and reform Portland disappeared with the departure of Foster and his militant social scientists. The trustees were no longer concerned with offering a practical service to Portland to satisfy fully the spirit and terms of the original bequest, and they were eager for purposes of public relations that the staff and students tend to their business on campus. Community services proved to have a peripheral characteristic, easy to shake off. With the extension work removed, the college was neater and tighter than it had been previously and was now formed in almost a pure liberal arts mold.

## Conclusion

Reed was born under favorable circumstances of unfettered charter, autonomous trustees, and adequate endowment. Its first educational leader initiated purpose that was singular and clear. The college soon came upon financial hard times, however, its emerging practices and general style became suspect in the eyes of most who gazed upon them, and it was not long before it became an institution swimming against the current. In a context of nonsupport and hostility, the early staff continued to enunciate vigorously the singular purpose, to select and commit personnel and clientele accordingly, and to let the environment take the hindmost. When a second president brought some new ideas and new staff, the outcome was not an adaptation to outside interests but a more effective structure for the intended severity.

Such a college was bound to have serious difficulties. Even if a liberal millionaire had happened along to ease the financial agony, the divergence in values caused environmental strains from which there was little escape. The college soon won the hearts of those who thought that academic life should be pure and severe, but it then also appeared high

60. McKinley, *loc. cit.*

and mighty, a place given to superior ways and claims, an elitist cult in a land of popular democracy.

Out of this early intense strain between purpose and environment, the college began a tendency to turn inward upon its own human resources. This introversion, soon a habit, downgraded and warded off the hostile environment. As commitment formed around sharply focused intent, members of the organizational core depended on their own judgment and not on that of the outside. Any adjustment to environmental demands was then likely to be suspect as a denial of what was right. The college was on the road to becoming an unaccommodating institution.

# *Chapter 5.* Embodiment

THE CHARACTER of Reed became firmly fixed in a particular combination of values and organizational structures. The curriculum increasingly expressed the academic ideals of the early years. The students increasingly evolved a subculture that made them an independent force, while they also vigorously expressed values of academic excellence and individualism that were true to the rest of the institution. The public image of the college increasingly developed a sharp edge that in stereotyped and dramatic ways expressed its internal features. Most important, the faculty became wedded to a concept of the institution, determined to develop that concept, and possessed of the means of protecting it. Between the death of President Richard Scholz in 1924 and the beginning of World War II, the institution developed unusual tenacity in protecting a distinctive set of values. At the core of the tenacity was the power of the faculty to control campus affairs.

## The Authority of the Cadre

After William Foster and Scholz, the senior members of the faculty became the center of gravity at Reed. This group numbered hardly more than a dozen—eight to ten important figures brought in by President Scholz, together with the several senior men who had remained from the

Foster era. All had been involved in the struggle to rebuild the college in the early twenties, and a few had also been through the ups and downs of the first decade; the sources of personal commitment were many. They had been recruited and had come to Reed because they possessed educational points of view congenial to those of one or the other of the two presidents. They each had been close to a leader who, though now gone, had his ideals reflected in specific practices. The soul-searing intensity of the difficulties in the late nineteen-tens and early twenties had separated the believers from the nonbelievers. The senior men of 1925 were strongly conscious of a distinctive Reed point of view and were determined to see it prevail. The distribution of status and authority on campus supported and made dominant that determination.

Reed very early developed an unusual set of faculty ranks that enhanced the status of the full professor. Everywhere the rank of professor carries more status than the rank of instructor, but normally there is a reasonably smooth progression from instructor to assistant professor to associate professor to professor. The main break in the progression is at the point where tenure takes hold, normally between the assistant professorship and the associate professorship. Even with this break, the status of an assistant professor who has been in this rank for five or six years is usually not much below that of a low associate professor. At Reed, however, senior ranking was divided sharply from junior status because the rank of associate professor did not exist. From the day the college opened in 1911 until after World War II, the rank structure was instructor, assistant professor, then full professor.

This structure was a Foster scheme. In his rigorous eyes, the associate professorship had had unfortunate effects in American colleges. Too often, men who were not able scholars or teachers had been allowed to slide from assistant to associate professor; then, upon realizing the mistake, the college would freeze these men at the associate level. Hence, this rank had become a limbo category, one deeply unfortunate for the man as well as for the institution. The sensible alternative was to eliminate the category and to force all-or-nothing evaluation of the man when he was to rise above the junior ranks. This scheme took hold at Reed (beginning about 1916), and for thirty years the college had no associate professors, no one between the one or two full Professors in a discipline and the junior, non-tenured staff.

Whatever its manifest purpose, this structure had the clear consequence of promoting faculty oligarchy. A senior rank was sharply set off, the status of full professor was not part of an easy progression from the status of assistant professor. These top men numbered eight in 1920, in a faculty twice that size; thirteen in 1930, out of a total staff of twenty-six; and eighteen in 1940, in a faculty then totaling thirty-seven. The junior ranks of instructor and assistant professor suffered much turnover, a phenome-

non that was to persist as part of the nature of Reed long after the associate professorship was added. The unusual rank structure thus helped form
and protect a faculty cadre. A dozen to eighteen men monopolized status
in the faculty and the personal influence that flows from it all through the
years when a distinctive character was first being generated and then fully
institutionalized.

Even more important, however, in the structural underpinning of the
faculty cadre was the distribution of authority among trustees, administration, and faculty. By 1930 the organizational structure at Reed was an
extreme illustration of faculty authority; the influence of faculty in policy-
making very considerably exceeded that which obtained in other colleges
of average and above-average rank. When compared with the trustee dominance and presidential power usually found in colleges of below-average
quality, the structure of authority at Reed was like the other side of the
moon. That structure has played a crucial role in the history of the college,
and to review its operation and impact, as we shall do in this and the
following chapter, is to be instructed in the possibilities and functions of
strong faculty control.

It all began about 1915, a time when academic men were vibrating
about academic freedom. The particularly nasty affair that had occurred
at the University of Utah, as mentioned in Chapter 4, spurred an effort
already under way at Reed. The president had had the idea of a campus
constitution for some time and had requested the faculty to elect a committee, which they did, to draft a plan. The committee formulated a constitution that was adopted by unanimous vote of the faculty and then approved by the trustees. This faculty constitution of 1916 opened the door
to faculty control.

The constitution provided several radical features of college organization. It defined the faculty as consisting of the president as well as of the
professors and called the president chief executive officer of the faculty. It
put the faculty in charge of educational matters. It specified a welfare
committee, consisting of two trustees, the president, and two members of
the faculty chosen by the faculty, which offered the faculty direct access to
the trustees. Most important, it established a council of nine members of
the faculty, "consisting 'of the president, exofficio, and eight members
elected annually by vote of the faculty." The council would be involved in,
indeed would be the center of, deliberation on policy: The president's
recommendations to the Board of Trustees "shall [first] come before the
council for discussion." [1] Here, then, the faculty would have a central
group to confer with the president on all matters of personnel and budget.
President Foster believed that in establishing closer than usual contact

1. Constitution of Reed College in "William T. Foster, First Report of the President,
1910–1919," *Reed College Record*, No. 34 (December, 1919), pp. 46–48.

between faculty on the one hand and president and trustees on the other in policy deliberation, the college was occupying a middle ground "between the two great opposit [sic] evils of administration—an executiv [sic] vested with autocratic power and an executiv [sic] vested with so little power that he could not be held responsible."[2]

The idea and the form were thus under way, but Reed did not immediately plunge into faculty control. At this time, exodus of staff greatly weakened the hand of the faculty. Also the president was not temperamentally suited to easy give-and-take: As indicated earlier, faculty members grew restive under his autocratic ways. Then, after Foster left and an interim committee managed the college for two years, Scholz came in to dominate the scene for three years.

A portent of things to come, however, was the stiff battle given Scholz and his newly hired professors in 1921–22 by a few of the survivors from the Foster era who did not appreciate the second president's plans for reorganizing the curriculum and the faculty. The defenders of the practices of the nineteen-tens, two or three of the senior men, were not afraid to express themselves when the president brought his reform to the faculty. One Reed professor who saw it all described the debate as one in which "there were many vigorous differences of opinion." "So radical a departure from the laissez faire spirit of the elective scheme to the collective planning of the curriculum was bound to provoke controversy—not always good natured." [3] Others used harsher terms. One professor who stayed at the college for only one year (1923–24) wrote after Scholz' death of "a pitched battle." [4] A later president and critic of the college claimed that the squabbles of the Scholz period were an indication that efforts to change the college "tended to touch off devastating intramural conflict." [5] Clearly the senior faculty members by the early twenties had the habit of speaking their minds. Scholz prevailed over the opposition, however; the opposing ranks were thin, and he had brought his own troops.

After Scholz strong faculty control became operative. Upon his death the college for a few months again used the device of an interim committee of three professors. Then a third president, Norman F. Coleman, took office in 1925 and remained for nine years. President Coleman was a known element. He had been with the college as Professor of English from 1912 to 1920 and was the only senior member of the faculty in the early days with strong local ties. He had taught previously in the area; he became a popular extension lecturer; and he was liked by the timber

2. Foster, "First Report of the President," *loc. cit.*, p. 49.

3. Charles McKinley, *Report on Reed College Presented in Behalf of the Educational Policies Committee* (Portland, Ore., Reed College, 1934).

4. C. E. Ayres, "Scholz of Reed," *The New Republic*, Vol. XL, No. 516 (October, 1924), pp. 197–99.

5. Dexter Merriam Keezer, *The Light That Flickers* (New York, Harper & Row, Publishers, 1947), p. 33.

interests. Coleman left the campus during the unsettled days of 1920 to enter labor relations and conciliation in industry in the Pacific Northwest as president of Loyal Legion of Loggers and Lumbermen. He was not a well-known or bold educational reformer, and when he came back to the college as president, he did not bring grand schemes of new purpose or internal reorganization. He wished to inject a dose of piety into what was already known in local conservative circles as "Godless Reed" and was selected partly for this point of view by trustees worried about atheism in the college; but Reed was already immune to standard religion, and this effort caused little trouble. The president was also interested in Far Eastern affairs but was not able to find a place for such a program in the Reed scheme. He also considered the possibility of convincing some other private colleges to relocate at Reed to make a complex of colleges, but the only colleges that might have considered such a move were weak-sister institutions and the faculty wanted nothing to do with this idea.

The third president started with only small capital, anyway, in faculty support. When the presidency was open and various men were being considered, the faculty had developed a preference for a striking figure, Alexander Meiklejohn, who had just left the presidency of Amherst College (1912–24), had spent some time lecturing at Reed, and had not yet been tapped to be chairman of the Experimental College at the University of Wisconsin (1926–38). But the trustees were not eager for a third educational leader and moved to a more conservative, business-minded man who could work on finances and public relations and get along reasonably well with the faculty. The faculty, in turn, did not feel led or threatened.

During this period of consolidation, the faculty got into the habit of running the educational program and participating decisively in budget formation. The forms established by the 1916 constitution then became genuinely operative, tilting more and more toward faculty governance. In the late twenties and early thirties an established group of full professors, among them men of intellect with forceful personalities, controlled the internal affairs of the college. These men sat together on the council, on the welfare committee, and in the faculty meeting, with a single administrator who, in a sense, was up from the ranks and whose main strength resided in his capacity to restore the faith of local citizens and hence possibly to improve the financing of the college. In this mix strong faculty influence became institutionalized.

We can assert that the faculty moved into control during this period partly because knowledgeable faculty members, when later interviewed, said this had occurred; and in part, because the record shows no programmatic residues of the intentions and efforts of the president. During his period of tenure, 1925–34, annual reports spoke of "steadily augmented financial resources," of planning for a retirement fund, of a new library building almost completed.[6] No major sustained effort to change the curriculum, to reshape the faculty, or to reorder campus affairs was distinguishably the president's. An unsympathetic faculty easily beat back such hopes as that of bringing more religion to the college. Most important as evidence of faculty control, however, is what occurred when this third president stepped out of office to become again a professor of English on campus and a new man from the outside took up the presidency.

A fourth president, Dexter Merriam Keezer, had the ideas and the will to leave a significant educational mark on Reed College. Trained as an economist, having taught in several colleges, he had more immediate experience as a newspaper editor, a position which was to stand him in good stead with the local press, and as executive director of the Consumers Advisory Board of the National Recovery Administration in Washington. Energetic and forceful, even cantankerous, he was not one for tea and Plato. He symbolized, at the outset, his desire to cut the cake of custom on campus by turning his own inauguration into an educational conference, one designed to raise issues about the character of Reed and its appropriateness for the times. At the conference-in-lieu-of-formal-inauguration, discussion groups, with outside speakers, addressed themselves to such topics, selected by the new president, as the following: [7]

How, for teaching and study, can Reed College draw more effectively upon materials available in the City of Portland and the Northwest? . . . How can the social and recreational set-up of Reed College, characterized by the absence of formalized intercollegiate athletics, fraternities and other recreational and social devices conventionally employed by American colleges, be improved and made more generally appealing while continuing to escape the evils it has successfully avoided?

The new president had several aims. He thought the college was over-intellectualized, so he would strengthen extracurricular activities to provide balance in the life of the student. The course of study, in his view, was far removed from the real world, so he would bring in more practical courses oriented to the basic social problems of the day. The college was too detached from its immediate area and was suffering too much from local hostility, so he would work to reduce the self-imposed isolation and to improve opinion of Reed in Portland. The place had become set in a mold, so, above all, one way or another—through conferences, new courses, new personnel, personal dynamism—he would shake up the settled vision that faculty and students possessed.

6. Norman F. Coleman, "President's Report," *Reed College Bulletin*, Vol. 9, No. 4 (July, 1930), quotation on p. 1.
7. "Conference on Educational Problems, on the Occasion of Inauguration of Dexter Merriam Keezer as Fourth President of Reed College, May 15, 16 and 17, 1935," *Reed College Bulletin*, Vol. 14, No. 4 (November, 1935), p. 2.

The new president did not equivocate or wait. Two months after arriving, he was writing a long letter to the alumni: [8]

Intellectual development is not the sole interest of the College. . . . It is firmly committed to the cultivation of those generous and understanding attitudes toward fellow human beings which form the foundation of good manners. . . . And, as a wise teacher, it recognizes the value of social activities in providing joyful entertainment and in stimulating sensible regard for those amenities which make for more gracious living and more individual ease in dealing with the world.

The work in the social sciences was "too bookish"; majors in these fields were "preoccupied with a theoretical approach." [9] And by the end of his first year, in his unusual three-day inaugural conference, Keezer was arguing forcefully in a discussion of "the social and recreational set-up:" [10]

Reed College, as many of you know, lacks support. How is it to be obtained? Not by adopting a laissez-faire attitude and living in a vacuum, trusting in some beneficent spirit to provide those financial sinews of the lack of which I am so acutely and painfully conscious. I speak as a person having responsibility for a going concern and I say that laissez-faire would be a suicidal attitude. We have an extra-mural job of community relations and within the College we are going to be increasingly forced to deal with this personality question of social enjoyment for our students. . . .

The College has not made for itself such a place in the community that its stability is assured. One of the tremendous strengths of a college should be its alumni body. What have we to draw the alumni back? We need new and stronger contacts with them; we can't live here in a vacuum, and we cannot drift. There are certainly decent and friendly ways to make contacts without going into commercialized athletics.

Differentiating relatively informal intercollegiate athletics from commercialized sport, Keezer asked the athletic director of the college for suggestions of "what can and should be done." The director defended current practice, concluding that "we are struggling along lines in keeping with the educational program of Reed College." To that the new president retorted, "After all, many of the ideas now operative in our recreational and social scheme at Reed are twenty-five years old and a searching re-examination is called for." [11]

Full of ideas and energy, critical of a number of specific practices that seemed to him to lower the tone of Reed or to plague it with problems, Keezer was an agent of intended change, but his efforts were to come to nought. He ran contrary, not to the trustees—for they were in consider-

8. "A Letter to the Alumni from the President," quoted in "The First Quarter Century: Retrospect and Appraisal, 1911–1936," *Reed College Bulletin*, Vol. 15, No. 4 (November, 1936), p. 12.
9. "A Letter to the Alumni from the President," *Reed College Bulletin*, Vol. 13, No. 4 (November, 1934), p. 18.
10. "Conference on Education Problems . . .," *loc cit.*, p. 26.
11. *Ibid.*

able agreement—but to the ideals and practices of the faculty. Desiring an intellectual campus, the faculty did not share the president's concern about balance in the life of the student. They wanted solid studies and felt that any material on local problems should be carefully integrated with theoretical interests. They did not care to plan social life or to open the door to major intercollegiate sports. They were concerned little about public opinion that, to them, did not understand the college or criticized it from vulgar premises. They would defend the college as it was.

And defend it they did, against the outsider, a president who was a "challenge to intellectualism" [12] and who, in the faculty point of view, did not understand what distinguished the college. After a short honeymoon, opposition to the president from the faculty—and students—mounted rapidly, and the Keezer period became characterized by disagreement between a forceful, change-oriented president and an established faculty. The president later maintained—to take one issue—that in order "to bridge the gap between the college classroom and the workaday world" and "to extend the root structure of the college in its region," he had:

blocked out a course of study on the Bonneville development [Bonneville Dam on the Columbia River] which would enlist the co-operative efforts of students, faculty members representing half-dozen different specialized fields of study, and, from the community, managers of private and public electric power developments, engineers, and labor leaders.

The outsiders had been enthusiastic and the students came along, he claimed, but the faculty killed it: "From the outset, however, with a few exceptions there was an oppressive lack of professorial enthusiasm, and the course soon wasted away because of lack of support from that crucial quarter." On the demise of the course, he commented, "With it went what I remain convinced was an opportunity made to order to strike a real blow for liberal education." [13] The faculty, however, offered a different set of facts: The president suggested the course, two interested professors planned it, and the president then did nothing to implement it.

In any event, in the context any issue could become a contended one. When the president became convinced he had the wrong man in the gym for instilling competence in sports, he cut down to part-time work and salary the much beloved physical education instructor who symbolized the low-key approach to sports. But the instructor held on, backed by the faculty, and outlasted the president. The president also wanted to hire some men of practical experience in the social sciences. The faculty, in their turn, defined such men as incompetent and drew a line of no retreat

12. A tag placed by a Reed professor on the Keezer administration. The president agreed, saying that he had "a positive concern for all phases of the life of the college." Dexter Merriam Keezer, "Annual Report of the President of Reed College to the Trustees and Regents," *Reed College Bulletin*, Vol. 17, No. 4 (November, 1938), pp. 1–2.
13. All quotations from Keezer, *The Light That Flickers*, pp. 46–48.

around the appointment and reappointment of nonacademic men. The last straw for them was the appointment in 1941 of a man as professor of sociology and dean of men who had been in Indian Affairs in the federal government and, before that, in "social service, advertising, and manufacturing." [14]

Keezer also was active in outside affairs, away from the campus part of the time in labor arbitration and government service, and the faculty saw this deflection of effort as a lack of presidential commitment. One unsympathetic faculty member kept book on the president's absences and claimed he was away seven out of twelve months during one period. There were also head-on encounters at faculty meetings and occasions when trustees had to mediate between the president and the faculty. Any issue would do. The president intended to reform weaknesses as he saw them, and he would not cease the attack; the faculty saw his efforts as a serious threat to Reed virtues and would not back down on defending the college as it was. With a growing and acute sense that he was in the wrong post, Keezer stayed until 1942, when he took a leave of absence to go to Washington, D. C., on war work and then some months later resigned.

In retrospect, Keezer had little chance. The key instruments of change, personnel and power, were not among his resources. There was little hiring to be done in those depression years and hence little chance to bring in men of his own. Years later, in his critical assessment of Reed as "the light that flickers," Keezer lamented this unfavorable condition: [15]

In almost eight years at Reed College I had occasion to make only one professorial appointment. . . . There are few more important indicators of the chances that a new president has of making a substantial educational imprint on a college than the number of key faculty appointments he will have a chance to make relatively soon. It is an indicator, however, which I innocently overlooked.

Equally important was the location of power in faculty-dominated bodies. The faculty council, in Keezer's view, gave "political expression to the extreme conservatism of the faculty, both in matters of educational policy and any others which might affect job tenure." This outlook "tended to solidify the obstacles in the way of getting ahead effectively" and anchored the college firmly to the *status quo*.[16] Keezer discovered that the faculty influenced educational policy to a degree probably not exceeded anywhere in the country. The faculty was able to conserve the Foster-Scholz values and the practices they defined as the expression of those values because they not only believed strongly in them but also had the tools of power. Given what was by then a fixed belief in faculty control, and especially the specific device of the faculty-dominated administrative council, a change-minded president had little room in which to maneuver.

14. *Reed College Notes,* Vol. 4, No. 1 (October, 1941), p. 3.
15. *The Light That Flickers,* p. 71.
16. *Ibid.,* p. 32.

## Curriculum as Embodiment of Purpose

The academic ideals of the first fifteen years required, for their fulfill-ment, close attention to the curriculum. This attention was forthcoming in unusual degree: The faculty persisted in certain critical ways of ordering their work and their instructional relationship with students. They and the students become inordinantly conscious of a distinct Reed curriculum, holding firmly through decades to given practices as the essence of the college. Tough basic requirements, established by 1925, as indicated earlier, were still central in 1960: the harsh sequence of Junior Qualifying Examination, senior thesis, and oral thesis examination, which dominated the student's thought and behavior in the last two years of study; the heavy hand of the humanities program, which brought the whole fresh-man class to the same lecture room and then plunged freshmen into small groups for intensive seminar discussions. These requirements spelled academic seriousness across all fields of study. They helped generate a community of experience for both the students who were in attendance at a given time and the students of other generations. The physics students of 1960 shared these compelling features with the student majoring in English thirty years before. Students as well as faculty also soon learned to use these requirements in arguing with themselves and others about the uniqueness of Reed.

A consensus emerged and became fixed that these tough mandates alone gave Reed a special place in American higher education: [17]

> In the development of the curricula of American Colleges of liberal arts in the last twenty-five years [1920–45], Reed College has played a significant part. Reed has worked out methods of handling broad and yet individual programs in fields of concentration and has made provisions for general education through courses of distinctive content and method at the underclass level. . . .
>
> The college seeks thereby to challenge the students to explore and to interpret materials and problems for themselves firsthand in conference discussion, in lab-oratory and in studio, in writing, and in research. Such is the rationale of a cur-riculum that proceeds from the basic courses of the freshman year to the senior thesis and oral examinations.

Professor Rex Arragon, sometimes known as the high priest of the human-ities program, wrote often about this program and its techniques of group discussion.[18] And any review of general-education curricula was likely to turn its eye to Reed.[19]

17. Rex F. Arragon, "The Development of the Reed Curriculum," *Reed College Bulletin*, Vo., 24, No. 1 (November, 1945), pp. 3, 19.
18. E.g., "The Humanities Program at Reed," in Earl J. McGrath, ed., *The Human-ities in General Education* (Dubuque, Iowa, Wm. C. Brown Co., 1949), pp. 261–75.
19. E.g., Russell Thomas, *The Search for a Common Learning: General Education, 1800–1960* (New York, McGraw-Hill, Inc., 1962), pp. 221–29.

If these features did not fully satisfy a sense of distinction, the grading system was likely to complete the picture. The practice of recording course grades but not reporting them to the student, perhaps a simple and innocent difference in the eyes of outsiders, became weighted with hoary significance. For the faculty not to speak to students in a language of grades, for the college not to issue a report card, for the student not to know his letter grades became a bold and lonely venture to reduce the caring for grades. It symbolized thought for thought's sake as against the crass pursuit of grades at other places:

Grades are not released to the students. The college believes that letter grades become artificial goals for education, and that learning should be encouraged for its own sake.[20]

The student must find in himself and in his associations with faculty and fellow students the incentives to steady, disciplined work, and learn to measure his success, not by letter grades, but by his grasp of a subject, and by his gradual intellectual growth.[21]

Faculty and students became inordinately proud of this policy. Reported in the annual catalogue through the years and touted in other publications of the college, the nonreporting of grades also became a specific element of a reputation that caught the eye of intellectual high school seniors looking for a college where learning came first. Admissions officers of the college noted time and again in their visits to high schools that this feature of the campus had external meaning, attracting intellectually adventuresome students while repelling the more routine types. The grading policy thus internally and externally came to stand for intellectual purity.

But the purity could be harsh since the nonreporting of grades fed directly into a general severity in grading that was at the very soul of the college. Reed ideals early and strongly discouraged the coddling of students. The thrust in practice was increasingly to involve a small number of young people so intensely in academic work that they would develop the intellectual concentration, as well as the specific skills, of the scholar. Early presidents and sustaining senior faculty were not inclined to induce such motivation by heavy praise and abundant rewards. With a bright student body accustomed to high grades from earlier schooling, austere grading became a faculty tradition. Even in the late fifties, with a nationally recruited student body of high selectivity, the recommended distribution of grades for freshman and sophmore courses was 40 per cent A's and B's and 60 per cent C's and D's. In the freshman humanities course required of all, the instructors were grading even more severely than that, e.g., giving less than 30 per cent of the students A's and B's. This system

20. *The Reed College Handbood* (student handbook), (Portland, Ore.: Reed College, 1959), p. 40.
21. "Catalog, 1959–60," *Reed College Bulletin*, Vol. 37, No. 11 (August, 1959), p. 14.

led to greater grade deprivation than would normally obtain in highly selective colleges.

In this context, the nonreporting of grades did not ease the pressure but reduced further the rewards of academic effort and increased the penalties. Students earning good grades did not receive much information: [22]

> Twice each semester the standing of all students is reviewed by the faculty. . . . The adviser presents each student [freshmen and sophomores] with a "white slip" informing him in general terms of the quality of his work and makes any additional remarks he deems necessary.

Upperclassmen were free to consult their advisers or not. The verbal assessment given the student could remain at whatever level of ambiguity the faculty adviser desired—e.g., "You are doing all right here", "you are doing very good work and are among the best students." Students getting marginal to failing grades, however, had to be told something specific: "You have failing grades," or "you are close to failing" or "you got an F." In personal conversation and by official memo, it was necessary to warn the student that his continuation was in danger: [23]

> Various faculty actions may be taken in dealing with deficiencies. These are: warning of noticeable drop, reference to advisor, official warning, probation, advice to withdraw, denial of registration, and dismissal from the college.

The faculty could issue special commendations at the end of the year for exceptional academic records, but these were kept in short supply; e.g., they went to ten students in the whole student body in 1959. The better students for their own satisfaction could often extract a letter grade from the ritualistic verbal statements of advisers, but this process was not concrete and elaborate. The result was that low grades were better communicated than high ones. On top of severe grading in a bright, competitive student body, the policy of not reporting grades made the college strongly punishment centered.

A third critical element that reflected and carried central values, was the purity of the curriculum in the liberal arts. There was no engineering, business, nursing, or pharmacy. Of all the applied fields, only education resided in the curriculum, and this in weak form. The performing arts, too, had only a weak place because the Letters and Arts Division gave a strong preference to the history of music, art, and theater over performance, e.g., "no degree credit is granted for instrumental instruction." The college had only one senior man in the arts, with one popular class in calligraphy long serving as therapeutic escape from the constant intellectual activity. With its boundaries tightly drawn, the college offered a small number of courses and granted the bachelor's degree in an unusually small number of fields:

22. *The Reed College Handbook,* p. 40.
23. *Ibid.*

e.g., in the mid-fifties, the curriculum totaled about three hundred semester courses, compared with five hundred at Swarthmore, seven hundred at Antioch, and over fourteen hundred at San Francisco State College. Degrees were being taken in about fifteen fields, compared with about eighteen at Swarthmore, twenty-nine at Antioch, and over fifty at San Francisco State.

In brief, the curriculum was exceedingly lean in the traditional disciplines of the liberal arts, strongly structured with requirements, and firmly muscled with hard grading. It became an operative definition of academic purity and toughness, bearing daily on the direction of the student and his definition of himself and the college. Because the curriculum was also an expression of the understanding among the faculty members that in the classroom, they knew what was best for students, it became a powerful instrument of faculty control over student effort. The Reed classroom became a site of intellectual challenge and logical reasoning. Curriculum and classroom became the components into which the faculty, having won control, poured their heart and soul; outsiders had this structure in mind when they spoke of Reed as having become a "model liberal arts college." [24] In curriculum, Reed became the liberal arts dream fulfilled.

## Student Commitment

The early staff wanted Reed to be a residential college housing virtually all its students and with many faculty members also living in the dormitories or taking up residence no farther away than the edge of the campus. But this condition was not realized. The Portland students often could not afford the luxury of a dormitory, and as the college got into dire financial straits, it had to depend heavily on student tuition, enrolling students without quibbling over whether they would live on or off campus. Commuting students, known as "daydodgers," then became numerous: By 1934, 86 per cent of the students were nonresidential.[25] This state of affairs did not rest easily with administrators, faculty, or students—among other things it left the dormitories partly empty—and beginning in the late thirties, during the regime of President Keezer, the college sought to develop a full residential character, with students drawn from the whole nation rather than just from in and around its home city. These moves took years to accomplish. In the late forties the daydodgers still outnumbered the students in residence, and the college was drawing only about one-fourth of the students from outside the Pacific Northwest. In the fifties the change finally took hold: By 1960 nearly all of the eight hundred

24. Frederick Rudolph, *The American College and University* (New York, Alfred A. Knopf, Inc., 1962), p. 456.

25. Keezer, "A Letter to the Alumni for the President," *Reed College Bulletin*, Vol. 13, No. 4 (November, 1934), p. 5.

students were in residence, with about one-third drawn from the Northwest, one-third from California, and one-third from states east of the Rocky Mountains.[26]

## THE STUDENT CULTURE

Whether the student body was composed primarily of local students living on campus, daydodgers, or nationally based students filling the dormitories, after the first few years students had a strong collective sense of being different from other groups and being apart from the rest of the world. President Foster and his early students self-consciously and earnestly worked to create normal student traditions around Campus Day, Christmas party, and Commencement. The specific practices they tried to establish were to come and go, often change form, and as we shall later see, largely disappear. But what early got under way among the students to become later strong and permanent was a general definition of who they were, a definition derived from and closely allied with the strident claim of the president and the faculty that Reed was different.

For the students as well as the faculty, the primacy of scholarship became a proud claim. As indicated earlier, the subordination of sports and social life had become so much a part of student thinking by 1919 that the students opposed the brief venture into intercollegiate sports at that time. By the thirties this sentiment was deeply entrenched in the alumni as well, which gave firm outside support for the policies that kept Joe College away from the Reed scene. In a 1932 alumni poll covering the ten graduating classes of 1915 to 1924, the alumni voted 185 to 15 against more intercollegiate athletics.[27]

The students as students and then as alumni used the avoidance of sports as an indication of complete commitment to serious matters. They were not "normal" students, they knew, and they were not about to become normal adults. As they developed a sense of specialness, as students, they cared little about associating with people in the surrounding society. With their collective self-concept, they turned their backs on the outside world. Although the center of Portland was only twenty minutes by bus, the Reed student, by the fifties, had stopped going downtown. What he wanted, he knew, was to be found on campus, within the confines of the student body. This turning-in tended to make the college a total institution that psychologically, socially, and physically encapsulated the student.

On the Reed island that the students themselves did so much to create, several giant oaks of student style grew from the small acorns of the founding years, eventually casting such large shadows that they pre-

26. Registrar's records, 1945–1960, Reed College.
27. "Reed Graduates Appraise the College," *Reed College Bulletin*, Vol. 11, No. 1 (January, 1932).

vented the saplings of competitive activities and norms from growing. One such giant growth was informality and individualism in extracurricular activities. Early classes were much interested in formal activities— establishing clubs, organizing all-campus dances—but the emerging central doctrines of the campus set little store in this round of activities. In due time the commitment to scholarship and study became, on the other side of the coin, an anticommitment to a regularized social life. The student culture moved steadily toward highly individual use of the time not devoted to study. The drift was slow over the first two decades but sped up in the thirties and then came to full tide after World War II. By 1960 virtually all formal social occasions had vanished, killed by attenuation of interest through the years.

The Reed students in 1930, for example, were undoubtedly not a group centered on social life compared with students at other colleges at the time, but they still possessed regular social forms. Besides Student Council, the newspaper, and the yearbook, they also had such clubs and activities as International Club, Social Science Club, Debate, Chorus, German Chorus, Orchestra, Drama Club, Freethinkers Club, Letterman's Club, and Reed Women's Athletic Association. The commuting students had an association; those living on campus were self-consciously organized by residential house. The student body as a whole was still organized by classes. There were formal dances, such as the Daydodger Formal and the Women's Formal, and formal dinners, such as "House F formal dinner in the Commons." There was even a Junior Prom at the Portland Country Club. The calendar of events for a month, e.g., October, 1930, listed formal activities each weekend: a dance sponsored by House C; a tea given by the Amanda Reed Association (a women's group); a dance sponsored by the football men; a "hard-times party" given by the "Frosh"; and an open house held by House D.[28]

Ten years later, at the end of the thirties, there was still such a phenomenon as a "Central Dance Committee . . . composed of two representatives from each class . . . delegated to plan all dances, each class being responsible for one formal and one informal dance during the year." The yearbook was still a class or group production—nowhere in it was authorship attributed to an individual—and otherwise ordinary, including the pages of advertising in the rear that helped cover the cost of printing.[29] And still, in 1950, some annual dances remained: Along with one square dance and a folk dance, there was an evening of dinner-dancing in the commons and a Junior Prom with an Alice in Wonderland motif. There was some lingering class organization, and the annual Campus Day remained an occasion when students helped to clean up and repair the

28. *The Griffin* (Reed College yearbook), 1930.
29. *Ibid.*, 1939.

campus, sometimes topping off their labors with a tug of war. But the regular participation in clubs had thinned considerably: Alongside several political groups—Young Democrats, Young Progressives, United World Federalists—just a few social clubs—Camera Club, Outing Club—remained.[30]

By 1960 the trend to informality had killed virtually all formal student organizations. Class organization had vanished, and dormitory groups no longer held scheduled events. Clubs other than several volatile political groups were almost completely gone. Scheduled teas, dances, and bonfires were not to be found. The yearbook became a personal art form, given to one or two students for expression of their creativity. The student newspaper had moved to the posture that the most important news was individual opinion. The style of social life was not to make arrangements ahead of time but to decide on an activity on the spot. In short, the social forms expressed an extreme individualization. The freedom from planned event and scheduled occasion was almost total.

The students wanted it this way. When queried about their interest in student government and extracurricular activities, Reed students as sophomores (1959) and again as seniors (1962) showed little interest relative to students in other colleges.[31] For example, among the eight colleges in the Berkeley study, Reed was lowest in student self-assessment of how active they were in extracurricular activities. Only one in seven sophomores considered himself quite interested in student government (compared to one in three at Antioch), with over a third claiming no interest at all. Seniors were even less interested than sophomores.

A second trend was one toward rulelessness. The seed here was an early conception of honorable behavior that emphasized an abstract principle, a spirit, over specific rules. By the time the first class graduated, the students, under the urging of the first president, who wanted to encourage self-discipline, formulated an honor principle: [32] "There is no 'honor system' at Reed College, devised to cover certain hours or certain exercizes [sic]; there is a principle of honor which is regarded as sufficient to cover all phases of student life at all times." With the principle, however, went some specification of honorable behavior. The president was no laissez faire libertine, and the students, a relatively homogeneous lot from the homes of Portland, assumed, as students elsewhere, that honor meant some agreement on proper and improper behavior: [33]

30. *Ibid.*, 1950.
31. Sophomore and senior questionnaires, entering classes of 1958. Unpublished study of student development, Center for the Study of Higher Education, University of California, Berkeley.
32. "Fourth Annual Catalog, 1914–1915," *Reed College Record*, No. 19 (January, 1915), p. 12.
33. *Reed College Annual* (first student yearbook), Vol. I (1915).

In scool work [the students also used Simplified Spelling!] the Honor Spirit requires earnestness, frankness, and consideration for the rights of others in the use of library, laboratories and the like. In general conduct it includes especially respect for property rights of persons both in and outside the college, economy and care in the use of college property, the prompt payments of dets, and a regard for the reputation of the college abroad. In athletics the Honor Spirit means fair play and sportsmanship in the best sense of the word. In student government it imposes the duty of conscientius servis on the part of offis-holders, and a sense of interest in the welfare of the group on the part of individuals.

Thus, under the honor principle, there were to be all the homely virtues. The honor spirit was to be "a force in social control." It was a "point of honor" not to cheat in examinations. The students would also police their ranks, for they had "voted to relieve the faculty of the burden of enforcing honesty in these tests."

Through the first twenty years, Reed students did indeed give content to the concept of honor, specifying virtues and rules and punishing transgressions. In 1921, for example, reputed "violations of the library regulations concerning the circulation of reserve books" brought heavy condemnation in the student newspaper: This "gross violation" merits "summary disposition." "There are enough students hereabouts who sufficiently cherish the principle of individual responsibility to remove any moral defaulters who endanger it." [34]

In the thirties the rules of the game were showing strain as students began to move toward personal interpretation of appropriate behavior in the name of the principle. They were finding the honor principle "foggy" and were exhibiting a reluctance to play informer. But student leaders still believed the system had definite norms, and they were still willing to punish. In 1939, for example, the Student Council heard rumors of mass cheating in a large class.[35]

Members of the Student Council interviewed several people in the class who were willing to verify the rumors, but could find no one sufficiently interested in the preservation of the honor system to testify specifically as to the identity of the people engaged in the cheating.

The council members finally had to obtain their evidence from the instructor, in the form of identical answers. The student leaders then took the whole state of affairs to a campus assembly, where they ticked off the violations and read the riot act to the freshman class. The willingness to strike a strong moral posture still lingered: [36]

We got the system, but we ain't got the honor.
Each student [is] expected to take on certain responsibilities. . . . It is their

34. *Reed College Quest* (student newspaper), November 16, 1921.
35. *Ibid.*, November 22, 1939.
36. *Ibid.*, December 6, 1939.

[the students'] duty as individuals to uncover and report any offender of the honor system.

The principal duty of the student council is the administration of the honor system. If we don't administer it correctly, somebody else will.

Certain acts were considered a clear and definite violation of the honor system: "cheating, stealing, intervisitation [mixing of the sexes in the dormitory], mixed drinking, and illegal taking of books from the library." [37]

That same year, a student leader, later a faculty member, became much exercised over his inability to keep the billiard table operative under the honor system. Shattered cues and torn felt were to him symptoms of "a rapidly flagging honor system" since the recurring damage to the pool table, annoying enough, did not stand alone. "Flagrant violations in the library, in the classrooms, and in the gymnasium, have already tended to undermine student faith in the honor system, as well as the utility of the system." [38] Creeping violationism was throwing the honor principle into doubt.

The interruption of campus traditions by the radical alteration of the student body during World War II about ended the willingness of the Reed student to agree to a body of rules applicable to all and especially to report himself or others for violations. By 1950 students were in full cry against any policing requirements. If the Student Council punished or threatened to punish "if you break the rules again," students would reply: "This does not appear to me to be in accord with the Reed tradition of treating members of the community as adults." The "honor system is predicated on the assumption that the members of the Reed community are adult, rational human beings. Presumably, such persons would form a civilized society." [39] "The Student Council isn't placing enough faith in the honor principle. Their handling of the library reserve book situation was unnecessary and harmful to the Reed tradition of freedom for the individual." [40] "We didn't come to Reed College to be pushed around! . . . The very thought of rigid regimentation for one day—or for one hour or one minute—in Reed College, is not only disgustingly repulsive but absolutely unnecessary." Find the violators, "but leave the rest of us alone." [41]

The move from local to national recruitment in the fifties, producing a more heterogeneous student body at a time of growing student sophistication, moved the student culture further in this direction. The freedom aspect of the honor principle was highlighted, while individual and collective responsibility were washed out. For some, honor meant no rules. The student ideology approved great personal freedom and protection of the

37. *Ibid.*
38. *Ibid.*, April 19, 1940.
39. *Ibid.*, October 31, 1949.
40. *Ibid.*, November 14, 1949.
41. *Ibid.*

individual against the controls of community. Some adult critics on campus charged that this interpretation of the honor principle was a cover for license. A student in 1956 portrayed it as a laissez faire honor principle: "I'll be honest by myself, and you be honest by yourself, and never the twain shall even consider each other." [42]

A third development in the Reed student culture, one that fitted closely with the evolution toward informality and the attenuation of rules, was an increasing amount of autonomy and authority for student government vis-à-vis the administration and the faculty. As at other colleges, student government began as administrative machinery that would help create a social order among students, relieving the faculty and administration of the work of direct control and giving the students some chance to participate in governance. The student council would, of course—in standard collegiate language and understanding—be a co-operative partner, toiling happily in the hot fields of rule-making, rule enforcement, and rule adjudication, alongside the dean of students and the faculty members currently serving on committees charged with student affairs.

Student officeholders in American colleges have always been men in the middle to some degree, serving between administration and student body, operating as the lowest rank of "management" and as the highest rank of "workers." The role is tolerable as long as there is some consensus about behavior and regulations; but in the face of striking disagreement and disaffiliation, the student leaders come under exceedingly heavy pressure to abdicate or to fall toward one interest or the other. As the norms of student life at Reed moved toward great informality and freedom from adult control, the Student Council became both a weaker organizational unit and an antiadministration force. A regular council, serving in part as an instrument of administrative control, did not fit the emerging individualism and informality. The basic function of a council had to be to protect the student in his personal interpretation of how to behave. Student leaders willing to write rules and apply sanctions increasingly encountered resistance and abuse and gradually fell from office. The promise of the successful candidate for office became maximum freedom; the performance of the successful officeholder that of struggling to widen individual discretion and to weaken collective controls. From the standpoint of the nonconformist student, that government was best that governed least. From the standpoint of the administrator and the concerned faculty member, this was, at best, government by discontents and, at worst, no government at all. As nonconformity spread in the student body, the role of the Student Council became that of guarding students against the play of standard adult morality.

Thus, by the early sixties students seeking election to the council com-

42. *Ibid.*, April 23, 1956.

monly ran on a platform emphasizing the antithesis between rules and the honor principle: [43]

Student A:

Reed people are sufficiently mature and responsible to govern themselves intelligently by the honor principle without recourse to rules and decrees instituted by an authoritarian body such as the present Student Council.

Student B:

I am running because I believe that Reed students are capable of acting in a mature and responsible manner. Recently this attitude has been absent from the Council. They have made rules which diminish the Honor Principle's importance as a guide to behavior. The honor principle can only be as effective *as people think it is.*

Student C:

The guide for the behavior of the student is the Honor Principle, which presupposes and depends upon the responsibility of the individual. This code, to me, is the verbal expression of the unique character of Reed among American colleges and universities, and should form the basis for all Council action and disciplinary procedures.

Student D:

Laws are without a function in an intellectual community. And, in fact, laws as functional entities simply do not exist on the Reed campus. There is no invariably binding practice. . . . In practice what do exist on the Reed Campus are suggestions misstated as rules, tendered by the Student Council, concerning specific aspects of student conduct which are to be accepted or rejected as the individual deems fitting. . . . Reed tradition asserts the primacy of the honor principle. In practice it is this principle of individual decision that does govern.

As the Reed student culture reached its maturity after World War II, having developed the potential opened by the ideals of the nineteen-tens and twenties, it raised as a significant model the free spirit whose natural habitat was outside the classroom. The informality, the personal autonomy, and the normative system that shielded the student from rules led to a well-anchored nonconformity so salient that it was able to recruit and sustain supporters. This nonconformity, a part of the campus often confused with the whole in the minds of outsiders, always had a quiet rival, however, in the model of the young scholar-scientist whose home was in the classroom, library, and laboratory. The serious academics among the students took Reed for its faculty and classroom and ignored or offered broad and friendly toleration to those who based themselves in noncon-

43 *Ibid.,* December 4, 1961.

formity. Through these two orientations and models, the student culture of the college became an important carrier of the original central values of intellectuality and individualism. The academic orientation of the students embodied a high order of academic intellectuality, a serious and often stern quest for knowledge. The nonconformist orientation also carried intellectuality of the free-swinging variety, but it became especially the upholder of the right to great personal freedom and radical dissent.

On the small, tight island that Reed became, this imposing student culture could not, over a long period of time, have developed and have been sustained if its direction were markedly contrary to faculty values. The students' academic orientation was one naturally favored by faculties. The students' nonconformist orientation could not have become strong at most other colleges, but it did so at Reed because the faculty had long been ruggedly committed to the ideals of individualism and had chosen to leave students alone outside the classroom. When the honor system of the campus had reached the extreme of ambiguity in the fifties, fuzzed beyond the point where rule and sanction could apply, central figures in the faculty [44] still philosophized that it was a

system of living paradoxes and contradictions. Clarification would be the death of the system, however, since it would then become a machine that would limit the wide range of freedom that it presently allows. . . . The system gives Reedites a sense of community because of their loyalty to the system under which they live. The honor principle is a myth to be taken not literally, but seriously.

And when faculty members were asked (in the 1963 faculty survey of the Berkeley study) about the interest of their colleagues in students, they answered in a distinctive pattern: that the faculty was strongly interested in the academic problems of students, as in some of the other small colleges and in contrast to the self-assessment of the Berkeley faculty; but that the faculty was not interested in the students' lives outside the classroom, here appearing similar to the faculties of large campuses rather than to those of small colleges. (See Appendix 2.)

SURVIVAL AND MORTALITY

Students may leave a college because of incidents in their lives that have nothing to do with the campus. Father's business goes bankrupt, and the student is suddenly without funds; the parents' marriage breaks up, and the student feels he is needed at home; illness or death in the family forces him to interrupt or to discontinue his education. Most withdrawing, however, is not due to such incidents but to the interaction of students with a campus. Reasons for dropping out relate to the academic pace of a college, its expense, its social life, or its structure of rewards and satisfaction.

44. A senior professor in *ibid.*, April 12, 1954.

Withdrawal is *the* breaking point in the fit of students and a college to each other. In examining the student who leaves and the one who stays and why, we inform ourselves about the character of a college.

Reed early acquired a high mortality rate, one greatly in excess of that found in the selective colleges and universities to which Reed was increasingly compared and with which it increasingly competed. Harvard has long retained almost all its students, graduating 90 per cent or so of an entering class. A completion rate of about 75 per cent became characteristic of Swarthmore. The Reed figure has long run to less than 50 per cent: Of the entering class of 1915, 34 per cent graduated; 31 per cent of the 1926 entering group finished; and 42 per cent of the combined entrants of 1936 to 1939 finished.[45] Consistently throughout the forties and fifties entering classes were soon decimated: A third would be gone by the sophomore year, over a half by the junior year, and 75 per cent would often not make it into the senior year on normal schedule. Even with delayed graduation, the proportion of an entering class that would ever finish at Reed was only about one-third (Table 5-1).

*TABLE 5-1. Student Mortality, Reed College*

| Year of Entrance | Percentage Returned as | | | Percentage |
| | Sophomores | Juniors | Seniors | Finally Graduated |
| --- | --- | --- | --- | --- |
| 1940–41 | 69 | 46 | 11 | 34 |
| 1941–42 | 57 | 18 | 14 | 30 |
| 1942–43 | 25 | 9 | 10 | 30 |
| 1943–44 | 34 | 21 | 13 | 26 |
| 1944–45 | 37 | 20 | 18 | 29 |
| 1945–46 | 39 | 17 | 9 | 16 |
| 1946–47 | 63 | 36 | 25 | 36 |
| 1947–48 | 64 | 47 | 31 | 44 |
| 1948–49 | 65 | 36 | 29 | 35 |
| 1949–50 | 57 | 34 | 24 | 35 |
| 1950–51 | 60 | 34 | 21 | 30 |
| 1951–52 | 59 | 40 | 29 | 35 |
| 1952–53 | 62 | 37 | 30 | 33 |
| 1953–54 | 63 | 36 | 27 | 32 |
| 1954–55 | 71 | 47 | 35 | 36 |
| 1955–56 | 67 | 44 | 25 | 21 |
| 1956–57 | 78 | 47 | 31 | — |
| 1957–58 | 64 | 44 | — | — |
| 1958–59 | 72 | — | — | — |

Source: Registrar's records, 1940–60, Reed College.

The causes of this staggering mortality in a selective college are not entirely clear, but some informed explanations are available for parts of it, and we can estimate the rest. When the daydodgers bulked large in the

45. "Reed College Self-Study Program," Reed College, 1953, p. 31.

student body, the attitude and practice developed on their part of using Reed as a junior college—that is, of taking one or two years of college nearby while living inexpensively at home and then transferring to another college or to a university away from home for the remainder of the four years. President Coleman took note of this phenomenon in a 1930 report: [46]

A first group of students graduating from high school wish to enter Reed and are qualified for admission, yet do not contemplate taking the full four years' course that Reed offers. Some are residents of Portland and say frankly, "We are not yet ready to leave home, but at the end of one or two years, for the sake of wider experience and greater independence, we may wish to get away from our families and accustomed surroundings and enter a college or university in another part of the country." This desire is accentuated if the students develop definitely an urge toward vocations, such as music or business management, for which a college of liberal arts does not clearly prepare.

In addition, academic severity was at work. The place was rigorous, as Coleman also noted: [47]

A second group of students discover that the upper years at Reed require too rigorous or too specialized a course of study and either content themselves with a partial course or choose to take their final year or years at some institution where requirements for graduation are more easily met.

For many students at Reed, academic stress became the name of the game. They studied very hard. The Berkeley survey showed that in hours per week spent studying, the mode at Reed (and Swarthmore) was thirty to fifty hours, compared to ten to twenty hours at San Francisco State College.[48] The academic monkey was on the back nearly all the time. Then, too, as mentioned earlier, the faculty was tough in its evaluation of students, and the policy of not reporting grades meant in operation that good grades went relatively unpraised while low grades were expressed verbally and in writing to warn students about the trouble they were in. In academic punishment and reward, there were many sticks and few carrots. Those with failing grades were likely, in their own eyes and in the eyes of friends, to be wearing black bands. There was also little of the feeling often found in selective colleges that if the student was good enough to get in he was probably good enough to graduate. Without any trace of old Eastern Seaboard patterns of sponsoring gentlemen, the Reed faculty poured on the work, graded hard, and rationalized the high mortality as being due to the students' not being good enough.

46. "President's Report," *loc. cit.*, p. 4.
47. *Ibid.*, p. 4.
48. Sophomore and senior questionnaires, entering classes of 1958. Unpublished study of student development, Center for the Study of Higher Education, University of California, Berkeley.

The academic stress led to a pattern of students dropping out voluntarily, rather than through formal eviction. Once behind in his course work, with the books piled high on all sides, a student would feel that he could never catch up and decide to pull out. Receiving several warnings about low grades, the student would decide he was not good enough for Reed and choose to go to some lesser place, such as Berkeley. Having gotten through the first two years, the student would look ahead to the Junior Qualifying Examination and the senior thesis and decide that he did not want to face these third- and fourth-year hurdles. Having persisted to the senior year, the student would block on his senior thesis—anticipating by four years a common psychological problem of doctoral candidates —drop out while a senior or fail to graduate on schedule. Commonly a half of the withdrawing students were in satisfactory formal academic standing.[49]

Interacting heavily with the academic pressure was the social stress of life outside the classroom. The students were tough on one another, first in what they expected by way of academic and intellectual performance. Their personal expectations, together with the Reed ideals they quickly absorbed, were high. Students were "on" a high proportion of their time outside the classroom, a situation which led to weariness as well as to excitement and to diminished as well as to exalted self-concept. Second, conformity to nonconformity, in such things as dress, beards, and bare feet, irked the socially moderate students who on occasion wanted to put on a coat and tie or a dress of some color other than black or brown. Students who thought they were liberal found themselves defined as fraternity boys and took off for campuses where they could again be considered liberal. Third, the anomic quality of individualism at Reed was too much freedom psychologically for some, especially if their previous family and community life had not been heavily permissive. Such students either could not appropriately decide for themselves how to behave or had their sensibilities shocked by the decisions that others were making. Then, finally, some students were so nonconforming or artistic in interest that they found Reed too structured! Some who came to the campus in search of maximum freedom for self-expression had not perceived the old-fashioned sternness of the Reed classroom. When they came up against the severe academic demands, they decided they did not want to try to match up and took themselves elsewhere. An unusual student perceived Reed as conservative and square, but then precisely such unusual young people picked Reed out of hundreds of alternatives as the college of their choice.

With so many students withdrawing from a college to which so many were intensely drawn, several patterns of dropping out developed that allowed students to leave formally without leaving totally. One was to

49. Reports on withdrawing students, registrar's records, 1960, Reed College.

withdraw from formal student status but to remain living on the fringe of campus life, still with friends, and to use the campus as much as possible. Following this route, one could continue to see oneself, and to be seen by friends, as a student and a part of the campus community. Such dropouts even managed on occasion to sleep in the lounge of a dormitory and have food served to them, as their friends shielded them from critical eyes and sought to have the informal definition of student status take precedence over the "administrative" or "bureaucratic" one. This problem of separating student from nonstudent in the use of campus facilities was normally faced by only a few major universities, such as Chicago and the University of California (Berkeley), and usually, up to the sixties, at the graduate level. But Reed, like Antioch, developed such intense commitment in many of its students that, upon dropping out, they did not want to remove themselves physically. The result was a fringe community.

A second way to leave without leaving was to find a Reed colony, one peopled by other dropouts as well as graduates, in Berkeley, San Francisco, or elsewhere. To transfer from Reed to the University of California, Berkeley, was not to leave Reed behind since one could slip into the Reed student body already in residence there. This pattern offered many advantages, to some students the best of all possible worlds. One could taste whatever delights one wanted of the large university campus, including faculty luminaries as well as artists and coffee shops, and at the same time escape the sharp eye of the Reed professor. At Berkeley, since the professors are not close to the students, one could easily hide in the interstices of a loose structure, remaining in the meantime surrounded with Reedies and continuing to identify with Reed. Reed dropouts often have had as much loyalty to the college as graduates. To have been at Reed was the important criterion.

## Image, Social Base, and Isolation

The *reputation* of high academicism initiated by the first two presidents became firmly institutionalized in the three decades following 1930. Alongside this characteristic, another gradually emerged—political radicalism and social nonconformity—and by the fifties it was equally strong and fixed. Around these items the college developed a sharp and salient global image that helped produce a relatively tight self-selection by prospective students and a relatively narrow social base in the outside population.

In every decade the college continued to receive substantial praise from afar. The attention given Reed by national magazines and the national press during the quiet periods between crises in governance was almost always favorable in tone. *School and Society*, for example, reported on the college during the thirties as follows: An article in 1931 by a Reed professor pictured the college, now twenty years old, as experimental and distinctive; a note in 1934 reported on the selection of Keezer as the fourth president; an article in 1935, again by a Reed professor, claimed that Keezer's conference-inauguration had been most unusual, with gratifying results; in 1936 there was a report on an interdivisional curricular plan; and then in 1937 an article by President Keezer on "putting college athletics in their place." [50]

Beginning in the mid-thirties *Time* magazine repeatedly paid attention to Reed as an unusual, eye-catching place. In 1935 *Time* portrayed President Keezer as a dynamic new president who shocked the "bookworms" of the campus by inaugurating a carnival and skiing trips and telling them, " 'You don't live on intellect alone.' " In 1939 a fun piece entitled "Husky Reed" claimed that in the face of an annual football budget of $100 a patched-together team had broken campus traditions by scheduling and winning some games. Over a decade later, in 1952, in an article on the appointment of a president, *Time* commented that the previous president had "succeeded in pulling Reed out of the red, but he has never quite finished the job of pulling its reputation out of the pink." Among the local citizens, "some still labor under the false suspicion that Communist John Reed founded it and that its first president, William T. Foster, was really Communist William Z." In 1962 a long article, entitled "A Thinking Reed," suggested that the college might well have the "smartest body of undergraduates in America." [51]

*School and Society* and *Time* were not the only national magazines paying attention. Reed never received the kind of concentrated coverage that Antioch under Arthur Morgan gained from the eastern press—that had been a veritable windstorm—but it certainly proved far more newsworthy than all but a handful of colleges and universities. Its values were a long way from those of *Time*, but *Time* found Reed the kind of college that it liked to highlight in its educational news. And so it was for other magazines. In the early fifties, for example, Reed received a large spread in *The Saturday Evening Post* in the form of an article by the late senator Richard L. Neuberger entitled "School for Smart Young Things." Neuberger, then a state senator, spoke of the college as having had a record as "a fortress of scholarship" and claimed that "this academic anarchy produces more big brains than many big universities." [52] In the early sixties *Look* did the same kind of thing, with a major article on the college as

50. *School and Society,* Vol. 33 (February, 1931), pp. 289–94; Vol. 39 (July, 1934), p. 838; Vol. 42 (September, 1935), pp. 382–83; Vol. 43 (May, 1936), pp. 730–31; Vol. 45, (February, 1937), pp. 261–66.
51. *Time,* Vol. 26 (November, 1935), pp. 49–50; Vol. 34 (December, 1939), p. 57; Vol. 59 (June, 1952), p. 47; Vol. 80 (December, 1962), p. 38.
52. "School for Smart Young Things," *The Saturday Evening Post,* Vol. 225 (October,) 1952), pp. 36–37, 95–101.

"Portland's academic gadfly." The article quoted the Reed president as saying that "Reed is about as controversial a place as exists in higher education"; it headlined the point that "Reed College is 'far out' in some regards, and many Portlanders wish it were 'far away' too." [53] Meanwhile, newspaper articles usually carried the same message; e.g., *The Christian Science Monitor* in 1957 headlined a major spread "Reed Stresses Academic Exploration and Is Proud to Be Different"; *The Seattle Times*, the same year, went to its headlines with "Take Heed of Reed—A College Where Learning Comes First." [54]

As indicated earlier (Chapter 4), even by the end of its first decade Reed was able to gather glowing testimonials from well-known educational statesmen, college presidents, and professors elsewhere any time it sought them. On its twenty-fifth anniversary in 1936, for example, the college was able to draw on an impressive array of academics to testify about its development, achievements, and character.[55]

And finally the most eloquent testimony of all came from research. If the Reed image had not carried the day up to the fifties, it surely went over the top with the publication of two national rankings of undergraduate colleges, widely used thereafter, based on the undergraduate origins of American scholars and scientists.[56] In these ratings on the proportion of graduating seniors who achieved later distinction (e.g., receiving the doctorate, being recognized as among leading scientists), Reed came out extremely well. In various categories (e.g., humanities, social sciences, natural sciences), the college appeared at or near the top of the list. In the proportion of male seniors who later received the Ph.D. or at least a graduate fellowship, Reed stood second in the social sciences, fourth in the natural sciences, and tenth in the humanities. For all the fields combined, Reed ranked second, behind Swarthmore and ahead of such substantial and noted institutions as University of Chicago, Oberlin College, Haverford College, California Institute of Technology, Carleton College, Princeton University, Antioch College, and Harvard University—to complete the first ten. Among colleges with only a small number of women graduates, Reed ranked third. The researchers, in interpreting their results, spoke glowingly of Reed, Oberlin, Antioch, and Swarthmore as the top cases of a very limited kind of institution in which there was "singular hospitality to intellectual values." Terming them institutions of "general intellectuality,"

53. Sam Castan, "'Portland's Academic Gadfly," *Look,* Vol. 26, No. 7 (March, 1962), pp. 77–80.

54. *The Christian Science Monitor* (Boston), March 23, 1957; *The Seattle Times,* April 18, 1957.

55. "The First Quarter Century," *loc. cit.*

56. Robert H. Knapp and Hubert B. Goodrich, *The Origins of American Scientists* (Chicago, The University of Chicago Press, 1952); and Robert H. Knapp and Joseph J. Greenbaum, *The Younger American Scholar: His Collegiate Origins* (Chicago, The University of Chicago Press, 1953).

the researchers suggested strongly that on these campuses "the climate of values sustained by the institutions elevated the scholar and the intellectual to the position of 'culture hero.' " [57]

Such rankings and such descriptions would be pleasing to any college. In external affairs alone, they were the kind of credible information that could not be manufactured by a public relations office at any price, and Oberlin, Antioch, and Swarthmore were not loath to use the findings in their own bulletins, newsletters, and news releases. But such an independent, "objective" confirmation was especially valuable to Reed, which, more than the other top-rated colleges (and approached only by Antioch in this regard) had the character of a beleaguered outpost.

For at the same time that distant national opinion gazed largely with eyes of admiration upon Reed, local opinion, building from *its* beginning in the nineteen-tens, remained steadily hostile to the college. For the comment of a Portland newspaper in 1919 that "Portland did not take kindly to the boasted self-righteousness" (reported in Chapter 4) one could find the direct descendent in 1952 in "many Portlanders get a little tired of the theme that Reed is an oasis of scholarship in a vast area of ignorance." [58] In highly favorable coverage of Reed in a national medium, usually invidious comparisons, at least implicitly and often explicitly, downgraded the home area as well as other Oregon colleges. Thus, the positive comment from a distance irritated the negative attitude of the local community: The above 1952 newspaper comment was stirred by the Neuberger article in *The Saturday Evening Post*.

It was almost in the cards, then, that when an institute designed to induct new college presidents into the mysteries of college administration turned to the topic of the college and the community, the institute organizers would select the president of Reed as one eminently informed and qualified to speak on the topic. In 1961, at a Harvard institute, the president of Reed suggested he had been invited as the expert on this topic "because Reed has at times had about the worst possible relationship with its local community. Almost every conceivable misunderstanding has arisen at one time or another." The president concluded his remarks with the hope that no other college or university might have "quite the same complication of relationships with its own community that Reed has had for half a century." [59]

Indicative of the negative opinions of local citizens were the reactions reported in a small survey made in 1961 of the local reputation of several

---

57. Knapp and Greenbaum, *op. cit.*, p. 97.
58. *Oregon Journal* (Portland), October 27, 1952.
59. "Excerpts from 'Community and College: Mutual Interests and Mutual Tensions,' " a guest speech by Richard H. Sullivan, June 27, 1961. The Institute for College and University Administrators, The Presidents' Institute, Harvard University.

colleges in Portland.[60] The researchers simply asked Portland adults what they knew about colleges in the area and what they thought of them. Reed drew much comment, and some of it was appreciative—"high academic standards" and "good education provided" but the bulk of the free responses indicated sharp dislike of the reputed ways of the college: "free thinking without guidance"; "extreme political attitudes"; "teachers may be communistic"; "no socials and sports"; "beatniks"; "too progressive"; "seems to cater to odd type of students"; "their students dress in a sloppy way"; and, finally, "I don't understand some of the things Reed students get excited about." The other colleges in the area, in comparison, had less salient images, with favorable comments of "nice campus" and "students courteous on the bus" and unfavorable ones in the order of "they have Saturday classes" and "I do not like Catholics."

When students entering Reed in 1958 were asked about the special qualities of the college, their reactions were in line with the public reputation that had been developing so consistently for so long a time. In reply to the question, "Do you see this college as having some special quality that distinguishes it from other colleges and universities? If so, what is it?" nearly all entering students at Reed, as also at Antioch and Swarthmore, claimed a distinctive quality (99 per cent at Reed, 99 per cent at Antioch, and 96 per cent at Swarthmore). In comparison, in several church-related colleges of less renown, the proportion of the entering students claiming a distinction was somewhat less (87 per cent at St. Olaf, 74 per cent at the University of the Pacific, and 71 per cent at the University of Portland); in the University of California, Berkeley, the proportion was 77 per cent; and in San Francisco State College, less than half (46 per cent) perceived a special quality.[61]

What were the imagined or imputed qualities? Six major categories cover the characteristics mentioned frequently in one or more of the eight colleges in the survey: (1) curriculum, (2) high academic standards and reputation, (3) liberal climate of the campus, (4) close contact and friendliness, (5) religion, and (6) pragmatic features of convenient location, attractive physical facilities, and low cost. The replies at Reed fell largely in just two of these categories. The students first stressed liberal climate, and here they were similar to the entering students at Antioch. An answer typical of this reaction was "the freedom of thought and action in intellectual and social areas." Second, they pointed to high standards and academic reputation, and here they were similar to entering students at Swarthmore. A typical answer was "more emphasis on academic matters."

60. J. Boddewyn, "What Do People Know and Think of Major Portland Colleges and Universities," *The University of Portland Review*, Vol. XIV, No. 1 (1962), pp. 34–37; and same title, unpublished paper, University of Portland, 1962.

61. Unpublished study of student development, Center for the Study of Higher Education, University of California, Berkeley.

Actually, students often coupled the two characteristics in attempting to identify the most distinctive quality of the college: "emphasis on intellectual efforts, personal freedom for students"; "besides superior intellectual quality, an air of freedom, honor, and respect for individuals"; "high standards, freedom"; "academic atmosphere, individual freedom, high academic rating."

When entering freshmen at Reed were asked what was particular about the students of the college, they emphasized the serious intellectual, the kind of person deeply interested in his education rather than in the social life: "more concerned with 'truth' and knowledge than superficials of 'college life' "; "less anxious to learn in order to make a living but for the sake of learning"; and "more intellectually oriented than average student body." The freshmen also commented on the maturity and liberality of the Reed student body.

Newspaper and magazine articles, samplings of adult opinion, college publications, and the impressions of entering students indicate that for a college of its size Reed has had for several decades a public image second to none in its salience. Reputation has cut and cut sharply through potential applicants, repelling very large numbers and attracting a few. The college has had a high-quality but relatively small group from which to select students. This selection has, in turn, given the college the kind of students who support the historic values and practices and thus help ensure that public impressions, favorable and unfavorable, continue much as they have in the past. The college has long obtained an academically promising student body without being able to exercise much direct selection—that is, without having a high ratio of applicants to students accepted. In the fall of 1958, for example, after all the glowing reports of the early fifties had had time to take full effect, Reed had to accept nearly four out of five applicants (375 out of 475 completed applications, or 79 per cent), leaving only narrow possibilities for purposeful selection. In many of the years before 1958, Reed struggled to fill its freshman class. But the students who applied, on the average and in generous measure, had many characteristics valued by the best college faculties. They not only had high scholastic ability but also scored very high in tests designed to measure originality, complexity of outlook, cultural sophistication, and concern with national and world affairs.[62] Thus, public image has done a tremendous amount of work for the college. In affecting input alone, the fixing of stubborn public impressions has been a critical component of over-all organizational character.

Beyond input, public image has consistently through the decades affected the inclination of the college to relate to its surrounding community, to "go downtown." Hostile local opinion has ensured that the

62. *Ibid.*

disdain of some of those on campus for those on the outside would not be kindly overlooked but would be returned many times over. The resulting pervading sense of strain between the college and the community has contributed to the social isolation of the campus. With local opinion hostile, with selection operating within narrow tolerances, with campus ideals and practices at great variance with those of the community, administrators, faculty, and, particularly, students became firmly habituated to turning inward, toward each other and toward the resources of the campus. The intellectual walls around the campus have been high and wide, a part of the character of the college.

To an important degree, this intellectual and social isolation served the formation of distinctive character, warding off environmental influences while persons on campus first nurtured and then institutionalized values and practices deviant from those of the surrounding culture. But as the isolation became engrained in character, it could not be readily abridged or modified whenever it served the interest of the college. The isolation remained, even after it was no longer so functional as a condition of character formation, and ensured community suspicion and the disadvantages for the spirit of a siege mentality.

# *Chapter 6.* Persistence

OVER THE thirty-five years between 1925 and 1960, Reed College remained close to the ideals and organizational practices of its first two presidents and its early faculty. It was relatively single-minded and integrated, with faculty perspectives, student values, curricular practices, and other features of its organization fitting closely together and sustaining an over-all character of remarkable persistence. The previous chapter therefore treated central features as continuously unfolding over the three to four decades that followed the death of the second president. Primarily these features were the intensification of academic norms, the growth of a nonconforming and rebellious spirit, and the development of a high degree of institutional autonomy.

Another important development, a trend toward science and research, will be reviewed briefly here as an issue of the years after 1945. Also, some soul-searing events in this latter period testified strikingly to the character of the institution. A crisis in governance in the early fifties caused more strain and grief than had occurred at any time since the late years of the first president's tenure. It was in the nature of Reed to be vulnerable to civic strife since the strain between the dominant faculty and student values and those of the surrounding society was expressed directly, forcefully, and specifically in the structure of control and in the process of administration.

## Evolution Toward Science and Research

If we examine the fields in which students took their degrees over the years and group them by the divisional structure of the college, we readily identify an evolution from the humanities to the sciences. In the first ten graduating classes (1915–24), 33 per cent of the graduates majored in the humanities (later organizationally defined as the Letters and Arts Division), 29 per cent in history and social science, 22 per cent in natural science and mathematics, and 16 per cent in philosophy, psychology, and education (Table 6–1). If the graduates in history and philosophy are grouped with those of the Letters and Arts Division, then the proportion graduating in the humanities was about 40 per cent, or approximately double that in the natural sciences.

TABLE 6–1. *Degrees Awarded, by Fields of Study, Reed College, 1915–59, Per Cent*

| Subject Field° | 1915–24 | 1925–34 | 1935–44 | 1945–54 | 1955–59 |
|---|---|---|---|---|---|
| Natural science and mathematics | 22 | 36 | 35 | 44 | 48 |
| Letters and arts (humanities) | 33 | 29 | 19 | 13 | 12 |
| History and social science | 29 | 28 | 33 | 27 | 20 |
| Philosophy, psychology, and education | 16 | 7 | 9 | 10 | 14 |
| Other | 0 | 0 | 4 | 6 | 6 |
| Total | 100 | 100 | 100 | 100 | 100 |
| N = | 398 | 422 | 774 | 859 | 440 |

°Subject fields are grouped by the divisional structure of the college.
Source: Registrar's records, 1915–59, Reed College.

The percentage of majors in natural science rose in the second and third decades of graduating classes (36 per cent in 1925–34, 35 per cent in 1935–44) and then, after World War II, pushed to 44 per cent in the 1945–54 period and to 48 per cent between 1955 and 1959 (Table 6–1). Meanwhile, the graduates in letters and arts fell steadily, from the original 33 per cent to 12 per cent. Thus by the late fifties, the science departments were graduating four times as many students as the Letters and Arts Division (48 per cent compared to 12 per cent). Even when all the graduates in history and philosophy were added to the humanities group, the proportion did not exceed one-fourth of the graduates, compared with one-half in the sciences. The percentage of graduates in English and literature had declined through the years from about 20 per cent to about 10 per cent. Of the four departments in the late fifties having 10 per cent or more of the graduating seniors, three (physics, biology, and chemistry) were in the natural sciences. The interest in science was also apparent at the point of intake: In the fifties one-half of the entering students commonly had a declared interest in the sciences and were eager to get into science courses as soon as possible. With the growth in enrollment went growth in faculty, so that by the late fifties the natural science departments had up to six to eight men each, compared with two or three in earlier periods.

With the trend toward science, by the fifties the humanities faculty possessed the student for one-fourth to one-half of his first two years, in the required freshman course and in an optional sophomore one, but then lost him to the science faculty as majors were declared for the specialization of the last two years. This common pattern, the build-up of faculty in the sciences, and an impression on the outside that Reed was particularly appropriate for bright boys in the sciences threw the humanities component somewhat on the defensive. The split between science and the humanities was a real one on the Reed campus since the rise of one meant to some significant degree the decline of the other on all levels—from the personal pleasure of having student disciples to the rank and salary offered young faculty members. On large campuses the differences in rewards that are bound to occur within a faculty are somewhat hidden by physical and social separation and in the confidential files of central administrators. But on a small campus, informal exchange of information reveals such differences to a significant extent; and in a college with such full faculty participation in governance there are few secrets.

The build-up of the natural sciences was bound to increase faculty affection for research and publication. This tendency fed into a larger trend in which these university-centered interests invaded all the disciplines of the liberal arts college. A growing share of the faculty in physics, chemistry, and biology wanted the facilities and the time to engage actively in meaningful research. Professors in these fields in the fifties had contact with such federal agencies as the National Science Foundation and the Public Health Service and were able to bring grants to the campus for new science buildings as well as for research equipment and supplies. The scientists moved out of their dingy, cramped rooms in the basement and garret of the main academic building into the sunlight of modern quarters. The new buildings gave physical expression to the research interest, with laboratories for professors and their research assistants part of the mix of interior design.

As the interest in research and publication deepened and spread across the campus, some faculty members felt it undermined a vaulted and cherished commitment to teaching. Some senior men, and not alone those in the humanities, considered the fact that they had published little or nothing in their careers an indication of their full commitment to undergraduate teaching and of their personal capacity to resist the dominant values of American academic life, specifically the publish or perish spirit that they considered to be in full control in the universities. Guardians of teaching, they could hardly look kindly upon advanced and career-related research that pulled the professor away from the undergraduate. Whatever their thoughts and resistance, however, research by the late fifties presented a picture qualitatively different from that which had obtained in the college before World War II. Research and publication became necessary in an increasing number of departments, as the senior men in the natural and social sciences and then finally in the humanities struggled to create the work conditions attractive to the better trained and more specialized young men coming out of the best graduate schools. Here, finally, the issue was not whether research should go or stay but whether effective teaching could and should remain a necessary condition of being hired and promoted.

In a very good liberal arts college, then, competing with first-line universities for faculty, some adaptation had to be made to the dominant trends toward specialization, research, and publication. The evolution toward science within the college deepened the pressure to adapt. Anti-research sentiments in the faculty had to give way. The 1963 faculty survey, reported earlier, indicated that the Reed faculty had published considerably less than their scholarly counterparts at Swarthmore and slightly less than the Antioch faculty (see Appendix 2). The proportion who had not published a book, 81 per cent, was not far from the proportion of the faculty innocent of book-writing at colleges of lesser academic standing—St. Olaf, University of Portland, and University of the Pacific. But in plans to publish a book, the Reed faculty moved considerably away from the three faculties just mentioned and ahead of Antioch. Only 19 per cent had published a book, but 43 per cent were "preparing a book for publication"—an increase greater than that of the other seven faculties in the survey. Thus, a campus that had been exceedingly teaching-centered was evidently moving toward the combination of teaching and research that seemed compelling for effective recruitment in the academic market place.

## Faculty Control: Continuity and Crisis

The backbone of the stubborn character of Reed, as Chapter 5 made clear, was the capacity of the faculty, and secondarily of the students, to uphold certain values. This capacity was grounded in a tenacious personal commitment to historic values—arising from an integrated and salient definition of the institution—and in a collective power to ward off reform. For this backbone to remain strong, there would have to be a successful transference of commitment and power from the original senior men to a new group as retirement, death, and transfer decimated the first generation.

FACULTY SUCCESSION

The transference of personal commitment from the first-generation to the second-generation faculty was so even, unconscious, and unchallenged at Reed that it did not become problematic. At Antioch, it will be remembered, during the late forties and early fifties recruitment of faculty was so "sloppy" with respect to traditional values that senior faculty members felt that there had clearly been some mistakes. Little of this feeling occurred at Reed.

As seen in Chapter 5, there was little hiring to be done at Reed during the slow days of the depression, much to President Dexter Keezer's growing dismay, and such matters were also a little slow during World War II. A certain amount of catching up had to be done in the decade after 1945 since the faculty of the twenties were approaching retirement. Expansion also created more openings. And when Reed finally developed the rank of associate professor in the years after World War II, openings had to be filled from the outside or from the ranks of the assistant professors to give substance to this middle layer.

Alongside the Arragons and Cerfs of the twenties, a sizable group of men quickly moved into or near the seats of influence. New faculty members who would soon be senior men or among the several senior men in their fields included: in 1941 Richard H. Jones in history; in 1943 William L. Alderson in literature; in 1944 Donald MacRae in literature; in 1945 Frederick A. Courts in psychology and Arthur H. Leigh in economics. In 1946 a large group was added: Charles C. Bagg, in history and humanities; Edwin N. Garlan, in philosophy; Herbert B. Gladstone, in music; Maure L. Goldschmidt, in political science; Lewis H. Kleinholz, in biology; Frank Munk, in political science. Then in 1947 David H. French in anthropology; in 1948 Kenneth E. Davis and William L. Parker in physics and Arthur H. Livermore in chemistry; in 1949 Howard D. Jolly in sociology; in 1950 Frank S. Fussner in history and humanities, Kaspar T. Locher in German and humanities, and Roger B. Oake in romance languages; in 1952 Marshall W. Cronyn in chemistry. Others were added throughout the fifties, but the above group alone numbered twenty major staff additions.

Such an infusion of new blood could easily have upset established ways, diverting the college by drift or design onto a different path. With only one or two exceptions, however, the new men were as much committed to the developed character of Reed as were the men who had originally shaped it. Again and again the new men had decided to come to Reed precisely because they liked so much what the college had become and what it stood for. In interviews men spoke often, and almost with a physical shudder of revulsion, about the colleges at which they had taught before, where the academic standards had been soft, the students dull, and the faculty not interested in intellectual affairs. They came because they wanted the academic severity of Reed, its eager students, its intellectual zest. The image of Reed was, in short, a powerful factor in attracting faculty, and a large proportion of those who came at the critical time when the first-generation faculty was stepping down were appropriately oriented to carry on the traditional ways. Then, too, inbreeding played its role in the continuity of Reed tradition. Some of the men of the second generation were already strongly socialized to Reed and intensely committed to it because they were graduates. Among the twenty major appointments reviewed above, occurring between 1941 and 1952, five had taken their bachelor's degrees at Reed between 1930 and 1940. One became the senior professor in psychology, another an active, influential professor in political science. The other three, in chemistry and physics, returned to the college to staff it in fields where recruitment was especially difficult and in which they could have done far better financially in universities or industry.

And, finally, there were the sifting and the strengthening of personal commitments that always take place to some degree in a small college in the turnover of young men in the faculty, with some being asked to stay and wanting to do so, while others are asked to move on or want to escape. Reed long has had heavy turnover in the junior ranks, especially in the humanities staff. Many, although drawn by the name, found that they did not like the intensity of Reed or the teaching styles of some of the senior men or the close and critical scrutiny they received from the older professors in their fields. Or, liking Reed on balance and wanting to stay, some young men found they could not do so because the senior men thought they did not measure up or fit in or because no more tenured positions were open. In a college so poorly financed and with such a long tradition of a small staff of full professors supported by a larger staff of instructors and assistant professors, a heavy turnover of young men became a latent financial subsidy. Thus, compared with the number that went out, few went up. This system allowed, almost guaranteed, careful selection, in which a man was fully assessed for how he fitted the institution.

With powerful and interlocking mechanisms of recruitment and socialization at work, the faculty of the fifties continued to represent well the basic ideas of the founding fathers. But the consensus was not unanimous and did not embrace all the basic issues. Two types of dissenting factions arose: One was a small group of conservatives at odds with the political and social liberality of the majority of their colleagues and their students. More conservative in politics, even Republican, a few in this bloc were eager that the faculty work with the trustees and the community to remove the black eye the college had in Portland and surrounding towns. They were willing to go downtown, to sit with businessmen and community leaders, to improve town-gown relations. They were also eager to see the authority of the administration strengthened, to give more administrative order to the campus, to curb the excesses of students, and to obtain a larger voice for a neutral or conservative administration in the delicate issues of tenure that otherwise were decided by the liberals serving on the faculty council. This conservative bloc, however, was never large, numbering usually about half a dozen men.

A second and larger group of dissenters, the Young Turks, were much closer than the conservatives to the dominant liberal senior faculty in their appreciation of the Reed character but were critical of one or more of its basic components. Young men who came to the college in the fifties did not always see the point, particularly the sacredness, of requiring the senior thesis, of not giving out grades, of excluding research, or of giving students complete social freedom. They argued rationally that the college could do even better what it wanted to do in general if it changed some of its specific attitudes and practices. In the open discussion of Reed faculty meetings, the younger men were heard, frequently and sometimes endlessly. Within their ranks were some tenured men who would in all likelihood be part of the future senior faculty and some who could argue the head right off a pin, let alone specify how many angels were dancing on it, outtalking anyone in sight. The young Turks were partly co-opted to the senior camp and could always be outinfluenced, but their critical attitudes were the cutting edge of evolution in the dominant faculty point of view. They tended to be in favor of research or at least permissive about it. Some of them were close to the personal problems of the students and upset that the particular inputs and stresses of Reed led to human breakage. They had always to be partially accommodated by the senior faculty and administration, and in the accommodation to their interests and criticisms lay part of the potential change in the college.

CRISIS IN GOVERNANCE

After Keezer left Reed in 1942, having filled the president's chair for eight years, the college returned to the previous pattern of governing through interim committee and short-term presidents. During the war years (1942–45), the senior professor of chemistry, Arthur F. Scott, served as acting president. Then, Peter Odegard, a political scientist at the University of California, Berkeley, came to the presidency, only to leave three years later (1948). Odegard was sympathetic to the spirit of Reed, easy in his relations with faculty and students, and well accepted and supported on campus in his few years there, but the fund-raising component of the president's work, compelling and worrisome in a college in such dire financial straits, was not to his liking, and when the attractions of his former university campus beckoned, he returned. At this point, the college had another interim government, with a staunch former trustee,

Ernest B. MacNaughton, serving as president. An important banker, newspaper publisher, and community leader in Portland, MacNaughton came into office saying, "We need money, we need students, and we need to be interpreted better in the state." [1] He assigned himself the financial and outside affairs of the college, matters always in need of attention. The faculty was left with almost full responsibility for internal policy and administration. MacNaughton's appointment was intended both to improve financing and community support and to fill the gap until an appropriate academic man could be persuaded to take the position. That man, Duncan Smith Ballantine, then an associate professor of history at Massachusetts Institute of Technology, assumed the presidency of Reed in 1952.

Like Keezer in the thirties, Professor Ballantine came as an agent of change. He waited neither for time nor sociability to smooth the way—or tie his hands—but plunged right in with word and deed. At the outset he indicated that he saw the college "only on the threshold of its promised greatness" and soon made clear that getting beyond the threshold meant not moving ahead on the path already established but changing direction substantially. He obtained twenty-five thousand dollars from the Ford Foundation Fund for the Advancement of Education for a Reed self-study, and before the end of the first year the study was questioning virtually every sacred component of the college. President Ballantine defined the special concerns he felt needed to be faced.[2]

*On "the Reed program":*

Does the pursuit of academic distinction lead us away from the achievement of other desirable goals?

Do we have a proper balance in emphasis between the curricular and extracurricular aspects of our program?

Does the quality and quantity of academic pressure permit our students to make full use of available extracurricular opportunities to find enjoyment, recreation, and avocational skills? In this context we are interested in particular features of our program such as the freshman year program in Humanities, the Junior Qualifying Examination, the Senior Thesis, balance between courses of a specialized nature and liberal arts courses, the policy of not revealing grades to students, the athletic program, the creative arts program, student government, and so forth.

*On "the social environment":*

Does [the] balance, or imbalance, of freedom and authority actually contribute to the social and emotional maturation of our students . . . ?

1. "President's Report, 1949–1950," *Reed College Bulletin,* Vol. 29, No. 1 (November, 1950).
2. "Report to the Ford Fund for the Advancement of Education," a preliminary report, mimeo, May 25, 1953. Reed College.

How is the so-called permissive atmosphere at Reed structured by the students? Do the prevailing patterns of behavior and belief as distinguished from the official rules and mores of the community, act coercively upon the student, and is there in this sense a rigid structuring of the environment?

## On "the administrative structure":

How can the administrative processes of the college be made more efficient without damaging their democratic character?

## And, finally, to sum it up:

A better understanding of these problems will allow us to appraise policy questions of different orders of magnitude with greater insight and foresight of possible consequences. Are our standards too high? Shall we lower our standards, or can we devise ways of attracting a student body more appropriate for our program? Should the work load in the freshman year be reduced? Shall we have an honors and "pass" program instead of our present program, which in essence is an honors program for all students? . . . Should we have more precisely defined social rules and regulations?

At the end of his first year in office, Ballantine felt that the self-study had clearly identified student attrition "as a major problem requiring judicious remedial action." He felt, further, that the study had served "as an impetus to new experimentation in curricular matters." The president wanted the college to be interested in the "whole personality" of the student. He wanted it to prepare students for fields other than scholarship—"careers in commerce, industry, the professions, or in marriage and motherhood." In this regard, "the College has become more aware of its strength and weaknesses in this broader area, and is now considering how we can better meet the needs and desires of these diverse groups of students." [3]

Unfortunately for everyone's peace of mind, the president's concerns were not shared by the vast majority of students and faculty, who were simply not interested in whole personality, vocational preparation, or avocational skills. They did not see reason to question, from these premises, the long-standing and honored humanities program, the Junior Qualifying Examination, and the senior thesis. And the presidential initiative inherent in the attempt to probe and reform traditional character soon brought the president into conflict, first, with the students, and, then, with the faculty.

With the students, the fight centered on the "permissive atmosphere." Ballantine felt there was too much freedom, that the "operation of the honor system is threatened by a laissez-faire attitude, which makes stu-

3. "President's Report, 1952–53," *Reed College Bulletin*, Vol. 32, No. 1 (November, 1953), pp. 3, 9.

dents indifferent to or unwilling to take action against their fellows."[4] He felt the administration should share the responsibility for student affairs, through his own office and that of a dean of students. A simmering conflict between the president and the students broke into the open in the spring of his second year, when he disciplined a boy and a girl who took leave to California, only to have student leaders object that any punishment should have been decided by the Student Council. The senior class went as far as to send a letter to the alumni association protesting administrative performance in this case. With this incident, the break between the students and Ballantine passed the point of no return. The students had come to define the president as unsympathetic to the honor principle and student-faculty community government and hence as a mortal enemy of the dearest part of Reed.

With the faculty, the strain centered on presidential prerogatives in the face of faculty control. Ballantine maintained that "by nature" he was "unable to be just a figurehead," a mere executive secretary of the faculty. He wanted not only more responsibility for administrative officials in student affairs and in some curricular experimentation but also some changes in organizational structure that would enhance the power of the president, e.g., to have the president appoint the chairmen of the four divisions and then to have these men serve on the central faculty council along with the men elected by the faculty. As Ballantine reviewed the matter, he saw as the first among the bad traditions of the college the "domination of policy and politics by the faculty control." He had worked, he said, to "restore the balance between faculty council and administrative control over appointments. . . ." He had "asked particularly that the faculty council not determine salaries." He[5] maintained that

Reed's faculty power over who is hired, who gets raises, who is fired or placed on tenure includes the obvious: That it can build a patronage system, lead to self promotion, the kind of inbreeding that tightens into oligarchic dictatorship.

The faculty rejected Ballantine's basic ideas and proposals one by one. By the time of his open rupture with the students, matters were, to say the least, going badly with the faculty as well. The majority on campus had become firmly set against him, and their feelings were becoming public knowledge; but the trustees and a conservative minority in the faculty lined up behind him. The campus was becoming seriously split.

And then matters took a sudden and dramatic turn for the worse. The Velde Committee (the House Un-American Activities Committee of the United States House of Representatives) came to Portland in June, 1954, to hold hearings on communist infiltration of the local institutions. They

4. Portland *Oregonian*, May 23, 1954. Article by Wilma Morrison, an excellent education editor and observer of the Reed scene.

5. *Ibid.*, October 2, 1954. Article by Wilma Morrison, education editor.

promptly identified three Reed professors as prime suspects, using the testimony of a former Reed student and of the director of admissions (also dean of students) of Reed, who had resigned just a few weeks before. One of the accused professors was to teach in a summer session at the college, and in the context of the committee's accusation, President Ballantine, backed by the chairman of the Board of Trustees, "removed," or suspended, the professor from the faculty of the summer session. Two days after this action, the faculty issued a bitter protest, and one day later voted thirty-eight to nine (with thirteen absent or not voting) to ask the trustees to "review and reverse" the suspension. The president's action, they said in their resolution, had caused "a grave weakening of [the faculty's] confidence in presidential leadership at Reed." [6] Seven of the eight members of the faculty council signed the resolution. Students and alumni soon took similar public positions. A group of students sent letters to all the other students, dispersed for the summer, asking them to write letters to the chairman of the board and the faculty council in protest of the president's action. All new students who were to arrive at the college in the fall received letters that summer from a student group urging them to oppose the president. The alumni in San Francisco chimed in with a heavy (seventy-seven to nine) endorsement of the faculty position.[7]

The division, the bitterness, over this one act of Ballantine was enough in itself to rip open the campus, but there was more to come. The college had to take some position on all three men accused by the Velde Committee, in a context of great community hostility and pressure. As reported later by an investigating committee of the American Association of University Professors:[8]

The House Committee hearings in Portland received wide local coverage and were televised if the witnesses did not object. There was much adverse reaction to the conduct of faculty members invoking the Fifth Amendment before the Committee. The prevailing mood is illustrated by the fact that there was a suggestion that the Reed College campus might be condemned for a Portland city college. Some persons of acknowledged maturity and judgment felt that the College might not be able to open the following year, or at least might suffer a severe setback, unless prompt measures to assure the public of its educational integrity were taken by the Board. It was the opinion of some members of the College community that the fact that the future of the college might be in grave peril was entitled to weight, and that it was the responsibility of faculty members to help "save" Reed by disclosing the facts with which the college had to deal.

6. Faculty action, as reported in the *Oregon Journal* (Portland), June 24, 1954. Also stated in a report of an investigating committee of the American Association of University Professors, "Reed College," *AAUP Bulletin*, Vol. 44, No. 1 (March, 1958), pp. 102–36.
7. Portland *Oregonian*, July 8, 1954.
8. *Loc. cit.*, p. 110.

One of the accused professors, a vigorous and popular teacher, chose not to co-operate with the trustees in their investigation of him but instead to argue his case forcibly and publicly. The trustees asked for reports from the faculty and the president, and through July and into August, the faculty council, the president, and a committee of trustees conducted three separate investigations of the issues, the charges, and the positions of the professors. The faculty council recommended to the trustees that all three professors be retained and, with respect to the nonco-operating professor, that "no charges of misconduct be brought" and "that no disciplinary action of any kind be contemplated." [9] The president, on the other hand, recommended to the board that the case of the most recalcitrant professor go to a formal hearing before the trustees. The Board of Trustees decided that the two faculty members least in question should be retained, with no formal action, but that the recalcitrant one should have a formal hearing. That hearing was held, in mid-August, and on the basis of the testimony, the trustees directed that the professor be removed from the faculty.

Ballantine's position on campus was untenable from the time in June when after his action of removing the accused professor from the summer session, the faculty had, at a dramatic meeting, voted no confidence in him. The later events of the summer, full of tension and bitterness and culminating in the firing of a professor, deepened and solidified that opposition. There was then no waiting on amenities, a timing of one's departure to serve personal grace and institutional health. In September, at the beginning of the work of the academic year, Ballantine announced his resignation. A few weeks later a trustee who had served twelve years resigned in fury, claiming that he could not live with the attitudes of the faculty toward communism and the office of the college president, or, translated into newspaper headlines: "Brand Quits Reed: Says 'Too Red.'" [10] A few months later the president of the Board of Trustees, who only a year before had given the college $100,000 (the largest bequest in over twenty years), resigned. When another trustee followed suit, the college had lost three trustees in three months as a result of the conflict and Ballantine's resignation.

Perhaps the newspapers of the area could be pardoned for describing the campus conflict as "total war," [11] for even the papers that tried to be fair had a dismal story to tell; and to the others, Reed was dangerous, fair game, and deserving of its lumps. The attention it received won it the award, in the end-of-the-year roundup of news, of being "the top story of 1954 in the state's educational news." [12] And the academic statesmen of the

9. Quoted in *ibid.*, p. 114.
10. *Klamath Falls Herald and News*, October 7, 1954.
11. *Oregon Journal* (Portland), September 21, 1954.
12. *Ibid.*, December 26, 1954.

nation, who serve as placement officers for administrative personnel, could perhaps also be pardoned for firming the rumor that Reed was a grave-yard of presidents since indeed the mortality had been impressive and the root cause of presidential instability was deep in the character of Reed.

Sex orgies and other social hanky-panky can cause inordinate trouble in a college, taking it over the brink of strife in a canoe of scandal, but such issues are child's play compared to the depth of trouble battles of power can cause. The crisis in governance at Reed in the summer and fall of 1954 took it to the lowest state of institutional health that it had been in since the early twenties. The president had been driven out, the trustees' anger led to resignations and mutterings about closing the college, the sur-rounding community was implacably hostile. For the faculty there was no victory since the events left men personally scarred, broke open a division between the liberal faculty majority and the small conservative minority, and all in all left as a residue the feeling that turmoil had gone too far and was now threatening the immediate and long-run viability of the college.

To begin to repair the damage, Reed called to the presidency a retired professor of mathematics, F. L. Griffin, who had joined the faculty when the college opened in 1911 and had been a part of it ever since. Respected by trustees and faculty alike, with a record of commitment and service second to none, Professor Griffin was the ideal choice for an interim president whose purpose was to reduce conflict and to restore confidence to the point at which a man from the outside could be attracted to the office. At the outset of his two years as president, Griffin and the trustees obtained an important concession from the faculty: The hallowed faculty constitution of 1916, of which Griffin had been one of the five framers, was suspended.[13] In a memorandum on presidential responsibility, for which he was able to obtain wide faculty approval, Griffin[14] established the operating philosophy that

Administrative decisions should be made by administrative officers and that the faculty should not feel aggrieved if an occasional decision runs counter to majority preference, provided there has been fair consultation. The president is expected to function as the executive officer in full charge of administration, not to serve as an agent of the faculty.

The faculty would continue to have a large role in governance—that was in the spirit of Reed—but there would also, perhaps, be an administrative role, and the central faculty committee was in the last analysis to advise rather than to fully control the president. The eight-man elected faculty council was changed to a ten-man advisory committee, of which five members were elected directly by the faculty and five were appointed by the president from a list of ten nominated by the faculty.

13. *Reed College Bulletin,* Vol. 33, No. 2 (November, 1954).
14. Reported in "President's Report, 1955–1956," *Reed College Bulletin,* Vol. 34, No. 12 (August, 1956), p. 3.

Griffin then felt he was able to say to the outside world: "It is clearly understood that the presidential function is re-established. We may talk of things informally, but the president initiates things administratively." [15] And public reassurances were needed: The president reported at the end of his first year that "there has been a substantial shrinkage in applications for admission from the Eastern states," and he felt that this was "an unfortunate residual effect of misunderstanding of the events of last summer." [16] A local newspaper, in reporting a drop of 7 per cent in Reed enrollment in the fall of 1955, "while other independent colleges in Oregon all showed increases," editorialized sarcastically, "It's just possible that these communist teacher and political picketing episodes are affecting Reed enrollment." [17] The following year Griffin was able and pleased to report that the college was experiencing "a renewed influx of applications for admission from even remote parts of the nation." [18] To hold enrollment at its peak was absolutely necessary, for the college lived close to the subsistence line. In 1955 its endowment yielded only eleven thousand dollars more than it had the year it was founded, while the cost of living had almost trebled; its endowment per student was a thin twenty-seven hundred dollars compared to twenty-four thousand dollars at Wesleyan University.[19]

Then, a new president was found: Richard T. Sullivan, a vice-president of the Educational Testing Service, agreed to come to this "graveyard of presidents." Sullivan had had a good look at the college in 1954, while studying administrative-faculty relationships across the country under a Ford Foundation Fellowship, and had been impressed with the values and spirit of the place. With his attitudes, the conditions were relatively favorable for his incumbency. His broad acceptance of the Reed character, including its nonconformity, was soon assessed as genuine by the faculty. He had not come to make basic changes; he announced no platform of reform at the inauguration or a few years later. Easy in personal relations with faculty and students, he became and remained much liked by the faculty. The shattering events of 1954 had put the staff on their best behavior in relation to the president's role, and the interim regime of President Griffin had begun a process of accommodation whereby it was possible for the trustees, president, and faculty to work relatively well together. This accommodation effectively continued under the new president. Sullivan stayed at Reed for ten years (until 1966), giving the college some peace in its governance and sustaining the first important presidential reign since 1923.

15. Portland *Oregonian*, February 5, 1955.
16. "President's Report, 1954–1955," *Reed College Bulletin*, Vol. 33, No. 12 (August, 1955), p. 3.
17. Portland *Oregonian*, October 9, 1955.
18. "President's Report, 1955–1956," *loc. cit.*, p. 2.
19. *Oregon Journal* (Portland), May 15, 1955.

But peace for a president at Reed must be understood as a relative thing since it is in the character of the institution that the presidential role be difficult. Faculty stubbornness on academic issues had so long helped to sustain the place that it was not easily turned off. More than the usual amount of individual consultation and persuasion had to take place before even minor alterations were made. Faculty authority remained real, a proud and noteworthy tradition. Then, too, the financial problems never seemed to abate—if anything, to get only worse; to expand the faculty, pay higher salaries, or otherwise raise financial commitments was to take grave risks in financial overextension. The Reed endowment in 1958–59 was $3,500,000 for seven hundred students, compared with $15,000,000 for nine hundred students at Swarthmore.[20]

And then among the students there were inescapably those for whom the man in the president's chair had to be a representative of the forces of reaction, suppression, and retrenchment from all that Reed had stood for. When the retired professor, Griffin, had taken his emergency stint in the office, his Taft-Republican and Highland-Baptist ways had drawn loud and caustic criticism in the student press and the college assembly, let alone in the byways of conversation. One sarcastic letter to the student newspaper referred to the president as "Brother Griffin," with his "Baptist flavor of Christianity," and concluded: "I wish conservative Griffin the same luck in instituting his brand of authoritarianism that liberal Ballantine had with his. One knows the Bible and the other knows Mill." [21] President Sullivan, supported in the faculty for a sustained period in a way not afforded any president from the outside for thirty years, was not immune from student criticism and ridicule and from the anticipation and preparation that goes into frequent battles with students. In the strong subculture of nonconformity that had evolved in the student body, anti-authority was a prime ingredient, stronger than at other liberal and sophisticated liberal arts colleges. When Reed sophomores were asked in 1959–60 "What role do you think the president should play in academic matters—a dominant role, a leadership role, an advising role, or little or no role?," 83 per cent gave the president the two weaker assignments of advising or little or no role, compared to 52 per cent at Antioch, 56 per cent at Swarthmore (and 47 per cent at San Francisco State College). A full quarter (24 per cent) of the Reed sophomores chose the weakest category of little or no role, compared with 7, 10 and 3 per cent, respectively, at the other three colleges. These Reed students as seniors (1962) felt even more strongly about it: 87 per cent chose the two categories;

20. *American Universities and Colleges,* 8th ed. (Washington, D. C., American Council on Education, 1960), pp. 860, 918.
21. *Reed College Quest,* March 5, 1956.

38 per cent, the bottom category.[22] Thus, whether the issue was a tuition increase, a new building, or a new social rule, the odds were high that the students would not only vigorously speak their minds but also take the president to task for acting out of turn and diminishing the institution. In presidential wear and tear, a year at Reed was hard to duplicate elsewhere in small-college circles.

## The Character of Reed: 1960

If any one characteristic stood out from all others in the intentions of the first president of Reed and the spirit of its first faculty and students in the nineteen-tens, it was surely intellectual vigor. On this central characteristic, the college never seriously wavered. Through all the years of operating on a financial shoestring, the periods when administrative conflict seemed about to tear the place apart, the times when threats were posed to all financially insecure colleges by war, depression, and inflation, Reed was an academic center of the intellectual life.

This defining characteristic was a product of academic rigor plus—or even multiplied by—the mix of student attitudes and values. A student at Reed not only learned a great deal from the faculty but also learned as much if not more from his fellow students. Not every college that is academically able, with a fine faculty offering good instruction, has intellectual zest. The old days in the Ivy League testified to this point. To have zest, a college must have students seriously interested in ideas. And so Reed students were through the Roaring Twenties, the depression years of the thirties, the war and postwar years of the forties, the McCarthy era and the "silent generation" years of the fifties; and they still had this quality as this small but noisy college turned into the sixties.

Virtually on a par with intellectual vigor as an institutional characteristic of Reed was the sense of independence and nonconformity. This characteristic was also one instituted at the outset, in the high-minded divergence of the first president and the faculty from traditional academic ways and the normal life of the Portland community. As we have seen, the Reed posture of normative divergence later came to center on political radicalism and especially on social nonconformity as increasingly symbolized by the manners and dress of the students. By 1960 some faculty members and many students were using Reed as an institution of rebellion, as the locale of a nonconforming sect within modern American society. The norm of nonconformity, in general, supported the vigor of the intellectual life, while the intellectual vigor, in turn, encouraged the critical attitudes that supported the spirit of nonconformity.

22. Sophomore and senior questionnaires, entering classes of 1958. Unpublished study of student development, Center for the Study of Higher Education, University of California, Berkeley.

And, third, Reed remained in 1960 a virtually unparalleled example among American colleges of the unaccommodating institution. A place captured by intellectual vigor alone could be an accommodating enterprise, following the dictates of rational discussion, even of scientific planning; but a college of great intellectuality equally possessed by an institutionalized rebellion is not free to adjust easily to changing social demand and environmental alteration. The autonomous sect in a hostile world is suspicious of every move that appears to be an accommodation to worldly pleasures and pressures. The spirit of rebellion demands that the outer world be held at arm's length, that the group continue to hold itself apart and to define itself in ways antithetical to those of outsiders. As we have seen, the sense of difference has long been strong at Reed, and it was continuing strongly as Reed entered the sixties.

Such institutional stubbornness often has unwanted consequences. Appropriate numbers and types of students and faculty continued to make their appearance at the doors of the college, but that other important resource, money, was chronically undersubscribed. Many persons in the system had an exhilarating involvement in campus issues because of the strong student and faculty participation in decision-making, but when the system of governance fell into deep crisis or interim doldrums, the psychological and social stress on faculty and administrators reached levels no one desired. The openness of the social life offered great freedom and unusual opportunity for self-development, with the contingency that the lack of formal structure and the informal pressures to conform to non-conformity would lead to considerable mental anguish for some students and would help make dropping out of college a normal expectation in the student body. Such major contingencies of the distinctive Reed brand of success were its vulnerabilities, the chinks in the institutional armor through which the blows of future crises might force a fundamental shift in character.

Thus, Reed remained, at the end of this coverage of its development, a fascinating example of the many faces of commitment. William Trufant Foster's theme for a commencement address at the college in 1948, "Pay the Price and Take It," was still an effective point, an apt description. In 1960 the college was still holding to a striking commitment. Proud of having done so, the individual professor and the college as a whole were richly rewarded with academic and intellectual esteem. But the college was still undergoing much personal and institutional suffering occasioned by the unwanted contingencies of its successful commitment. Vigor and rebellion at Reed would not have been easy achievements under the best of circumstances; and at times the college labored close to the worst of conditions.

In the drama of college-building on the American scene, Reed thus appears as a heroic actor, propelled to the front of the stage by its pure expression of widely admired purposes. But the character of the college has been complex and double-edged, and we understand it well when we comprehend how much pain resides behind the noble face. If this college is a bold figure in American higher education, it is one that has steadily courted tragedy. The willingness to take *that* as part of the price, to continue on a high road of unbound danger, is the final indication of the intensity of the institution. The development of Reed vividly indicates that distinctive colleges can rival the most striking religious, political, and military organizations in the devotion of the individual and the collectivity to deeply cherished ideals. As at Antioch (and, as we soon see, as at Swarthmore), we find organizational life an imposing saga.

# PART III
## *Swarthmore*

# *Chapter 7.* Foundations

AT FIRST GLANCE, Swarthmore is simple in character. One surmises that it is easier to understand than Antioch or Reed since it is closer in character to the Eastern Seaboard Ivy and quasi-Ivy liberal arts college whose style has long typified the nature of the American college in conventional thought. But those who know it best consider it significantly different from Wesleyan and Williams, Vassar and Wellesley, and not merely in its co-education. They have good reason to think so. Close and persistent observation of the college uncovers subtleties that easily elude the hasty visitor and leave any but the experienced observer unsure of his touch and comprehension. The campus in its educational practices is at once noisy and quiet, experimental and traditional, bohemian and conformist, college and university. It is related to a church and yet it is not, affected by Quaker morality yet directed by secular commands.

To begin to understand the character of this college in the middle of the twentieth century, we turn to its early history. Whereas Reed had no nineteenth century and the radical break at Antioch in 1920 obliterated the imprints of earlier ways, Swarthmore had a significant fifty-year development before its critical redefinition in the twenties, and revolution never wiped away the past. Certain elements of Quaker influence can be seen clearly if we study both their historical roots and the clearer and more vigorous forms in which they were expressed before academic quality be-

171

came the controlling criterion. We then turn to the transformation that occurred under Frank Aydelotte, a period of twenty years in which new purpose entered, important changes were initiated, and the whole scheme was then firmly institutionalized. Finally, we look at the problem of the college after 1945 and its capacity to conserve its character in rapidly changing times. As much as any other college on the American landscape, Swarthmore was by that time both a model of undergraduate education and a promise that the better colleges could maintain their vigor in an age of mass higher education.

## The Originating Intent

Higher education in the United States at the time of the Civil War was carried on by very small colleges. With the majority of colleges less than two hundred strong, Harvard, Yale, Virginia, and Michigan were the giants of the day with five and six hundred students at the end of the eighteen-sixties. The colleges were a product of churchly interests: The early splintering factions of Protestantism—Congregationalists, Scotch Presbyterians, Episcopalians—had established the colonial colleges, and a revival of denominational competition and zeal between 1800 and 1860 added measurably to their population. The fast-growing Methodists and Baptists joined the fray, helping to ensure that the nineteenth century would be a time of competitive anarchy in American higher education. The Christians, with the establishment of Antioch in 1853, as we have seen, entered the college business late in the day. Also late were the Quakers, the Society of Friends, with Haverford School in 1833 (later to become Haverford College), Earlham College in 1850, and then Swarthmore in 1864.

Swarthmore was not easy to establish. The Quakers of the day were not evangelistic, and the hot blood that pulsed behind the founding of many another college had here a cooler flow. The Quakers were also prudent economically and given to doubt the relevancy of a college education to the orderly and ordinary concerns of life. Then, too, in the Great Separation of 1827, the Quakers had split into Orthodox and Hicksite branches,[1] and the larger and wealthier Orthodox branch had invested in Haverford. The smaller and less wealthy group of Hicksites, and but a few among them, contemplated Swarthmore from the early eighteen-fifties, incorporated it in 1864, and opened its doors for the academic year of 1869–70.[2]

1. Robert W. Doherty, *The Hicksite Separation: A Sociological Analysis of Religious Schism in Early Nineteenth Century America* (New Brunswick, N. J., Rutgers University Press, 1967).
2. Homer D. Babbidge, Jr., *Swarthmore College in the Nineteenth Century: A Quaker Experience in Education.* Unpublished Ph.D. dissertation, Yale University, 1953, p. 48. This unpublished manuscript is a fine source of information and insight on the development of Swarthmore before 1900. Other basic sources are Emily C. Johnson,

Although they were not evangelists, the founders of Swarthmore did have denominational defense on their minds. They wished to protect the flock from both secular influences and the prosyletizing of the more aggressive churches. The institution would board Quaker children and prepare Quaker teachers with whom, in the lower schools, "Friends' children could be safely and advantageously entrusted." [3] The first declaration of intent (1854) put it all in a title: "Report of the Committee on Education of Baltimore Yearly Meeting of Friends, on the Subject of a Boarding School for Friends' Children, and for the Education of Teachers." [4] These twin purposes persisted as discussion spread from Baltimore to groups in Philadelphia and New York and were reiterated in a "Joint Address" of "Some Members of the Society of Friends to Their Fellow Members" in 1861. [5] The purposes also contained the basic problems: What should be the extent and nature of Societal control? and how advanced the curriculum, for boarding "children" and educating teachers? The 1861 Joint Address of the interested Hicksite groups recommended that the proposed institution be "guarded" by Quaker men and Quaker thought, but it was not easy to reach a consensus among the sponsors, who varied in their religious and social liberality, on the scope and intensity of the guarding. In order to start the institution, decision on this critical issue was simply suspended, pragmatically left for the later days of actual operation. It proved difficult also to obtain agreement on the level of study: Some supporters wanted a college, while others formed their vision primarily around a preparatory school. This issue, too, was handled pragmatically by opening an institution that was both preparatory school and college. With these divisive problems temporarily pushed aside, only the matter of physical location demanded immediate action, and this proved relatively simple. The Hicksite group in Philadelphia became the most active center of fund-raising and finally contributed two-thirds of the subscription. The first president, Edward Parrish, selected four years before the doors managed to open, was also from the Philadelphia group. And so the school was located near Philadelphia, on three hundred acres of open farm land ten miles out from the heart of the city in what later was to be Swarthmore Borough. The name of the college was taken from Swarthmoor Hall in England, the home of George Fox, the Quaker leader.

When the college opened in 1869, it was prepared "to admit all over

*Under Quaker Appointment: The Life of Jane P. Rushmore* (Philadelphia, Pa., University of Pennsylvania Press, 1953); Edward Hicks Magill, *Sixty-five Years in the Life of a Teacher, 1841–1906* (Boston, Houghton Mifflin Company, 1907); Edward Parrish, *Education in the Society of Friends* (Philadelphia, Pa., J. B. Lippincott Company, 1865).

3. Babbidge, *op. cit.*, p. 54.
4. *Ibid.*
5. *Ibid.*, p. 59.

twelve years of age who apply, until the necessary limit is reached," [6] and to place the entrants, according to their achievement, in the Collegiate Department or in one of three grades of the Preparatory Department. The young Quaker applicants came low in achievement, and 173 out of 199, or 85 per cent, were duly enrolled in preparatory work. Thus, with the campus both a preparatory school and a college, the entering enrollment indicated that Swarthmore initially would be largely a prep school. The first staff consisted of twenty teachers and officers, with a former submaster of the Boston Latin School, Edward Hicks Magill, directing the Preparatory Department.

In its control and financing the campus was all Quaker. However, Swarthmore was significantly different from most church-related colleges in that it did not come directly under the authority of an official body of its parent church but was the instrument of a privately organized stock company started and controlled by the parental Quaker groups. A few stockholders were not Friends, but all managers had to be members of the Society.[7] The constitution of this stockholder association gave entire authority for the governing of the school to the managers (thirty-two in number, sixteen of each sex) and made them a self-perpetuating board.

The board immediately proved to have a conservative view of discipline and care. The environment of the student, it was decided, would be heavily guarded; the first president of the college was gone within two years, partly as a result of his leniency in discipline, to be replaced by the sterner principal of the Preparatory Department.[8] The second president, Magill, remained for a long period (1871 to 1889) during which he cooperated with the managers in carefully supervising the thoughts and actions of the young. The governing board itself maintained a close interest in daily affairs. It established a sixteen-member executive committee to operate between regular meetings. It chose to decide on quite specific administrative matters, e.g., in 1877 whether female students would be allowed to go boating. It even required in 1878 that each request of the boys for a game of baseball come to it for approval.[9] The president, in turn, impelled by board mandate, personal inclination, and a desire to avoid embarrassing incidents in the dangerous practice of coeducation, developed rules, one hundred in number, that came to be known as the "Laws of Swarthmore College Relating to Students."[10] In short, the guides imposed from the top were plentiful. The college was almost totally, at the outset, an agency of its parental religious body.

The board also had to consider carefully the original promise that the

6. Original statement of admission policy, quoted in *ibid.*, p. 87.
7. *Ibid.*, p. 72.
8. Magill, *op. cit.*, p. 153.
9. Babbidge, *op. cit.*, p. 127.
10. *Ibid.*, p. 164.

college would prepare teachers for the young children of Friends. Teacher training, as an organized field, was just becoming popular throughout the nation, and between 1870 and 1890 more than fifty state normal schools were founded in the United States.[11] In 1878 the college established its own Normal Department. The step toward teacher training, however, was shortly to prove more a gesture than a prime commitment.

## Emerging Patterns: 1880–1900

The college in its first decade, then, was heavily a preparatory school, closely guarding the Quaker youth in its care, and in the process of testing its promise to prepare schoolteachers. Drawing from Quaker families of eastern Pennsylvania and nearby Maryland and New Jersey, with a conservative board, it was a tight little island, Quaker style. In the next two decades, the eighties and nineties, the outside social base, the controlling board, and the financial dependence of the college on a handful of families all remained about the same, but life inside the college underwent considerable change.

First, the student body shifted from the preparatory to the college level. President Magill, for one, wanted a college not a prep school.[12] In the early eighties, the prep school enrollment was still dominant, but in 1885, the college enrollment was, for the first time, the larger, and by the time Magill left the institution in 1890, the college students outnumbered the prep students two to one.[13] After 1892, the Preparatory Department was no more.

Second, student life moved from guided care to fun. The college was neither geographically nor intellectually isolated from the main academic stream, especially as it developed the normal desire of an institution to be thought well of by others, and the characteristics of other colleges increasingly affected the campus in the eighties and nineties. Those characteristics spelled Joe College. Social fraternities, begun in the nation in the eighteen-twenties and thirties, and sororities, begun several decades later, had entered a period of major growth and, along with their equivalents in exclusive eating clubs and social clubs, were taking charge of the life of the student outside the classroom. Football also had come into its own. Kicked off by a few intercollege games (Princeton-Rutgers, Harvard-Yale) in the early seventies, the game charged over one campus after another with almost explosive force in the eighties and nineties,[14] serving the many purposes of student involvement, alumni interest and loyalty,

11. James Mulhern, *A History of Education* (New York, The Ronald Press Company, 1946), p. 491.
12. Babbidge, *op. cit.*, p. 144; Magill, *op. cit.*, p. 189.
13. Magill, *op. cit.*, p. 196.
14. Frederick Rudolph, *The American College and University* (New York, Alfred A. Knopf, Inc., 1962), pp. 373–93.

and general public relations. By 1882 Harvard had a twenty-eight game schedule, with nineteen games played away from Cambridge, and the Big Game weekend was fast becoming the most important event of the year for thousands of alumni, sportswriters, and innkeepers.

Quaker Swarthmore, along with other small colleges, was not immune. It, too, leaned to the collegiate way of life. This turn to the worldly concerns of other colleges was not to the liking of those supporters, managers, and staff members who were most concerned about guarded care of the young, but their resistance did not have much solid footing. The college was not endowed and was paying its way from tuition revenue alone. Thus, financing was directly dependent on students, a clientele that could easily go elsewhere. In an increasingly diverse and competitive market, college officials almost everywhere were listening carefully to popular demand. With this leverage the undergraduate student after 1880 increasingly made the American college what he wanted it to be. At Swarthmore the guarding of enrollment became more compelling than the guarding of morality. Potential applicants and students on campus viewed the administrative "laws," one hundred strong, and the close hand of the managers as unnecessarily stern and arbitrary authority. In the late eighties the college experienced a crisis of dropping enrollment out of which emerged more permissive policies than had previously been in effect on athletic activities, student organizations, and social life.

In came the fraternity alongside the literary society, the student publications, and the glee club. The student editors of the campus yearbook noted in 1891 that " 'the increased number of the college organizations . . . has necessitated a contraction of the literary department' " and offered the opinion that this change would "be of no detriment to the book." [15] The Board of Managers turned in the eighties from opposition to intercollegiate athletics to sympathy. The nineties saw the college go big time in football, to take on giants such as Princeton and the University of Pennsylvania, as well as small colleges, all then competing in the hiring of itinerant professional players in the hope of ensuring victory. Directed by students and alumni the rapid move of the college into the larger society through extracurricular activities is symbolized by a note one alumnus wrote to a fellow graduate in 1904: " 'I enclose check to help along football on the understanding no players are to be bought this year. It was no advantage last year. . . .' " [16] The Quaker students were fast becoming youth of the world; the alumni, organized in an association after 1875, were fast becoming worldly like alumni elsewhere.

The curriculum also was sensitive to changes brought about by the new freedom: The elective system—the right of students to choose their

15. *Halcyon* (1891), pp. 16–17; quoted in Babbidge, *op. cit.*, p. 235.
16. Quoted in Babbidge, *op. cit.*, p. 149.

studies—was then sweeping the country. The college from the beginning had been interested in science. However, the interests of the men students began to turn from science to engineering: In the ten-year period from 1873 to 1882, the enrollment of male seniors was twenty-six in science and six in engineering; in the following ten years (1883 to 1892), the engineering seniors predominated fifty-one to twelve.[17] The interests of the girls, in turn, encouraged the development of a literary curriculum demanding less mental exercise than that required in the classical curriculum or in the theoretical sciences. The relation of curriculum to enrollment weighed in the scales of adaptation: "Several young women have left us without completing their studies, who would almost certainly have stayed to graduate had this arrangement then existed." [18]

As a third point of change, the college, with many zigs and zags, evolved away from a normal school posture. President Magill was hostile to the normal school idea: To go this route, he said, would have a "disastrous effect" on standards and the standing of the college.[19] The Normal Department, initiated in 1878, never became effective and was discontinued a few years later (1886). But the break with teacher training was not as definite and complete as was the dropping of the prep school. The college continued to educate some young men and women who would enter teaching and made attempts in the nineties and after the turn of the century to increase the output of teachers; but after the failure to assume teacher education as a major commitment in the first two decades, the college became too fixed around other ideals and practices to evolve later into a normal school for Quaker teachers.

These important changes in the seventies and eighties did not institutionalize a firm, coherent pattern, however, and after Magill's resignation in 1889, the strains in the character of the college were revealed by a decade of indecision. The ideal of serving the Quaker society, through moral and religious training, remained active, particularly in the minds of managers. The ideal of the quality college was in contention, particularly in the ambitions of the faculty. The ideal of Joe College was very much present on campus, strongly entrenched in the attitudes of the students.[20]

After Magill, a scholarly professor and cultural leader of the campus, William H. Appleton, became acting president and president for two years (1889 to 1891), but he did not want the job permanently and neither did his immediate successor (William D. Foulke) who, for personal reasons, withdrew between the time of his appointment and the date for assuming the post. The man who took over for the next seven years was Charles DeGarmo, a professor of psychology from a normal

17. *Ibid.*, p. 203.
18. *Managers Report* (1875); quoted in *ibid.*, p. 205.
19. *Op. cit.*, p. 189.
20. Babbidge, *op. cit.*, p. 235.

school in Illinois. DeGarmo agreed with those managers who thought the college should reinvest in teacher training, but he also wanted to maintain intellectual standards equal to those of universities and the physical facilities necessary to compete more effectively with other colleges. He was not able to obtain the funds necessary for these steps or to attract a full student body, and he left in 1898.[21] The next man to try, William W. Birdsall, had been principal of the Friends' Central School in Philadelphia. His intention was a Society-oriented administration, and he was soon busy speaking to and corresponding with groups of Friends throughout the country. He symbolized Quaker faithfulness and a return to earlier simplicity and piety. His efforts brought some increase in enrollment from the traditional families, but he was considered plodding by those of scholarly intent, and antiquated by those who had found college to be fun. In the face of outspoken criticism he resigned after four years (1902).[22] Thus in little over a decade, the college had had four men elected president and three who had served. There was some bad luck in this turnover, but it reflected mostly the incapacity of men connected with the college to find the formula of reconciliation in a period when the old ideals of a conservative sectarianism were put forward, for what proved to be the last try, against the trend to a more worldly college.

## The Solid Base

In 1902 indecision came to a halt. The managers went outside this time, and they went big. Their selection was the president of the University of Indiana. It took considerable Quaker persuasion to move Joseph Swain to Swarthmore (enrollment 225) after nine successful years at a major state university. In making such a move, he had an unusually strong bargaining position, and he asked for much in the way of money and authority. The money was to come in a promised endowment drive, and the authority came specifically in the form of power to appoint and dismiss faculty and to veto salary changes made by the managers. In his background and experience, Swain combined the major thrusts of the college. He was Quaker and could be true to a Quaker heritage; and he had been president of an important university and could be true to the urge to build and stake out a larger and more significant claim for Swarthmore on the vast terrain of higher education.

The Swain solution to the strains of the college was to modernize its traditionalism. First, he kept the college firmly anchored on its traditional Quaker social base. He maintained close ties with the Friends' schools in the Middle States and Maryland, and with dependable feeder schools like Friends' Central School (Philadelphia), Swarthmore Preparatory, West

21. *Ibid.*, pp. 237–42.
22. *Ibid.*, pp. 242–45.

Chester Friends' School, and the George School. Quaker students came every year from such nearby public schools as Swarthmore High, Chester High, West Chester High, Philadelphia Boys' High, and Wilmington High.[23] Scholarships were assigned on a regular basis to a dozen or so co-operating Friends' schools in Pennsylvania, New Jersey, New York, and Delaware.[24] Affiliation between the college and specific Quaker groups was preserved by such means as encouraging them to provide money for certain programs or activities, as in the case of The Educational Committee of the Conference of the Seven Yearly Meetings, which provided financially "for the continuance of the courses in education. . . ." [25]

Second, President Swain strengthened the applied fields of study at the college. Pointing to the "demand of the times for practical studies," he wanted Swarthmore to stand "both for a liberal and a practical education." [26] Engineering, already strong at the college, was steadily enlarged. An Engineering Shops building, completed in 1907, allowed for courses in concrete, drawing, electrical railways, foundry, machine design, machine practice, woodworking, and sewerage.[27] Swain repeatedly pointed out "the necessity for enlarged facilities in applied sciences and other courses attractive to young men at Swarthmore College";[28] and the young men came in increasing numbers. Engineering became the most popular major for men. The department offered more courses than any other—twenty-two in 1907 to nine in mathematics and seven in English, the next largest in number of courses. By 1915 there were twenty-seven courses in civil, electrical, and mechanical engineering and another nine in chemistry and chemical engineering; the course enrollment in engineering was surpassed only by that in English. In 1920, at the end of Swain's tenure, over one-half of the graduating male seniors (seventeen out of thirty-two) were in engineering.[29] Although engineering had become the symbol of practicality at Swarthmore, other disciplines were also given a practical component, again primarily to make them attractive places for practical young men. Swain wanted subjects "useful to a student preparing for a business career," like accounting, in the Economics Department. "There are 121 students now enrolled [course enrollment] in this department. The number would be larger if we had the courses suggested." [30] And before

23. "President's Report," *Swarthmore College Bulletin*, Vol. 4, No. 3 (March, 1907), pp. 36–37.
24. *Ibid.*, Vol. 12, No. 3 (March, 1915), pp. 24–25.
25. *Ibid.*, Vol. 5, No. 3 (March, 1908), p. 32.
26. "President's Report" (1907), *loc. cit.*, p. 49; and *Swarthmore College Bulletin*, Vol. 5, No. 1 (September, 1907), p. 3.
27. *Swarthmore College Bulletin*, Vol. 4, No. 3 (March, 1907), pp. 41–42.
28. "President's Report" (1908), *loc. cit.*, p. 45.
29. "President's Report" (1907), *loc. cit.*, pp. 39–42; "President's Report" (1914–15), *loc. cit.*, pp. 29–34; *Swarthmore College Bulletin*, catalogue issue, Vol. 18, No. 2 (December, 1920).
30. "President's Report" (1907), *loc. cit.*, p. 49.

the year (1907) was out, the president was able to announce "a new course, entitled Modern Business Practice. . . ." [31] With this broadening, economics became an important men's major. Biology also was given a practical twist to boost it as a men's major, with the establishment around 1910 of "preparatory courses in medicine, forestry and agriculture." [32] The college was also offering some work in law and was considering more.[33] And, finally, among the applied fields, there was education. The president worked hard to redeem this original promise. The work in education had sunk to almost nothing by the early years of his administration (1902 to 1906). First on his list of needs in 1907 was to put the Department of Education on a permanent basis, and 1910 found him trying to raise money for a Department of Pedagogy. He wanted $375,000, but a cooperating committee of the Friends' General Conference had come up with only $15,000.[34] By 1912, however, Swain was finally able to announce that a permanent Department of Psychology and Education had been established, with six courses in education and a teachers' course in each of another eight departments. He estimated that one-half of the senior class desired to teach.[35] No one could accuse Swain of not trying to provide college-educated Quaker teachers for the thirty-nine Friends' Schools in the Middle States and Maryland.

Third among the components of the Swain solution to the inherent strains at Swarthmore was to let the life of fun, of social activities and sports, continue to develop apace or ahead of that of other colleges. There was no pulling back toward a simpler piety but rather a willingness to live in the big time. The president early (1904) stated that he could live with an emphasis on sports:[36]

The friends of our College who are particularly interested in its athletic work will doubtless rejoice to know that Dr. W. S. Cummings is to return in the fall to devote himself to that careful training and general supervision of the physical condition of the young men in which he has proved himself so efficient. . . .

To Swarthmore's athletes, past, present, and future, it may be said that with the new cinder track, the resoiling of Whittierfield, the six new and carefully graded tennis courts, and with the record of last year's scores in foot-ball and lacrosse as an inspiration to further victories, Swarthmore's athletic future is bright.

Swain could hardly have guessed upon making these remarks in 1904 what publicity was in store for Swarthmore. The college, as mentioned

31. *Swarthmore College Bulletin,* Vol. 4, No. 4 (June, 1907), p. 45.
32. *Swarthmore College Bulletin,* catalogue issue, Vol. 8, No. 2 (December, 1910), p. 4.
33. "President's Report" (1907), *loc. cit.,* p. 49.
34. *Swarthmore College Bulletin,* Catalogue issue, *loc. cit.,* p. 3.
35. *Swarthmore College Bulletin,* Vol. 9, No. 4 (June, 1912), pp. 46–61.
36. *Ibid.,* Vol. 1, No. 4 (June, 1904), p. 4.

earlier, was playing football against university teams—this in the heyday of brutality and unbridled professionalism. It happened in 1905:[37]

In Philadelphia during the Penn-Swarthmore game Bob Maxwell, an outstanding Swarthmore player, was subjected to a beating so systematic and thorough that a photograph, showing him tottering off the field, his face a bloody mess, became a news sensation. That photograph called into action the President of the United States. From the White House Theodore Roosevelt thundered that if the colleges did not clean up football he would abolish it by executive order.

After coaches and physical directors met with President Roosevelt at the White House, they launched a campaign to clean up some of the brutality and professionalism. Some universities and colleges went so far as to give up football for a decade or so.[38] (Columbia University, also a football powerhouse, stopped for nine years.) Swarthmore was among those that found a year of suspension enough.

In going ahead with intercollegiate sports, Swarthmore took a stand on principle. In 1907 the fantastic news was received that the late Anna T. Jeanes had bequeathed to the college her coal lands and mineral rights in Pennsylvania, rumored to be worth one million dollars (the rumor later proved an exaggeration), *but* "on the condition that the Management of the aforesaid Swarthmore College shall discontinue and abandon all participation in Intercollegiate athletics, sports, and games. . . ." [39] Here was a chance to be seduced to purity, and many observers advised the college to take the bequest, restriction and all. The Jeanes gift was not a bribe, the magazine *The Independent* pointed out, it merely offset the pressure from the other side. Since the gift did not interfere with basic academic freedoms, *Outlook* claimed, the college could accept the gift. Rejection of the gift would be little short of a calamity, shouted a good citizen in *The Nation*, for the choice was whether Swarthmore would become a football school or turn toward the academic.[40] But the bequest obviously represented close earmarking of funds by a donor, the bane of institutional autonomy. The president was against accepting funds under such narrowly specified conditions, and within the year the college turned down the bequest.

Swain took the occasion to say that professionalism in football had indeed become a problem at the college and to admit that "there have been some abuses from time to time at Swarthmore, as at other colleges,

37. Rudolph, *op. cit.*, pp. 375–76.

38. *Ibid.*, p. 376.

39. "Papers on the Bequest of the Late Anna T. Jeanes," *Swarthmore College Bulletin*, Vol. 5, No. 2 (December, 1907), p. 4.

40. "The Olive or the Laurel," *The Independent*, Vol. 63 (October, 1907), pp. 887–88; "Conditional Gift of Miss Jeanes," *Outlook*, Vol. 87 (October, 1907), p. 280; "Gift to Swarthmore," *The Nation*, Vol. 85 (November, 1907), p. 491.

and as there will always be where there is good, warm, American blood. . . ." But, he maintained, the past abuses had been corrected, the college had eligibility rules as strict as any, the rules were being carefully carried out by the athletic committee of the faculty, and athletes should not be discriminated against: "I do not share the opinion of those who think that financial assistance to a student should make him ineligible to represent the College in any intercollegiate contest." [41]

Football was legitimate, and Swarthmore returned to the pleasant excitement of the big game on Saturday. The college also continued to play over its head, against universities, as well as to maintain traditional rivalries with smaller schools such as Haverford. In 1916 Swarthmore beat the University of Pennsylvania *and* Columbia University. (Later, in the early thirties, a noted sociologist of education chose Swarthmore to exemplify the point that schools often win moral victories while suffering defeats: "Pennsylvania wins, but Swarthmore triumphs." [42] The week before President Swain's successor was formally inaugurated in the fall of 1921, Swarthmore managed to tie the University of Pennsylvania in football, a matter of sufficient moment to warrant mentioning by a speaker at the inauguration ceremonies. [43]

As big-time sports became deeply institutionalized at the center of student life, so did the associated social activities. Fraternities and sororities dominated the social life of the campus, institutionalizing their exclusiveness and their rituals. [44] Freshmen were physically hazed for violation of such rules and customs as wearing a garnet cap with green buttons and tipping the cap to all seniors. Freshmen and sophomores had class struggles, "with elaborate rules for governing keg fights, poster fights, tugs of war, and the like." [45] In these matters, the campus varied little from the typical small private college of the day.

A fourth element in the Swain solution of modernizing traditionalism was to make the college considerably larger by increasing its financing, developing the physical plant, and enlarging the student body and the faculty. The president was an effective fund raiser: Through endowment drives in 1902–6, 1909–11, and 1916–19, he brought the endowment from $400,000 in 1902 to $3,000,000 in 1920. By the time of the third drive, in 1916, in order to gain the leverage of poor comparison the college had to be pitted against such well-endowed schools as Haverford, Amherst, Bowdoin, Bryn Mawr, and Williams. Following after Haverford and Bryn

41. *Swarthmore College Bulletin*, Vol. 6, No. 1 (September, 1908), p. 11.
42. Willard Waller, *The Sociology of Teaching* (New York, John Wiley & Sons, Inc., 1932), p. 113.
43. "The Inauguration of Frank Aydelotte as President of Swarthmore College," *Swarthmore College Bulletin*, supplement, Vol. 19, No. 2 (1921), p. 26.
44. Everett Lee Hunt, *The Revolt of the College Intellectual* (New York, Human Relations Aids, 1963), p. 58.
45. *Ibid.*, p. 37.

Mawr, Swarthmore was the third best endowed college in Pennsylvania in support per student.[46]

By the end of his tenure, the president could point with considerable pride to his changes in the physical plant since seven new buildings and three athletic fields represented considerable expansion and renovation in a small college.[47] The college catalogue of the last Swain year devoted five pages to describing buildings and grounds down to the heating and lighting plant, which was "erected in 1911 at a cost of about one hundred thousand dollars" and was located "south of the Pennyslvania Railroad tracks" that ran through the college property.[48] Enrollment had increased from about two hundred in 1900 to over five hundred in 1920. The faculty expanded from thirty to about forty-five and the student-faculty ratio had moved to a favorable 11 to 1.

Swarthmore had had its days of worldly excitement and attention during those twenty years of a strong building president: the football scandal in 1905; the Jeanes bequest in 1907; the frequent dedications of new buildings; the announcements that the latest fund drive had gone over the top; the many exciting intercollegiate games played before large crowds; the annual commencements, in which the pleasures were many and the problems usually no more vexing than whether rain would drive the ceremonies indoors. In retrospect one of the unusual occasions in the life of pre-1920 Swarthmore was the forty-seventh Annual Commencement in June, 1919, when circumstances placed A. Mitchell Palmer, Class of 1891, and Drew Pearson, Class of 1919, at the center of the campus stage. Palmer, then attorney general of the United States, was generating the 1919–20 "Palmer Raids" that made his name a symbol of reactionary repression of civil liberties. This old grad, who had gone so far in almost thirty years, was on campus that day to receive an honorary doctor of laws degree from his alma mater and to deliver the Baccalaureate sermon. The stern attorney general was in such danger of physical assault by "the Reds," it was thought, that he was given special guards on campus. The young Drew Pearson, later to become, at least for a time, a symbol of liberal, crusading journalism, apparently could already talk as fast as he was later to write. Chosen to be the Ivy Orator, the student speaker, Pearson "stirred and inspired his audience as few Ivy Orators have done."[49] Whatever the elder fighting Quaker thought of the younger one that day, and the younger of the elder, the occasion certainly belonged to militant Quakers who were, or soon would be, men of the world. Swarthmore had moved far from the sway of simple pieties and the isolation of a small, cultural backwater.

46. *Swarthmore College Bulletin*, Vol. 13, No. 4 (June, 1916), p. 10.
47. *Ibid.*, Vol. 18, No. 2 (December, 1920), p. 5.
48. *Ibid.*, pp. 19–23.
49. *Ibid.*, Vol. 16, No. 4 (June, 1919), pp. 5–6.

# *Chapter 8.* Transformation

OVER FIFTY YEARS OLD, the Swarthmore College of 1919 had solid foundations. It possessed an excellent physical plant, it was in good financial shape, and its academic work would more than pass muster. Closely tied to a local Quaker constituency and heavily influenced by a few families, the college in return had a dependable social base for financial and moral support. Its participation in big-time sports was a special point of renown in the national press as well as among the nearby supporters. The Quaker community also knew Swarthmore to be "the little Quaker matchbox," where coeducation and the active social life of a Quaker student body helped ensure that the right girl would meet and marry the right boy. Swarthmore was not a shaky place on the brink of quiet bankruptcy as was Antioch or torn by dissension and weakened by inflation as was Reed. It was the solid college of fixed character, a seemingly unattractive setting for the educational reformer. Bold spirits would certainly pass it by as being too self-satisfied and too constrained by constituency to be open to change. Experts in administration would say: Better to establish a new college for a new program than to try to change a college so obviously enjoying its traditions and so closely tied to a founding group.

But then the philosophers of educational reform often have a poor sense of the organizational tools of action, and generalizing experts work with the probabilities of favorable conditions for change. The reformer who chose Swarthmore as his workplace in 1920 saw it differently. He thought he saw the conditions for which he had been searching; and he came to make fundamental changes. What he did in the twenties and thirties reveals the degree of openness that can exist in seemingly routinized colleges.

## The Goals of Change

If ever an American was taken with Oxford and willing to serve as its ambassador in the United States, Frank Aydelotte was the man. After taking a bachelor's degree at Indiana University (1900) and a master's degree at Harvard (1903), then working briefly as a high school teacher in Louisville, Kentucky, Aydelotte became a Rhodes Scholar, spent several years at Oxford (1905–7), and took a degree there. He returned to the United States to teach college English, first at Indiana (1908–15)—with a year off to return to Oxford—and then at Massachusetts Institute of Technology (1915–21). During these years he became increasingly active among Rhodes Scholars, seeking both to improve their selection and to widen their impact upon their return to the United States. He became secretary of the Alumni Association of American Rhodes Scholars and editor of the Rhodes Scholars' magazine, *The American Oxonian.* In 1917 he wrote a small book[1] subtitled "Articles from the Educational Creed of an American Oxonian," in which he praised Oxford for the freedom and responsibility given students, the informal life of talk and sport, and the academic work, "which, at its best, in the case of the honors man, is hard and thorough and independent to a degree which is rare with us." [2] His enthusiasm and devotion to the cause led to his appointment in 1918 as American secretary to the Rhodes Trustees, a position in which he was responsible for the administration of the Rhodes Scholarships in the United States and one he was to hold for thirty-five years, until 1953. As his reputation grew, he was bound to be considered for college presidencies. (As indicated earlier, the Reed trustees tried to get him to take the presidency there in 1919–20.)

Thus prepared, Professor Aydelotte was interested in intellectual distinction, English model. How did such a man come to the presidency of Quaker Swarthmore? Much is hidden in the shadows of history, especially in the privacy of a Quaker board room. The trustees of Swarthmore, after two decades of business-minded leadership, apparently were ready for someone who would turn directly to the educational program. The man who came to be interviewed was recommended as a promising educational leader; the retiring president, stepping down after twenty years,

1. *The Oxford Stamp and Other Essays* (New York, Oxford University Press, Inc., 1917).
2. *Ibid.,* p. 15.

apparently used these terms.[3] Aydelotte, in turn, saw a place attractive on the critical grounds of resources and permissive lay control. With buildings and finances in hand, he could concentrate on the educational program; with a liberal Quaker ethos as the climate of control, he would have some room in which to maneuver. After much hard work and some hard fighting, Aydelotte's success at Swarthmore proved his judgment correct. The conditions were amenable to his cause, but some of the trustees received more educational leadership than they bargained for.

The new president came in the door talking quality and higher standards. Speaking at an alumni dinner shortly before taking office, he suggested that the college put its money on quality:[4]

I know the pride you feel this year in the large additions to the college endowment fund. You will expect much from the College in return, not I think in quantity, but rather in quality. . . . Quality rather than quantity is the great need of American education today.

The increment of quality he had in mind was not small, he revealed. Throughout its history, Swarthmore had tried to raise the grade of its instruction, he maintained, and had become "one of the soundest of our small colleges," but "there is still room for further progress"; indeed, the college should strive for the top:[5]

In my opinion the standard of achievement required in the best American colleges for the A.B. degree can be, should be, and is destined to be gradually raised until it is practically equal to what we now require for the A.M. That will not be done in a moment. But progress is already being made in that direction, and it is my dearest wish that Swarthmore should be one of the institutions to lead in that movement.

In the fall of the year, at his inauguration, Aydelotte again emphasized quality, but now he focused on what could be done for a special group of young people, those truly interested in matters of the mind. He posed the question of how the best students could be brought up to higher levels of intellectual initiative and independence and thereby trained for leadership:[6]

The method of doing it seems clear: to separate those students who are really interested in the intellectual life from those who are not, and to demand of the former in the course of their four years' work, a standard of attainment for the A.B. degree distinctly higher than we require of them at present. . . .

3. Everett Lee Hunt, *The Revolt of the College Intellectual* (New York, Human Relations Aids, 1963), p. 51.
4. *Swarthmore College Bulletin*, Vol. 18, No. 4 (June, 1921), pp. 13–14.
5. *Ibid.*
6. "The Inauguration of Frank Aydelotte as President of Swarthmore College," *Swarthmore College Bulletin*, supplement, Vol. 19, No. 2 (1921), p. 23.

He went on to speak of "the separation of honors men from the main average body of students." Here were the values of Oxford, the intent to separate honors students from the pass men. This emphasis focused attention on a segment of the student body rather than the whole, offering the delightful prospect that Swarthmore could have it both ways—higher quality work for a few, traditional levels of work for the rest.

Yet, operationally, the campus as a whole would be involved and affected in many ways. As an honors program was constructed, it would have to be viably related to the general campus. If the president committed himself to educating the very best, he would not want to bring the honors effort down to fit the rest of the campus but would have to bring the rest up into a sympathetic relationship. In large colleges structural differentiation can protect a small high-quality program from being driven out by larger low-quality ones. But in small Swarthmore, life was too intimate for that. An honors program could be killed by the derision of a student body interested in fun and games, by the indifference of the faculty, or by the adamant hostility of the donors who provided financial stability. For the purpose of the honors program alone, then, Aydelotte needed to look across the many features of the campus and to select those where change would be essential. Once the main thrust had been conceived, the task of the institutional leader was to reduce the barriers and to fashion the supports in critical sectors of the organization.

The faculty, it turned out, was not a critical problem. The existing faculty, whose sentiments the president had canvassed before taking office, were mostly in favor of upgrading the academic effort. In addition, as he found the funds to staff his new program, the president also brought in men of his own choosing. Aydelotte was an engaging man, easy to admire and to follow and full of determination and drive. His charisma and his office made it difficult to oppose him effectively from within the faculty. He suffered little of the strain with faculty that presidents at Antioch and Reed experienced during some of the critical years of character definition.

The problems, as it happened, resided in the nature of the student body and in the external constituency. The students and the alumni were not academic men; their beliefs and practices were not those of high academia. Aydelotte had much to do before his goals would be reasonably approached. The most immediate consideration was the direction of effort in the student body. It would require considerable shifting of the ways of the students to bring about what the new president had in mind. The life of study had to be supported; the life of play had to be brought under control.

## The Supports for Study

HONORS PROGRAM

The primary means of upgrading the work for the brighter segment of the student body was, as Aydelotte saw it, an honors program for the upperclassmen, and he set to work immediately fashioning this tool, bit by bit, as various professors agreed to join it and plan courses. By the fall of 1922 eleven students had begun "reading for Honors in the Divisions of English Literature and of the Social Sciences." [7] The catalogue devoted two pages to honors courses. The following year, fifteen were reading for honors, three took degrees with honors, the Division of French and the Division of Mathematics, Astronomy, and Physics had now joined in, and the catalogue description ran to four pages. The news in the third year was that thirty students were involved and that the Division of Classics was participating. In the fourth year of steady expansion (1925–26) fifty-two, or one-fourth, of the juniors and seniors were in the honors program, and with the entry of German and chemistry, seven instructional divisions were participating.

The extension of the program continued steadily. In 1926–27 biology and education were added as fields for reading in honors; the description of the program in the catalogue had grown to ten pages. In the following year honors work was available in almost every field of study on campus, including engineering for the first time; the catalogue honors section had grown to fifteen pages. The college had no policy on the final proportion of students to be allowed in the honors program. In 1930 the president reported a wait-and-see attitude. That year nearly a third of the seniors graduated with honors. [8]

The annual catalogue faithfully mirrored the emphasis on the honors program. Many pages were devoted to honors courses, procedure for admission to honors work, and departmental statements of honors work, while the material on the social life of the campus was reduced to a six-line paragraph. The divisions of the college had been reordered into four— humanities, social sciences, mathematics and natural sciences, engineering —sometimes referred to as honors divisions. [9] When in 1932 about 40 per cent of each senior class took the honors degree, the program had reached the plateau of student proportion on which it was to rest. Thirty years later, in 1960, the program still incorporated about 40 per cent of the juniors and seniors, and in the intervening years participation in the program had not significantly increased or decreased. The president had

7. This and the following information are from catalogues and presidential reports of the respective years.

8. "Report of the President," *Swarthmore College Bulletin*, Vol. 28, No. 2 (December, 1930).

9. *Swarthmore College Bulletin*, catalogue issue, Vol. 28, No. 3 (March, 1931).

a strong sense of the institutionalization of the program: "It may now fairly be said that honors work at Swarthmore had passed the experimental state." [10]

OPEN SCHOLARS

Because the honors program required bright and serious students, to have changed the curriculum but not to have changed the caliber of entering students would have invited failure. Well aware of the importance of the student input, Aydelotte went out to obtain students who would set the pace in his program and attract others to it. His primary device, one he instituted immediately, was Open Scholarships. The scholarships, of which there were five a year, could be held for the full four years. They were not awarded to any particular feeder school and were not limited by geographical locality, subject of study, or religious denomination but were nationally competitive and in criteria attempted to follow the Rhodes Scholarships—intellectual excellence, character, and leadership qualities were essential. One significant limitation at the outset was that the scholars had to be men.

For the five scholarships open in 1922–23, Aydelotte reported 209 competitors from twenty-three states. He took quick note that some of the unsuccessful competitors had become interested in Swarthmore, and fourteen of them enrolled even though they had not won the coveted scholarship.[11] The following year over two hundred candidates were spread among thirty-two states, and twenty-nine of the unsuccessful as well as the five lucky ones entered the freshman class.[12] By 1925, the president felt the Open Scholars were making a difference in the caliber and tone of the student body:[13]

The success of the [Honors] plan among the undergraduates has unquestionably been due in part to the Swarthmore College Open Scholarships established four years ago. These scholarships . . . have given us a group of young men who combine intellectual ability with qualities which make them leaders in undergraduate life, and thus tend to increase undergraduate respect for excellence in intellectual work.

The president went on to announce a new companion plan, three Open Scholarships for women, which he felt confident would have similar effects of providing intellectual leadership among the coeds.

In later years Swarthmore did not always have as many applicants for the scholarships as it did during the flood tide of students in the twenties, but the number continued to be high, and the applicants were widely

10. "Report of the President," *Swarthmore College Bulletin*, Vol. 29, No. 2 (December, 1931), p. 9.
11. *Ibid.*, Vol. 20, No. 3 (March, 1923), pp. 10–11.
12. *Ibid.*, Vol. 21, No. 2 (December, 1923), pp. 10–12.
13. *Ibid.*, Vol. 23, No. 2 (December, 1925), p. 12.

distributed throughout the country. The plan was a spur for bright students, especially for men, to come to Swarthmore. It helped the college obtain male students who would number as many as the women, be as bright and serious, get good grades, and participate in the honors program.

## ADMISSIONS STANDARDS

Aydelotte also sought better students in the entering class as a whole. Student supply and demand was quite favorable in the twenties for such an effort. Expansion was taking place in higher education, and as in the sixties the average and above-average private colleges were receiving many applications. Even if the college had not had the honors program and Open Scholarships as special points of attraction, the raising of admissions standards would have been feasible. Swarthmore was undergoing a change in public reputation that helped to swell the numbers of applicants and hence make possible even greater selectivity. Very early (1922–23) the president remarked that competition for admission was among the important influences in "the improvement of the academic standards of the College." There were 800 applicants for 170 vacancies, a 4.7 to 1 ratio, and the president did not keep it a secret that "this pressure for admission . . . will serve in a few years materially to raise the level of character and intellectual capacity of our undergraduates."[14] Of course, with so many applicants, the college could have chosen to expand rapidly, but Aydelotte maintained it was not going to do so. It had definitely decided to go the other route, to follow "the policy of using the competition for admission as a means of raising academic standards." [15] For the country as a whole between 1921 and 1931, college enrollment went up over 50 per cent; at Swarthmore, it increased from 510 to 588.

The number of freshmen was, in fact, allowed to decline from 170 in 1922 to 150 in 1926, as dropping out declined among upperclassmen and the college sought to keep its over-all size "within the limits of numbers prescribed by the Board." The college chose the 150 freshmen of 1926 from "just under 1500 duly certified applicants"—a 10 to 1 ratio! And they were capable in academic work since 97 per cent of those chosen had stood in the upper quarter of their high school class in academic performance.[16] Not all the students were shining bright, however, when compared with later generations of students at the college. In 1931 the dean of the college reported the Scholastic Aptitude Test scores of students who had entered in 1927, grouped in categories of honors and non-honors as graduating seniors of 1931. The medium score for the students receiving highest honors was 624; for high honors, 571; for honors, 512;

14. "Report of the President" (1923), *loc. cit.*, p. 8.
15. *Ibid.*, p. 10.
16. "Report of the President," *Swarthmore College Bulletin*, Vol. 24, No. 2 (December, 1926), pp. 11–12.

and for nonhonors, 491.[17] Thus, by the norms of the colleges then a part of the College Entrance Examination Board system—a select group—the college still had a number of students of average ability.

Swarthmore did not always have ten applicants for every seat in the freshman class, but as the ratios declined in the thirties to 3 or 4 to 1, the chance to select high-caliber students remained unusually high, especially as the growing reputation of the college developed a sharper bite in attracting the good and repelling the bad. From its improving pool of potential students, the college engaged in very careful selection, using College Board test scores, high school records, and personal interviews.[18]

One major group stood to lose something important by all this change. The group was the alumni, and the important something was the guarantee that sons and daughters of the traditional, extended Swarthmore family would be admitted. Within a few years, grief began to build up in the alumni as the criterion shifted from family to ability and the requirements of ability became increasingly strict. The Quakers who were admitted would now have to be bright Quakers, and from the mid-twenties through the early thirties, Aydelotte went to great pains to find those good ones who would hold up the Quaker end on campus and, at the same time, would reassure the alumni that he was not deliberately de-Quakerizing the student body. In his annual report of 1925 he let go with a major lecture on Quakerism and higher education that referred directly to the growing apprehension:[19]

Academic standards at Swarthmore have recently been the subject of careful discussion in several meetings of the Board. . . .

Conditions at Swarthmore have brought the group of Quakers in the College (who, though they constitute less than one fourth of the student body, are nevertheless its traditional clientele) into comparison with a group of non-Friends comprising in their number many of the strongest graduates of the best schools in this and other parts of the country. In spite of some fatalities, the Friends make a favorable showing in this comparison. They exhibit wider differences of ability than the non-Friends, furnishing a larger percentage of those students who are dropped for not keeping up in their studies and of those who qualify for honors work. . . .

The failures which have occurred among Friends during the last few years have given rise to discussion as to the real purpose of the College, and the issue raised is of such fundamental importance that the Board of Managers has decided to draw up a considered statement of policy, to be sent to all members of the Society of Friends and all alumni and alumnae of the College.

This letter, which will be issued early in the New Year, points out the interesting fact that such improvements as has already been made in the academic

17. *Swarthmore College Bulletin*, Vol. 29, No. 2 (December, 1931), p. 45.
18. "Report of the President, 1939, Reviewing the Period 1921–1939," *Swarthmore College Bulletin*, Vol. 37, No. 3 (January, 1940), pp. 11–12.
19. "Report of the President" (1925), *loc. cit.*, pp. 6–8.

work of the College has tended to increase the number of Friends in the College and their percentage to the total enrollment. . . .

The object of this letter is to make clear that the Board approves unreservedly the improvement in the level of academic work which has already been made at the College, and stands solidly behind the Faculty in the effort now being made still further to raise the level. The Board asks that "parents and prospective students share its enthusiasm for a college that is a college and not a social club."

The president went on to indicate that the college was making special efforts to help Friends' schools improve their standards of work and thus "to add to the intellectual equipment of such students as come from them to Swarthmore." In 1928 Aydelotte[20] was pleased to report that

in seven years the number of Friends has increased from 113 to 155, from 22 per cent to 28 per cent of the student body. There are now more members of the Society of Friends at Swarthmore than at any time since the College opened its doors in 1869. The number of children of alumni has also shown a substantial increase, from 71 to 93, i.e., from 14 per cent to 17 per cent of the students of the College.

In 1929, after virtual completion of two major fund drives, the president noted that "misapprehensions and opposition were inevitable" in the alumni, that there was uneasiness about one's children getting in. Some "poorly prepared" had been excluded, he admitted, but some preference had been given and many good students had been attracted from the traditional sources.[21]

To fashion a new program, to fund some scholars, to select students appropriate for serious study—these are not easy administrative changes. They require imagination and determination, but they are what we expect of educational leaders, the items of reform to which our eyes are readily drawn. Equally important, however, if not more so, are alterations in the structure of affairs outside the classroom, changes usually made exceedingly difficult because they mean a diminishing or destroying of the practices of college spirit and song. The critical battles of academic reform at Swarthmore, in a sense, had to be fought on the playing field and in the fraternity lodge.

## Control of the Extracurricular

### THE DECLINE OF BIG SPORTS

Of all the features of the old Swarthmore that had to be subdued in order to place intellectuality front and center, big sports was undoubtedly the

20. "Report of the President," *Swarthmore College Bulletin*, Vol. 26, No. 2 (December, 1928), p. 7.
21. *Ibid.*, Vol. 27, No. 2 (December, 1929), pp. 12–13.

most important and the most challenging. Football was the kingpin of the old collegiate life; control it, and many of the other features of the fun subculture would abate. This fact was understood sooner or later by many educators. Robert Hutchins,[22] in explaining his decision to discontinue football at the University of Chicago in 1939, claimed that

since football is the symbol of the non-educational aspects of educational institutions, students do not come to the University of Chicago unless they want an education. . . . The abolition of intercollegiate football has done something to make clear what a university is.

Aydelotte also understood such facts of life in the identity of colleges. Solving the problem of football would be difficult because of the sentiments of the students and, far more important, the sentiments of the alumni.

The organizational dynamics of big-time sports at the time, and still today, have a nexus in gate receipts. Big sports require big money, and the historical pattern of raising that money, in the United States, is to get it from the spectator. Hence big crowds are needed, who in turn demand excitement and victory; and to provide *that,* one needs to recruit star athletes and to supply abundant muscles; and so on around the circle. The problem for those who wish to de-emphasize was, and is, to break the cash nexus. In a way, the problem was how to turn football from a profit to a loss.

At Swarthmore during the twenties the graduate manager of athletics made a report each year within the president's annual report. These reports tell the story. In the beginning (1922) football brought in fifteen thousand dollars a year and "with slight aid from basketball supports all other sports." [23] The football profits in 1923, 1924, 1925 ran between five thousand and seven thousand dollars. "Large crowds are attracted to Swarthmore" for the athletic contests, the manager reported, and the football profits were

chiefly the returns from the games with Pennsylvania, Princeton, and Haverford. . . . Under the present management, the problems of migration of athletes, professionalism, and unsportsmanlike conduct have disappeared, and a healthy atmosphere is encouraged and maintained.

In 1925 the manager was able to report that athletics "continue to hold a prominent place in the life of the students"; 198 out of 260 men in the college had reported as candidates for some varsity team, with 82 candidates for football. And "considering the fact that Swarthmore played with institutions usually much larger than itself the results of the play are

22. *The State of the University, 1929–1949, A Report by Robert M. Hutchins Covering the Twenty Years of His Administration* (no place or publisher, 1949), pp. 37–38.

23. This and following quotations and information on sports taken from presidential reports of the named years.

very satisfactory"—in all sports, thirty-six wins, thirty-eight losses, and three tied games. The manager was reassuring: "No important change in the policy of the Athletic Committee has been made during the year just concluded."

But some changes were being initiated. Eligibility rules were being tightened, and the tilt toward de-emphasis had begun:

One great advance is being made as the year 1926 opens. The men in charge of our most important teams will be resident coaches and members of the faculty. . . . The responsibility for the action of the teams is now placed in the hands of members of the Faculty.

Although coaching was taken away from alumni managers, financial control was still in the hands of an alumni athletic association that handled the gate receipts and whose dues of $15 per member were contributing another four thousand dollars of support.

That association was soon in distress:

Our present dependence on the proceeds of the Pennsylvania, Princeton, and Haverford football games is unfortunate in that we are not as free as we would wish to be in the matter of schedule formation. So vital are these three games, which provide approximately $9,500, to the welfare of the Association that the elimination of any one will leave the Association financially embarrassed. We are facing such a situation in the schedule for 1927, where it will be seen that two of these teams, for one reason or another have been omitted.

Princeton and Haverford had both been knocked off the schedule, the one permanently and the other, as it turned out, until 1941—the year after President Aydelotte left Swarthmore. The decision, in fact, had been made to drop big games and big gates and, in the case of Haverford, to cool off a traditional rivalry that had become too hot.

From here on, there was to be little or no profit in football. With its income diminishing, the athletic association, after the 1926–27 season, "was forced to borrow $2,000 and utilize a reserve fund of $450." The professor who had served as graduate manager for fifteen years resigned. The following year football lost money for the first time within memory, and the athletic association saw its over-all deficit zoom from $568 to $3,409. Now, "the problem of finances is the most troublesome one confronting the athletic authorities at Swarthmore."

Over the next two years (1928 to 1930), the athletic authorities were able to report "no financial loss" and we "held our own," this due to a "careful check on all expenditures and to a somewhat increased subsidy from the college." The issue of de-emphasis was now ready to come out into the open. In his 1930 annual report, after reporting success on a major fund drive, Aydelotte himself put it to friends of the college:

There is a growing feeling of dissatisfaction among undergraduates and alumni with our traditional policy of playing one or two football games against teams from large universities for the sake of the financial returns. Games of this type with teams outside our own class cannot be justified on any except financial grounds. . . . Furthermore, the newspaper publicity and the attitude of the spectators distort values and endanger true sportsmanship. . . .

The Athletic Committee is at the present time seriously considering a change in policy. In my opinion they would be wise to make our football schedule entirely with teams in our own class.

The graduate manager spoke also of "certain football games," the money-makers, as "questionable" in nature. The following year (1931) he noted that "attendance at the games has fallen off to a point where it is no longer sufficient to meet expenses."

In 1932 the old athletic controlling committee was discontinued, and the coaching staff was absorbed into the faculty. The graduate manager then said:

For the first time in the history of Athletics at Swarthmore, the College has assumed direct responsibility for the Athletic Program. The old committee of Faculty, Alumni, and Student membership has been discontinued and a new committee appointed by the president has succeeded it. All the Instruction Staff in the Department of Physical Education, including the staff of coaches, have faculty standing and are paid entirely by the College.

With the coaches paid through regular instructional funds, college subsidy had taken over from gate receipts. The coaches could now afford amateur sports; they could ignore the size of the gate and could lose games without losing their jobs.

The following year the college took the last big drawing card off its schedule. "After last Saturday's 54-0 game . . . ," *The New York Times* reported in October, 1932, President Aydelotte announced that Swarthmore, in a friendly parting, would end its fifty-four-year rivalry with the University of Pennsylvania.[24]

The king was dead. Henceforth Swarthmore would engage in friendly contests on Saturday afternoons with colleges such as Union, Amherst, and Hamilton. The college assumed complete financial control, settled "all outstanding debts," and readjusted "guarantees, salaries, and general costs" (1933). The football team had become a good loser, with win-loss records of 1 and 6, 2 and 5, 2 and 4. Admission fees at sports events were becoming only "an easy method of controlling the crowds"; by 1938 only "visitors from the outside" were charged a fee, and the president said, "It is only a question of time until all admission fees should be abandoned." Gate receipts had been reduced until they covered only 25 per cent of the cost of sports.[25] The cash nexus had been broken.

24. *The New York Times*, October 13, 1932.
25. Swarthmore College Faculty, *An Adventure in Education: Swarthmore College Under Frank Aydelotte* (New York, The Macmillan Company, 1941), p. 107

Here was de-emphasis long before its time. Slowly but surely during the twenties and thirties, Swarthmore robbed big-time sports of their dynamics. In his last report, reviewing the nineteen years of his presidency, Aydelotte said proudly:

Perhaps the greatest change in undergraduate recreation has been in athletics. We have entered frankly upon a policy of playing games for fun. We no longer compete in football against large universities. . . . Athletics, having become universal [for all the students] have ceased to be a problem.

## THE EROSION OF SOCIAL LIFE

President Aydelotte and his expanding band of allies in the administration, faculty, and student body also took out after the social life that was such a major obstacle to the use of the intellect. Joe College was a stubborn foe; there was much tradition and commitment in hazing, dancing, membership in exclusive sororities and fraternities, and the use of the campus as a Quaker matchbox. But the life of fun and games was nibbled to death. As early as 1922 Aydelotte began pressing for a more democratic social life. He later reported, in the mid-thirties, that the social life of the college was "the first undergraduate problem which I attacked." [26] He estimated also that for several years he made little progress, but in the first year of his efforts, he did get the students to rule out physical hazing as a punishment for violation of the "so-called Freshman rules"; the number of fraternity dances was cut, and a campus-wide annual prom was established; nonfraternity men were organized to reduce their feeling of being excluded from everything.[27] Two years later, to reduce physical violence further, the students abolished the Freshman-Sophomore Scrap. The following year, in a letter to alumni, the president got the Board of Managers to commit itself to the doctrine that Swarthmore should be "a college and not a social club." [28] From this point, the de-emphasis of the social was out in the open. Aydelotte pounded away on the theme of subordinating "social values" to "intellectual and spiritual values." He recalled Woodrow Wilson's imagery of social activities as the sideshows that had crowded out the main performance of academic life.[29]

The change taking place in social activities was evolutionary not revolutionary, however, and it was too slow for some observers. The father of a girl student who was at Swarthmore in 1927 wrote an article entitled "The Revolt of a Middle-Aged Father," in the *Atlantic Monthly*,[30] in which he castigated American colleges for using money to train playboys,

26. "Report of the President," *Swarthmore College Bulletin*, Vol. 31, No. 3 (January, 1934), p. 15.
27. *Ibid.* (1923), pp. 13–14.
28. *Ibid*, (1925), *loc. cit.* p. 8.
29. "Report of the President" (1928), *loc. cit.*, p. 12.
30. I. M. Rubinow, "The Revolt of a Middle-Aged Father," *Atlantic Monthly*, Vol. 139, No. 5 (May, 1927), pp. 593–604.

using "X College" (Swarthmore) as his case in point. The college he was referring to, he said, was small and had an excellent reputation. It had become difficult to get into and was not ostentatious. It could have a true college life. Yet after observing life there, he had to conclude that idleness was venerated, that the college was much like "a summer hotel in the mountains or at the seashore." The father's comments were reasonably justified, according to professors interviewed at the college in 1960 who had experienced the earlier period.

If any one event in the evolution of the twenties and thirties signified the demise of Joe College at Swarthmore, it was the abolition of sororities in 1934. Aydelotte increased the vigor of his criticism in the early thirties. He spoke of the student oriented to the extracurricular practices as one "cheated of his birthright." Those activities entailed "empty publicity" and "mediocre distinctions"; they pulled Swarthmore toward the stereotype of "the college of the moving picture screen, which is a travesty on education." Echoing the disgruntled father of the *Atlantic Monthly* article, he maintained that a college serving as "a playground or an athletic club is a waste which no nation however wealthy could or should afford"—hitting conservative Quakers and businessmen with their own prudence. He spoke of his regrets that "the men's and women's fraternities" (at Swarthmore sororities were referred to as women's fraternities) still had undue influence, that in fact both had been increasing in size to the point where about three-quarters of the men and women were in fraternities, making it very uncomfortable for the minority left outside.[31]

Under this sharp questioning and steady prodding and with the student body tilting away from sympathy to the fraternities, the students were ready to move. In 1933 the Women's Student Government by a vote of 160 to 108 recommended that women's fraternities be abolished—this, Aydelotte noted, after "eighteen months of discussion of a question which has been seriously raised half a dozen times before during the last twenty years." [32] Some alumni objected, and the Board of Managers debated the matter. They decided that the opinion of students should prevail but only after a second round of voting one year later. The vote came out to a similar tally in 1934, and the sororities were done. After years of nibbling, the students were ready for a major change. From that point, the men's fraternities, which remained in existence, were heavily on the defensive.

And so were any organizations and ceremonies that smacked of exclusiveness, secrecy, and fraternal ritual. A senior society, Book and Key, modeled after a Yale society, got under way early in the presidency of Joseph Swain and by 1910 had made itself the pinnacle of status on campus. Replete with endowment funds, influential alumni backers, and mausoleum, Book and Key invited only seven juniors a year to its

31. "Report of the President" (1931), *loc. cit.*, p. 8.
32. *Ibid.*, (1934), p. 11.

membership. For a number of years it was able to draw on the top student leaders: It had impressive alumni, including presidents of universities and some Swarthmore faculty and administrators. And through those years the rest of the students went along with its ceremonies, such as Tap Night in May, when senior members of the society tapped seven men, at intervals of seven minutes from among all junior men assembled on the lawn. But beginning in the early thirties, students increasingly turned away, repelled by its exclusiveness and its secrecy. They learned to laugh and to refuse membership. The society survived but as a pale imitation of what it once had been.

With the decline of big sports and the steady erosion of the traditional social life, the major on-campus barriers to Aydelotte's intentions were removed. In their place, practices that supported his ends arose. Following Oxford, Swarthmore provided ample playing fields, equipment, time, and staff for the afternoon exercise of the amateur athlete. It fielded teams in many intercollegiate sports, becoming particularly proficient for its size in track, soccer, and lacrosse. Also part of the picture was a more low-key social life. The college did not push all the traditional forms of sport and fun out the door, as did Antioch and Reed. Rather, it kept those that would integrate with the academic-intellectual emphasis of a small, modified Oxford.

## Alteration of Social Base

### FROM LOCAL TO NATIONAL CONSTITUENCY

During the years of transformation Swarthmore did not dwell, in public discussion, on the changing geographical distribution of its students. Since the sensibilities of the alumni were so directly involved, public utterances were designed to reassure them that Quakers and children of alumni were still being admitted, as was true, in large absolute and relative numbers. But if the trend toward national recruitment was unspectacular, it was steady (Table 8–1). Approximately two-thirds of the students in 1920 were from Pennsylvania alone, and four-fifths were from Pennsylvania and New Jersey combined. The proportions from these states had increased during the Swain period, in line with his effort to keep the college on its traditional social base. But after 1920 the proportion from the home area decreased in each of the next four decades, with the sharpest decline occurring in the twenty years of Aydelotte's tenure, while the proportions from New York, the New England states, and the rest of the country rose. Between 1920 and 1940 the percentage of students from Pennsylvania declined from 64 to 30 per cent, and the percentage from New Jersey declined from 15 to 10 per cent. Thus, while the percentage of students from New York increased from 6 to 23 per cent, from New England from 1 to 7 per cent, and from the rest of the country from 14 to 30 per cent, the percentage from Pennsylvania and New Jersey combined dropped from 79 to 40 per cent. At the same time the number of states from which students were recruited steadily increased, until at the end of the fifties it was up to forty-two. By that time, students from Pennsylvania composed only one-fifth of the student body.

*TABLE 8–1. Geographical Distribution of Students, Swarthmore College, 1900–1958*

|  | 1900 | 1910 | 1920 | 1930 | 1940 | 1950 | 1958 |
|---|---|---|---|---|---|---|---|
| Entire student body | 183 | 372 | 507 | 588 | 765 | 915 | 892 |
| Percentage from |  |  |  |  |  |  |  |
| Pennsylvania | 60 | 57 | 64 | 47 | 30 | 29 | 21 |
| New Jersey | 10 | 16 | 15 | 14 | 10 | 9 | 9 |
| New York | 9 | 6 | 6 | 12 | 23 | 25 | 21 |
| New England | 1 | 1 | 1 | 3 | 7 | 7 | 10 |
| All other states | 21 | 20 | 14 | 23 | 30 | 30 | 38 |
| Number of states |  |  |  |  |  |  |  |
| Represented in student body | 16 | 27 | 22 | 34 | 33 | 39 | 42 |
| With more than five students | 5 | 8 | 8 | 10 | 17 | 22 | 24 |

Source: Registrar's records, Swarthmore College.

The proportion of students who came from Friends' schools (e.g., George School and Friends' Central in Philadelphia) and from the three major public high schools near the campus held to the previously established level all during the twenties, but the college increased the numbers

*TABLE 8–2. Freshman Students from Friends' Schools and Local Public High Schools, Swarthmore College, 1920–58*

| Year | Number of Entering Students | Friends, Schools, Per Cent | Three Local Public High Schools*, Per Cent | Total, Per Cent |
|---|---|---|---|---|
| 1920 | 156 | 13 | 15 | 28 |
| 1930 | 179 | 22 | 5 | 27 |
| 1940 | 239 | 13 | 1 | 14 |
| 1950 | 243 | 7 | 3 | 10 |
| 1958 | 275 | 7 | 2 | 9 |

*Swarthmore High School, Chester High School, West Chester High School
Source: Registrar's records, Swarthmore College.

from the Friends' schools, while the share from the public high schools fell sharply (Table 8–2). The proportion then slipped considerably in the thirties as the trend toward national recruitment had its major impact. By 1940 the local public high schools had only a slightly greater claim on Swarthmore than did other schools in the country and, together with the

Friends' schools, supplied only one out of seven of the entering students. Schools that in the earlier years of the century had sent a student every year to Swarthmore, and in some cases an annual cluster of students, were now completely outside the feeder system or supplied only an occasional entrant. West Chester High School, for example, had six graduates entering Swarthmore in 1920, one in 1930, none in 1940; students from Chester High School declined from seven in 1920 to none in 1930 and one in 1940. From among the many schools of the traditional social base, only Swarthmore High School and the George School were to persist as major feeder schools up through the fifties, and their improvement in academic quality had somewhat kept pace with that of Swarthmore.

THE SHIFT IN FINANCIAL BASE

As previously indicated, the college in 1920 was in solid shape financially as a result of President Swain's efforts. His third major fund-raising drive had just been successfully concluded, and endowment stood at a reasonably attractive three million dollars; but this financial situation was appropriate to Swarthmore as Swain left it, not as the new reforming president wanted it. The honors program needed money. With a small student body, a two-track curriculum was much more expensive than a one-track course since even within small departments classes had to be divided into honors and regular courses. The honors classes also had the smallness of seminars, so that an hour of a professor's teaching assignment might relate him to only a third, or a fifth, as many students as usual, i.e., a seminar of seven students in place of a class of twenty or thirty-five. More money was an essential component of the experiment. Without it, the odds on floundering would rise sharply.

With the growth of the honors program, the resentment of traditional supporters began to increase. There were major pockets of doubt about the wisdom of giving one's money when there would be no preference in admissions. The issue went so deep that some influential, loyal followers decided to sit on their hands when contributions were sought. However, the capacity to bring new money to Swarthmore was one of Aydelotte's greatest initial strengths and was finally his trump card. Close to Abraham Flexner, he could always turn to him and the General Education Board, to other foundation executives who knew talent when they saw it, and to private donors who found the president one of the most forceful and convincing men ever to grace their drawing rooms. The Swarthmore experiment, in turn, was precisely what Flexner and other educational statesmen had in mind when they turned to general reform in American higher education. Aydelotte did not offer the far-out, utopian talk of Arthur Morgan or the threat of vulgar vocationalism that many thought inherent in the Antioch work-study program. Swarthmore did not present the multisided risk of Reed, where so much could—and did—go wrong. Here was a solidly established college with a new president whose purpose was to lift it to the highest possible standards and whose model was the best in British higher education. With this marriage of friendship and ideals, Swarthmore was soon cast as a favorite of those whose role was to finance educational reform.

In 1925, when the proportion of juniors and seniors working in the honors program had grown to 25 per cent, Aydelotte noted that the high cost of the program "began to be apparent last year":[33]

That we are able to carry on the experiment is due to the generous subsidy granted to Swarthmore College by the General Education Board for this purpose. Under the terms of this grant the College is to receive $20,000 for the year 1925–1926, $40,000 for the year 1926–1927, and $60,000 per year for the next three years [1927–28, 1928–29, 1929–30], provided those amounts are needed to provide extra instruction for honors students, and provided furthermore that the results of the work justify this extra expenditure. This grant has been made on the understanding that the Board of Managers of Swarthmore College will by the end of the five-year period provide additional endowment to continue the work upon the same scale of expenditure.

Here was the money needed to sustain the new program for its second five years, given at a time when its growing size made cost an important factor and generated unease in the ranks of the old supporters. The funds could be spent only on the honors program—"to provide extra instruction for honors students"—and the program would have to show results. Then, too, the trustees were warned that at the end of the five-year period the General Education Board expected them to undergird the program with endowment.

Thus from 1925 to 1930 the college received $240,000 in direct grants from the G.E.B. Then came the day of decision: Additional endowment had to be found or the whole experiment could go under. An endowment campaign was initiated in 1929 to raise $2,750,000 altogether, with $2,000,000 for educational endowment. The heart of the matter was $1,200,000, which would annually replace the subsidy of $60,000 from the General Education Board. Other sums were sought for an addition to the library, a new men's gymnasium, athletics, and improvements at the power plant. Toward the educational endowment, the G.E.B. itself immediately pledged $675,000, which was one-third of the total and over one-half of the sum needed to replace its own annual subsidy. Outside sources— mainly two wealthy private donors—gave another $680,000 and alumni, undergraduates, and parents acquitted themselves with gifts totaling over $700,000, to put the drive over its lower target of two million dollars—all between May 1 and June 3 of what must have been a very lovely spring! This was victory for the experiment.

33. "Report of the President" (1925), *loc. cit.*, p. 11.

And then, just to make sure, the victory was sealed twice over. In spite of the Wall Street crash and the depression, Swarthmore turned around the following year and went straight back to the donors for another two million dollars. The new endowment secured in the first campaign had indeed "assured the continuance of the present standards of academic work," the president said, but it left "only a small margin for the further strengthening and improvement." [34] The second campaign was also successful. The General Education Board gave another $675,000. The Julius Rosenwald Fund and another foundation made sizable contributions, and the two private donors who had given handsomely ($550,000) to the first drive now gave $850,000. Thus $1,825,000 was raised from foundations and two individuals—all outside money—leaving only $175,000 still to be raised from traditional sources. After the second campaign Aydelotte was pleased to say that Swarthmore was "in a secure position financially for the next decade at least" and that the campaign had ensured "the continued development of our academic work in a way commensurate with its importance." [35] Here was truly a pot of gold for the year 1930—handsome funds raised quickly from impeccable sources and all for the Aydelotte experiment.

The General Education Board had a very clear role in the critical 1925–30 period. In spite of the large funds contributed in the first campaign by those close to the college, a sense of profound strain might have cost Swarthmore deeply. In writing about this strain in the midst of the endowment drives, Aydelotte took the approach that "misapprehensions and opposition were inevitable" since "raising academic standards is never a popular procedure," and the honors program "was not widely understood by those who had not followed closely recent developments in the college program." [36]

The opposition was expressed by a sizable bloc of traditionalists who were in a fighting mood, angry over the loss of assured admission and the decline of big sports and social life in a college into which the loyal old families had put so much money, work, and moral support. When relations moved past sweetness and light into conflict, Aydelotte's opponents thought they had the means for bringing him down: dry up the financial wells. However, the monies put up by the G.E.B. and the several other outside groups supported, defended, and finally institutionalized the leap forward at Swarthmore. The major grants in 1929 and 1930 put Aydelotte fully in control. The shift in financial base was a crucial step. After 1930 the alumni and local friends of the college were still important, morally

34. "Report of the President," *Swarthmore College Bulletin*, Vol. 27, No. 2 (December, 1929), p. 7.
35. *Ibid.*, pp. 17–18.
36. *Ibid.*, p. 12.

and financially, but general financial support was no longer concentrated in local families.

The level of support offered by the new funds also placed the college in a different financial category. Between 1921 and 1939 endowment increased from three to eight million and annual income from $470,000 to over $925,000. Within the yearly budget instructional salaries rose from $100,000 to $320,000; library expenditures, $5,000 to $52,000; and scholarship funds, $16,000 to $75,000. Expenditure per student had also risen substantially, from $934 to $1,381.[37] This level of support, based on endowment, measurably enhanced institutional security. How could any business-minded member of the Quaker community fault the enterprise? The Board of Managers managed the funds conservatively and well. The president had not proven a reckless plunger but rather had personally attracted large sums of money to finance his reform and then was content to live within the budget.

## The Building of Image

A modified and measurably enlarged public image of Swarthmore developed in the twenties and the thirties along with the changes taking place in the curriculum, student recruitment, and financing. Aydelotte, as much as Morgan, had a sharp sense of the importance of reputation in changing the operational character of an American college. In the short run a reputation of quality would ease his way; in the long run it would be essential to the institutionalization of his purpose and program. An articulate speaker and convincing writer, Aydelotte, aided by the professors, gave a steady flow of information to the outside world. The General Education Board offered public comment. Educational reformers gave public praise, and the national press and magazines were sympathetic. For a small place, much was said about it.

*The New York Times* was a veritable storehouse of information and praise. The East Coast business or professional man reading his *Times* on the commuting train, as pointed out earlier, would have encountered Antioch and could not have failed to have made the acquaintance of Swarthmore. Between 1913[38] and 1919, leaving aside the sports page, the *Times* had only three articles about Swarthmore; they referred to two public addresses and to the protection of armed guards given Attorney General A. Mitchell Palmer when he spoke in 1919. But then between 1920 and 1930 the *Times* had over 60 different pieces on the college, followed by over 150 in the 1930–40 decade. In eleven of those years, the *Times* averaged at least an article a month on Swarthmore. The message

37. "Report of the President" (1939), *loc. cit.*, pp. 16, 78.
38. The year that the *Times* began an annual index of its articles.

was honors and quality: the separation of brilliant from mediocre students urged (1921); the successful competitors for Open Scholarships named (1924); Rhodes Scholars elected (1924); a Yale professor whose resignation was "a surprise at Yale" appointed (1925); the grants from the General Education Board for the honors work announced (1925, 1929, 1930); the football series with the University of Pennsylvania ended, with the intention of limiting the schedule to smaller schools (1932); sororities abolished (1933);[39] and so on. Virtually every year there was an account of the Open Scholarship competition or the awarding of the honors degrees or both.

Similarly the journals widely publicized the new effort at Swarthmore as a praiseworthy experiment, as an attempt to do the very best. *School and Society* helped Aydelotte announce the Open Scholarship plan, pointing out that these awards were patterned after the Rhodes Scholarships at Oxford (1922). Later this educational journal came back with articles on General Education Board support (1925), housing for faculty members (1928), and the endowment campaign (1930).[40] An article in the *Atlantic Monthly* in 1931, by a book collector, praised the "keenness and intelligence" of Swarthmore students.[41] The *Literary Digest* allowed, in 1935, that the students were now serious and not so full of college spirit.[42]

Even more beneficial in granting prestige were public statements from eminent figures who placed Swarthmore at the top in the quality of undergraduate education. One such account in 1927 performed the service of coupling Harvard and Swarthmore:[43]

The reason the student attitude at Harvard and Swarthmore has been completely transformed within a decade is that seventy per cent of the Harvard eligibles are working for a degree "with distinction" and forty per cent of the Swarthmore upper classmen have a single clear-cut purpose that for twenty-four months remains fixed and compelling. Study is actually "the major sport" in these institutions, and it is so understood by those who are not, as well as by those who are, honor students.

And another account, by the president of the Julius Rosenwald Fund in the mid-thirties, placed Swarthmore first among small colleges:[44]

39. *The New York Times,* October 23, 1921; June 10, December 15, 1924; February 22 and 23, March 1, 1925; April 15, 1929; March 2, 1930; October 13, 1932; March 2 and 9, April 20, December 13, 1933.
40. *School and Society,* Vol. 15 (March, 1922); Vol. 21 (March, 1925); Vol. 28 (July, 1928); Vol. 31 (March, 1930).
41. *Atlantic Monthly,* Vol. 148 (December, 1931).
42. *Literary Digest,* Vol. 119 (April, 1935).
43. William S. Learned, *The Quality of the Educational Process in the United States and in Europe,* Bulletin No. 20 (New York, Carnegie Foundation for the Advancement of Teaching, 1927), p. 120.
44. Edwin R. Embree, "In Order of Their Eminence: An Appraisal of American Universities," *Atlantic Monthly,* Vol. 155, No. 6 (June, 1935), pp. 652–64, quotation on p. 662.

If I were picking a small college, I should place Swarthmore at the head of the list. Standing just outside the culturally rich city of Philadelphia, with a tolerant and intelligent Quaker background, this college is one of the few smaller institutions which has been able to appoint professors of distinction approaching those of the great universities, yet has never forgotten the fact that stimulating teaching is the first duty of a college. Under the able direction of President Aydelotte it has eschewed the temptations of bigness or any kind of professional training and has concentrated its very considerable resources on first-rate education.

The General Education Board, in annual reports of its activities, held Swarthmore up as a national model.

The Swarthmore experiment has already had a perceptible influence in raising the standard and ideals of undergraduate work in the country at large.[45]

The demonstration of honors work at Swarthmore College is so widely known as to need no detailed comment. In eight years of operation the plan has been studied at first hand by officers of many colleges. They have been able to learn how to use or to adopt the honors methods of Swarthmore within the limitations of their own institutions.[46]

For the G.E.B. Swarthmore was in effect a sponsored laboratory to which interested parties could be referred. Because of this relationship, the G.E.B. was interested in creating and disseminating the best possible impression of the campus.

The president had been busy from the start in shaping outside impressions. His annual reports were full and long, well written and interesting. In 1924 Aydelotte reported on the honors movement in forty-five colleges for the National Research Council of the National Academy of Sciences. An official of the council, in introducing the report, placed Aydelotte at the forefront of this movement:[47]

President Aydelotte's name gives the report a special prestige because of his well-known large personal knowledge of both English and American honors systems and his devoted efforts to introduce into American college and university practice more attention to the individual student.

The following year (1925), Aydelotte placed another article on honors courses in the annual publication of the National Association of State Universities.[48] In 1926 a senior Swarthmore professor wrote about honors for the Association of American Colleges[49] and then published a book,

45. *Annual Report of the General Education Board, 1927–1928* (New York, General Education Board, 1929), p. 11.
46. *Annual Report of the General Education Board, 1929–1930* (New York, General Education Board, 1931), p. 14.
47. Frank Aydelotte, "Honors Courses in American Colleges and Universities," *Bulletin of the National Research Council*, Vol. 7, Pt. 4, No. 40 (January, 1924), p. 2.
48. "Honors Courses in American Colleges and Universities," *Transactions and Proceedings of the National Association of State Universities*, Vol. 23 (1925).
49. Robert C. Brooks, "Honors Courses at Swarthmore College," *Association of American Colleges Bulletin*, Vol. 12, No. 3 (May, 1926).

*Reading for Honors at Swarthmore: A Record of the First Five Years, 1922–1927*, with the Oxford University Press.[50] Flexner wrote the introduction to this volume, offering his usual hard-hitting indictment:[51] "American Education plays down to the average; the elementary schools level down; the high schools level down." He concluded that "towards the Swarthmore campus many eyes are now turning in the hope of seeing an essential task fearlessly, thoroughly, and in the best sense, democratically performed." The president also had an article that year on "breaking the academic lock step." [52] So it went, year in and year out: a steady stream of writing about the honors concept and the progress of the honors effort.[53]

By 1939 persons in or close to Swarthmore had written at least thirty articles and a book about the honors work. These publicizing efforts were capped with a major volume in 1941, a tribute to Aydelotte by the faculty at the end of his regime.[54] To this list was added in 1944 a book by Aydelotte, *Breaking the Academic Lock Step*, written as his final review of "the development of honors work in American Colleges and Universities." [55]

With all this publicity, Swarthmore became publicly defined as *the* pioneer in honors work in the United States and came close for awhile to capturing the honors concept. To say honors was to think immediately of Swarthmore; and the honors image of Swarthmore had become part of the history of American higher education. To quote one historian:[56] "Most American colleges today offer honors work in one form or another. Swarthmore, under President Frank Aydelotte, a former Rhodes scholar, was a pioneer." And another:[57] "An educational movement of the 1920s that also expressed an aspect of the new spirit was the honors program which was pioneered at Swarthmore College in 1922."

Later, in the fifties and sixties, when something that could be considered

50. Robert C. Brooks, *Reading for Honors at Swarthmore: A Record of the First Five Years, 1922–1927* (New York, Oxford University Press, Inc., 1927).

51. *Ibid.*, pp. v–vii.

52. Frank Aydelotte, "Breaking the Academic Lock Step," *School and Society*, Vol. 26 (October, 1927).

53. E.g., Dean Raymond Walters, "Teaching Honors Students at Swarthmore," *Association of American Colleges Bulletin*, Vol. 14, No. 5 (November, 1928), pp. 419–24; Frank Aydelotte, "Honors Courses at Swarthmore," in *Five College Plans* (New York, Columbia University Press, 1931), pp. 59–70; Frank Aydelotte, "The Progress of the American College in Two Decades in Intellectual Achievement," *Association of American Colleges Bulletin*, Vol. 21, No. 1 (March, 1935), pp. 24–33.

54. Swarthmore College Faculty, *op. cit.*

55. *Breaking the Academic Lock Step: The Development of Honors Work in American Colleges and Universities* (New York, Harper & Row, Publishers, 1944).

56. George P. Schmidt, *The Liberal Arts College* (New Brunswick, N.J., Rutgers University Press, 1957), p. 234.

57. Frederick Rudolph, *The American College and University* (New York, Alfred A. Knopf, Inc., 1962), p. 456.

an honors program appeared in first dozens and then hundreds of colleges, Swarthmore was the defining figure. It was the initiator; it had made the honors program work, while others had let honors die on the vine. Typical of later comments were these:

> The British and Commonwealth universities have long made the distinction between Pass and Honors degrees. Frank Aydelotte at Swarthmore seems to have made the first conscious adaptation of the British practice to conditions in American Colleges.[58]
>
> Partly as a response to a post-war enrollment boom and partly because of Swarthmore's Frank Aydelotte, many colleges and universities instituted honors programs in the 1920s. . . . But after the founding committees had met for the last time and the initial enthusiasm for a new program had faded, most of these programs quietly slipped into the neat obscurity of catalogue prose.[59]

## Swarthmore 1940

Aydelotte was more fortunate than Morgan and William Foster, who initiated corporate identities but were not around to ensure their future. Aydelotte did not pack his changes quickly into the first several years of his presidency—the honeymoon period that presidents so often seize as the now-or-never time for action; they occurred with a rolling momentum. Made slowly in a stable setting and over a period of twenty years, the changes were well fixed in the character of Swarthmore by the time he departed, somewhat tired of alumni criticism, to become the second director of the Institute for Advanced Study at Princeton. In those two decades, most of the work of institutionalization as well as of initiating change was performed.

By 1940 Swarthmore had raised its head so clearly out of and above the mass of liberal arts colleges that it had one of the most distinct identities on the American scene. Honors was everywhere a symbol of excellence, and Swarthmore had become the symbol of honors. The self-image was strong; those who were a part of the college were likely to think it was a unique enterprise, and a Swarthmore instructor's self-esteem, based simply on being a Swarthmore instructor, was echoed by approbation from colleagues and outsiders. Public reputation for a small college could hardly be stronger. Everyone would rank it among the very best, many as *the* best, of the type of college—the private liberal arts institution—that in the face of the inroads of the university continued to stand high in public estimation. The 1920 Swarthmore was sound. The same college in 1940 was at the forefront of American education in reform and quality.

Basic to the leap forward was a change in the values that set the tone of

58. "On British Honors," *The Superior Student*, Vol. 4, No. 3 (April, 1961), p. 1.
59. Walter D. Weir, "That Honors May Flourish," *The Superior Student*, Vol. 5, No. 2 (November-December, 1962), p. 1.

student life and governed the direction of student effort. The college had moved from the collegiate life to intellectuality, changing its own climate by a concerted alteration of nearly every aspect of the campus. Recruitment and selection, the alternatives and pressures of academic work, the social rewards of extracurricular activities, the scholarship of the faculty, the day-to-day interests of the administration—all were so altered that the academic intellectual took first place on campus as a model of youth.

Thus, all the effort, all the hue and cry about honors work at Swarthmore, wrought changes far more reaching than those announced at the outset. The manifest purpose of the honors program was to provide a two-track curriculum, an internal differentiation. The long-run effects, however, were to obtain a student body bright and serious throughout. Honors did away with the pass man, a case of good coin driving out the bad. Although the college did, indeed, institutionalize two tracks, the honors and nonhonors, both came to possess able students, and the differences between the students became minor compared to the differences between Swarthmore students 1920 and Swarthmore students 1940 or between Swarthmore students and the students of an average liberal arts college. By the time the honors program had been made firm by correlated changes in such sectors as admissions and extracurricular activities, the major effect was an alteration of the college as a whole.

On a large campus, especially that of a university, honors and nonhonors courses can reside side by side without one necessarily controlling and radically altering the other, but on a small campus the same staff must be involved in both, and the students encounter both in their daily rounds. With so much interaction, one effort must inevitably tilt the other. At Swarthmore, Aydelotte left untouched no feature of the campus that would have sabotaged the honors program. The whole school was brought up into reasonable alignment. Whatever the labels on the curricular tracks, the entire campus was then for the bright and serious. Swarthmore never formally became a Balliol, a place where all students were in honors, but its character became so solidified around a talented student body that it became a place for the academic elite.

# *Chapter 9.* Conservation

WITH THEIR DIFFERENT institutional styles, Antioch, Reed, and Swarthmore after World War II encountered different problems of adaptation and continuity. Antioch had to adjust its character to the demands of academic specialization and to grapple with the perils of its permissiveness in student behavior. Reed had to struggle in the very depths of its soul with the stubborn tensions created by nonconformity and rebelliousness. Both colleges stood somewhat at odds with their settings, requiring substantial energy to maintain their characters in changing, demanding, and often hostile environments. Their tensions made them exciting, but exhausting—successful, yet flawed by one or more features that clouded their security and induced long periods of sleepless anxiety for those responsible and caring.

In comparison, Swarthmore was at ease. Here was the lucky institution: Its character was definite, its support was secure, and most important, its stance was right. What it had come to uphold and signify became prized in the larger society; representatives of the external world gazed fondly upon it and encouraged the college not to change but to conserve and enhance what it had already become. But the characterization of Swarthmore as a foremost instance of pleasing success in the fifties is from hindsight. It was not always that clear from up close in the day-to-day action of sustaining a faculty, suffering the errant ways of students, and soothing

209

parents and alumni unhappy with the ways of the campus. There was much to be done to ensure the vigor of the character that had come out of the Frank Aydelotte decades.

## The Commitments of Faculty and Administration

Central as always were the values of the faculty since what they defined as basic and right would prove in the long run to be the main support or the main source of erosion of the distinctive character that had evolved. As indicated earlier, transformation did not involve a radical departure from the academic ideals of professors, as did Arthur Morgan's scheme at Antioch, and it did not entail the risks of isolation in the provinces, as was the case at Reed. Honors was the kind of academic investment normally desired by professors, and the faculty of 1920 was for the most part ready to support an upgrading effort. The principal needs of the innovating president were to increase the size of the faculty in order to staff the new program adequately and to raise the scholarly level of the faculty to cope with serious and challenging students. While student values had to be transformed, faculty values needed mainly to be bolstered.

### THE BELIEF IN HONORS

The enlarged faculty that came out of the transforming years had a deep commitment to the honors concept and to the practices that had been established in its name. The commitment was as close to full consensus as is likely to obtain in a faculty. An occasional young man, putting on the mantle of Young Turk, would argue that there was too much specialization in the two years of honors and that students should be allowed and encouraged to choose more widely, but this point, in truth, was not very much to argue about as young men found again and again. They made no headway, in any event, against an overwhelming consensus that the honors program was right and was effective as it stood. Then, there were occasional twinges of conscience about the invidious distinguishing of the nonhonors from the honors students, usually stirred by a charge on the part of a student or an outside observer that the separation was undemocratic. But, in the face of over-all institutional success and no apparent damage to the nonhonors graduate, this doubt was so minor that it did not begin to disturb the deepening belief in the Swarthmore method.

Thus, when the faculty paid tribute to Frank Aydelotte at the time of his departure in 1940 with a full-length book,[1] they were able with great sincerity to praise the man and the college. Few presidents warrant or are

1. Swarthmore College Faculty, *An Adventure in Education: Swarthmore College Under Frank Aydelotte* (New York, The Macmillan Company, 1941).

given a departing book; when such publications do appear they are likely to be about new buildings and other items of local interest; but the Swarthmore faculty, in their volume, spoke of a man and a college whose efforts were of lasting national importance:[2]

This book is the record of an experiment in higher education. The experiment has proved a notable one. This not merely because it was novel, nor because it has been a local success, but because the ideas underlying it are making their way and producing similar enterprises in scores of other universities and colleges. The part played in this development by Swarthmore may have been great or relatively small; there is no means of measuring that. But it remains that what at the start was a local experiment is now a widespread and significant movement.

And they spoke proudly of the campus as a collective effort:[3]

Under Mr. Aydelotte's watchful eye, and inspired by his optimism and vision, the Swarthmore corporate state has gradually evolved its present educational program. From the start, policies were shaped through the deliberations of various groups, large or small, working in singularly harmonious cooperation. . . . The elder statesman of the faculty—so often an insuperable obstacle to programs for academic reform—showed themselves ready and willing to undertake an educational adventure.

Men were quietly but deeply conscious of a Swarthmore saga, one in which they had participated. At the core of the saga were the ideals and practices of the honors program. It had been the Swarthmore experiment, an educational adventure. A great leader and an unusually co-operative collective effort had produced outstanding institutional success that was still viable two decades later. The faculty belief in the college was a matter of fundamental emotion and pride.

THE SCHOLARLY MIX

A commitment to a university level of scholarship emerged alongside the commitment to honors. The faculty became an unusually scholarly group for the size of the college. With favorable conditions of work, including good salaries and a close relationship with students produced by a low student-teacher ratio and the seminars of the honors program, Swarthmore attracted and retained men whose points of reference and job alternatives included the major universities. The proportion of the faculty holding doctoral degrees in 1963 (74 per cent) was slightly *higher* than that at the University of California, Berkeley (70 per cent). In comparison, the proportion at Reed was 61 per cent, at Antioch 56 per cent, at St. Olaf 40 per cent, and at the University of Portland, 27 per cent (see Appendix 2).

2. *Ibid.,* p. v.
3. *Ibid.,* p. 26.

In his last annual report, in 1940, President Aydelotte proudly pointed to six books published by faculty members "during the last year," including Brand Blanshard's *The Nature of Thought* and Wolfgang Köhler's *The Place of Value in a World of Facts*.[4] Twenty years later, in the early sixties, the faculty had a publication record more like that of one of the leading universities in the country than like that of most small liberal arts colleges, including Antioch and Reed. When asked whether they had written a book, 36 per cent of the faculty reported having done so, ranking with the Berkeley campus faculty of the University of California, one of the most publication-conscious faculties in the country, where 40 per cent so answered (see Appendix 2). The more than one-third proportion at Swarthmore was considerably higher than the percentage at San Francisco State College, a semiuniversity by 1960, and the percentages at Antioch and Reed, the same type of small liberal arts college, and those at St. Olaf, University of the Pacific, and University of Portland, three church-related colleges. Nine per cent of the Swarthmore faculty had published four or more books, a proportion identical with that of Berkeley, compared with 3 per cent at Antioch and none at Reed. Higher proportions appeared for all the colleges when the faculty members were asked in this survey whether they were currently writing a book. The increase reflected both a national trend toward more publication and the hope that blooms eternal about one's unpublished manuscript. But the relative standings were about the same, with Swarthmore and Berkeley highest and similar to one another (see Appendix 2).

The Swarthmore faculty was active also in writing professional articles, definitely more so than the faculties at the other small colleges (Appendix 2), but here the level of professional activity fell below that of Berkeley. At Berkeley are all the pressures of quick publication—a necessity for faculty members, often in the short run for a salary increase, as well as in the long run for tenure and full professorship. At Swarthmore publication was more a norm than a necessity, and the norm included a preference for major, nonhasty publication.

In sharp contrast to attitudes at Berkeley, scholarly work was not supposed to get in the way of a concern for the student. When these faculties were asked in another question in the 1963 survey about their interest in students, for example, 87 per cent of the Swarthmore faculty estimated that over half of their colleagues were strongly interested in the academic problems of students compared to 34 per cent of the Berkeley faculty who made a similar estimate about their colleagues (see Appendix 2). The difference was even sharper when more refined categories are used: 60 per cent at Swarthmore thought that almost all of their faculty were strongly

4. "Report of the President, 1939," *Swarthmore College Bulletin*, Vol. 37, No. 3 (January, 1940), p. 11.

interested, compared to 9 per cent at Berkeley; while only 2 per cent of the faculty at Swarthmore replied that less than half or very few of their colleagues were highly interested in students, compared to 40 per cent at Berkeley. (These estimates of a very low level of faculty interest in students, made by Berkeley professors about their colleagues, occurred about a year and a half before the student uprising began there in 1964–65.) The Swarthmore faculty, in short, had an unusually high commitment to scholarship, one more normal to the university, along with the intense commitment to teaching and to students normal in liberal arts colleges.

MODERATE LIBERALISM

Besides the deep commitment to the honors program and the norm of productive scholarship, the faculty that helped to embody the Swarthmore distinction was also characterized by a quiet liberalism. For example, on political questions in the 1963 survey, only about one in six identified with the Republican Party; most had voted for the Democratic presidential candidates in recent elections: Adlai Stevenson in 1956 (68 per cent) and John F. Kennedy in 1960 (76 per cent); a third of the faculty members identified themselves as independent or Socialist (see Appendix 2). On questions about political investigations and the rights of political deviants, they were civil libertarian, not quite as much as the faculties at Antioch and Reed, but slightly more so than the liberal faculties at Berkeley and San Francisco State College and considerably more so than the faculties at St. Olaf, University of the Pacific, and University of Portland. The Swarthmore faculty favored, in this poll, considerable freedom for faculty members, under the principle of academic freedom, but their views on student rights and privileges were somewhat constrained—e.g., on students' writing as they please in their own publications without the censorship of faculty and administration. In short, the faculty was solidly liberal but not radical. Some Quaker properism was present. They were considerably more willing than their counterparts at Antioch and Reed to place limits around student behavior, here maintaining a connection with traditional Quaker thought on the guarding of the young.

On religious questions in the same survey, the Swarthmore faculty as a group was somewhat more religious than were the faculties at Antioch, Reed, Berkeley, and San Francisco State. They identified more often with a formal religion and more often regarded themselves as moderately or deeply religious (see Appendix 2); but they were considerably less religious than their counterparts at the three church-related colleges. Over a third (38 per cent) did not identify with a religious faith, compared with only 3 per cent at St. Olaf, 5 per cent at the University of Portland, and 15 per cent at the University of Pacific. Over a third (42 per cent) did not consider themselves moderately or deeply religious, compared with only 4 per cent, 14 per cent, and 15 per cent respectively at the three church-related colleges. Thus, in religious commitment, Swarthmore was a moderate version of the liberal faculty.

This moderate liberalism was framed by the gentle ethos of liberal Quakers. By the early sixties only about one in seven in the faculty were Quakers, but the trustees and the administration were largely Quaker, and the faculty members so identified were influential among their colleagues. As at Antioch, faculty men of varying religious persuasion, from atheistic to devout, found liberal Quakerism a congenial atmosphere within which to work and live. A few of the Quakers in the faculty were saintly men; as a whole, the Quakers were disinclined to sermonize and were willing to leave others alone while following their own moral vision. One faculty member, when asked to describe the character of Swarthmore, said of his Quaker colleagues:[5] "Their benign influence permeates the institution. I am not a Quaker, and have never been proselytized even in the slightest to become one. I appreciate this. Some day I may join the Society of Friends." As a result of the mutual tolerance and respect, the "religion" of the college was not challenged. Since the establishment of a distinctive character, no faculty group, young or old, large or small, has seriously attacked the Quaker spirit of the campus.

One specific practice reflecting this spirit was decision-making through "the sense of the meeting," a procedure common in Quaker groups. At a committee meeting or a meeting of the entire faculty the chairman would not commonly ask for a vote on an issue, and no one would rise from the floor to demand a count of hands or the use of a ballot. The expectation was that a common solution would arise through rational discussion, with each person first accepting for himself the rightness or appropriateness of a particular position. While the chairman and everyone else waited, there would be a search for the consensus; as the drift of opinion became clear, minority points of view often faded. The minority would see that the agreement necessary for policy and action lay in another direction, and if that direction seemed reasonable, they would go along with it. But a strong minority view that would not dissolve was taken seriously. Rather than vote it down, participants would continue the discussion or would table the issue so that further thought, discussion, and persuasion could take place outside the meeting room in the ensuing days and weeks. The matter might then be raised again at a subsequent meeting or, if a consensus was still missing, dropped.

This way of deciding on policy is, to say the least, not very common in American business or public administration. Its occurrence is rare in colleges. Professors in universities can hardly imagine it, so much do they become accustomed to interest-group representation within the faculty and parliamentary procedures in which one side votes down the other.

5. Response to question, "What have you found to be the central features of the character and climate of this college?" Faculty questionnaire, 1963 (see Appendix 2).

Outside cynics can quickly discern the weaknesses of the sense of the meeting, especially the leeway given to the chairman to declare agreement, and the system is not easy to operate. It requires an objective setting, such as a small college, in which informal discussion is the main means of co-ordination, and one in which men feel more unity than diversity. These and other favorable conditions existed at Swarthmore. The faculty numbered only one hundred and were in close contact with one another. They were united in their belief in the character and value of the college. The Quakers in the group were advocates and practitioners of the sense of the meeting, and the willingness of the non-Quakers in the faculty to accept this procedure, one they would not have known or used elsewhere, testified to the strong socializing power of Quaker beliefs and of their campus believers.

The attitudes and procedures involved in this style of administration put a premium on reasonable informal exchange and, if necessary, the slow working out of a compromise. Such decision-making curbs the impulses of activists in the faculty and blunts sharp disagreement. As a result, it is a conservative force, as well as a source of personal commitment and high morale. Each collective decision is, finally, one's own decision. Discussion, in this traditional form of group dynamics, involves each person in the decision before it is made and gains his support for what is finally decided. This style of decision is eminently suited for the old ideal of a community of scholars, and it has helped to make Swarthmore, in modern times, a good approximation of such a community.

ADMINISTRATIVE CONTINUITY

After twenty years of Aydelotte, institutional leadership in the sense of defining and embodying values was less needed in the presidency. With the character of the college so firmly formed around a successful formula, a second innovator hard on the heels of the first would have been inappropriate. If another bold and striking leader had chanced upon the scene, the faculty and other supporters of Swarthmore would probably have soon shown him the door. The leadership task of the next decade or two in so successful a place was to offer continuity in the president's chair, to consolidate and preserve the specific changes that had been made, and to make minor adjustments to a changing environment.

Few adjustments proved necessary, however, since the times were kind. The college had made the right changes: While elsewhere college life became serious and severe, Swarthmore had early adopted this attitude. Undergraduates everywhere increasingly defined college as preparation for graduate school; Swarthmore was almost perfectly oriented for this role. Undergraduate teaching faculties at other colleges became more specialized and research-minded; Swarthmore already had the inclination and the resources for specialization. The temper of the times had swung

American higher education toward what Swarthmore was doing. It was successful not only in its own terms and for its own supporters but also in much larger terms and for a much larger audience of educators and attentive laymen. The substantial resonance between its character and the larger system of elite liberal education after World War II helped to hold it in place. Once it had become what many other colleges would like to be, its visible and applauded success made it a leader among liberal arts colleges, an external role that exerted pressure toward conservatism.

The president who followed Aydelotte in 1940 came to the position, at the age of thirty-five, from within the Swarthmore administration. John W. Nason had been there for eight years, first as a philosophy instructor and then as assistant to the president. Married to a Quaker and having become a "Quaker by conviction," President Nason was temperamentally suited to sense of the meeting administration. He was thoroughly imbued with the ways of the college. Like his predecessor, he had been a Rhodes Scholar, a point of common background that helped to symbolize a continuity in administration, specifically the commitment of the president's office to the honors program.

Although a loyal member of the Aydelotte camp and considered by the faculty as one devoted to the Swarthmore experiment, President Nason was able to reach toward those in the alumni who had continued to oppose Aydelotte and to resist his program as a total definition of the college. Right up to the end of his tenure at the college, Aydelotte had remained for some a symbol of unwanted intellectualism. Although he had secured the honors program and his own position at the college by about 1930, the pressure of some alumni continued through the years, with charges that old-fashioned virtues were being lost because of a singular concentration on the academic. The president of the Alumni Association in 1935 had voiced it fully: [6]

There is abroad today in the ranks of the alumni the fear that men are being selected for Swarthmore on the basis of scholastic attainments without proper regard for the broader qualities of manhood. There is the fear that the purely academic functions of Swarthmore are crowding out those vital activities that have to do with the development of ruggedness, courage, determination and better understanding.

After Aydelotte left the presidency, it became somewhat easier for the college to deal with these fears. President Nason made minor adjustments that helped bring back those who were most distrusting. In his first annual report, he pointed out that "the resumption of football relations with Haverford College had already been announced." [7] The Haverford foot-

6. Everett L. Hunt, "Nason at Swarthmore," *Swarthmore College Bulletin*, alumni issue, Vol. 50, No. 6 (February, 1953), p. 55.
7. "Report of the President for 1940," *Swarthmore College Bulletin*, Vol. 38, No. 4 (January, 1941), p. 10.

ball team was not exactly Notre Dame, big-time sports were clearly dead at the college, and a campus rivalry that had grown too hot to handle before 1927 had become reasonable in the ensuing years. Now the game could be made to serve the ideals of amateur sports as well as to fulfill the fond wishes and to strengthen the loyalties of some alumni. Adjustments of this order did not disturb the character of the college, but they consolidated support and enlarged a consensus. As put some years later by a senior figure[8] of the college, in the phrasing of a eulogy:

It was one of John Nason's great gifts that he neither looked nor sounded like a professor. It was difficult to attack him as "academic" and impossible to abuse him as a mere salesman. The issue of intellectualism tended to fade away in his presence.

And so it went, for the greater part, through the forties and the fifties. There was always much to be done, from solving the annual problem of faculty salary increases through coping with the vexing limitations of library and dining hall space to battling state officials who, in their wisdom, envisioned a superhighway across the open spaces of the campus. But the work to be done was that of holding the college to the character it had developed and to the role of pacesetter that it had achieved.

When Nason stepped down after thirteen years (1952) to accept the presidency of the Foreign Policy Association, Swarthmore selected Courtney Smith, who as much as his predecessor was committed to the Aydelotte values. After graduating from Harvard, Smith also had gone to Oxford as a Rhodes Scholar. He then returned to Harvard, where he took his Ph.D. and taught briefly, and went on to Princeton, in English literature, there becoming the first director of the national Woodrow Wilson Fellowship Program. In 1953 he was appointed head of the American Rhodes Scholarships, directly succeeding Aydelotte in this honorable position; later in the same year, at the age of thirty-six, he became president of Swarthmore. Thus, the Rhodes Scholar Program in the United States again became headquartered in the president's office at Swarthmore, after some years up the road at Princeton in the office of the noted ex-president of Swarthmore and the office of the president-to-be. Reaffirmation of core values could hardly have been stronger. Formally, the new president was from the outside, but in basic values and personal background he was squarely in the Swarthmore tradition, more of an insider than many at the college.

Again, as with Nason, no major changes were intended or needed. For the second president after Aydelotte, the college was still very much on the right course except for some significant problems: Faculty salaries had been slipping and were brought up sharply by President Smith within a few years. Complacency was deepening, and it was useful for the

8. Quoted in Hunt, *op cit.,* p. 1.

president to be sensitive to and to warn others about the dangers involved. Faculty recruitment, particularly, required close attention to help the departments obtain excellent men in the face of strengthening competition. The steady increase in intellectual interest in the student body was also eroding the Rhodes concept of the well-rounded man, and Smith threw some of his weight on the side of physical vigor, broad concern, and character: "It is not enough to develop intellect, for intellect by itself is essentially amoral, capable of evil as well as good. We must develop the character which makes intellect constructive, and the personality which makes it effective. . . ." [9] But the basic problems were those of keeping the Swarthmore plan viable and protecting it from erosion. The administrative responses were effective. When Swarthmore celebrated its centennial in 1964, there was much about which to be happy and proud and relatively little to cause sadness and worry.

INTEGRATION AND AUTHORITY

Another point of steady continuity at Swarthmore was the high level of faculty contentment. For example, when asked in 1963 "In general, how do you feel about this college?" 80 per cent of the Swarthmore faculty responded, "It is a very good place for me," compared with 76 per cent at Antioch, 65 per cent at Reed, 68 per cent at University of California (Berkeley), and 61 per cent at San Francisco State College. Nine out of ten in the faculty considered it one of the top ten colleges. The proportion feeling they could not be "equally satisfied anywhere else" was surpassed at the eight colleges of the survey only by Antioch (see Appendix 2).

The steady ways also included a close integration of faculty and administration. As we have already seen, wide and firm agreement about the nature of the institution and specific techniques of discussion and persuasion joined men across the natural lines of disagreement and discord. Other devices testified to the care taken to integrate the staff. Nearly all the important members of the administration maintained a position in the faculty by teaching one or more courses. The administration was not even construed as a separate entity in annual catalogues and other publications, let alone listed first as is the usual style, but appeared under the broad heading of "The Faculty," with such descriptions of role as "Dean and Professor of Classics" and "Vice-President (Finance), Controller, and Professor of Economics." Such simple steps, taken alone in the face of adverse conditions, would probably have little meaning, but developed in the context of a gentle and unifying ethos and of the happiness of success, they added bit by bit to the capacity of the college to keep down the we-they sentiment that normally develops between faculty members and administrators.

9. From President Courtney Smith's inaugural address, quoted in Everett Lee Hunt, *The Revolt of the College Intellectual* (New York, Human Relations Aids, 1963), p. 9.

The high degree of informal integration softened the play of authority and power on campus. Meetings of the whole faculty operated about as elsewhere in the infrequency of their occurrence and in the amount of time devoted to routine matters of courses and degrees. Formally, authority became lodged considerably in the offices of the president and the department chairmen. No units represented the faculty with anywhere near the power of the faculty council at Reed or the Administrative Council at Antioch. Divisions were not key units as at Reed. The department became the basic unit of administrative and faculty structure, much as in universities, and the department chairmen had the power to deal directly with the president in the key matters of budget and personnel. A chairman was often long in office, and he could choose, as befitted his temper, to consult all hands in the department, the senior members only, or himself alone. A few chairmen held their cards very close to the vest— or the dress—but most followed the common academic procedure of consulting heavily with senior colleagues and lightly with the younger men.

Whatever the way he proceeded within the department, the chairman did not need to lobby his way past faculty-dominated councils, but he also did not relate to the administration from the strength of approval by major faculty bodies. Although the department chairman could be strong, the president also was in a strong position. The chairman recommended to the president; the president, with the advice of his staff, made the final decision—to add a faculty position or not, to hire this man or that one, to give the salary increase this year largely to the younger men rather than to the older ones. Thus, formally, the system at Swarthmore allowed for strong department heads and much presidential discretion. After the departure of the great reformer, Aydelotte, the faculty did not, as at Antioch and Reed, elaborate formal devices that would give the faculty great collective control and collective capacity to defend itself, if need be, against the president and trustees. The main formal defenses of the faculty were the individual chairmen, backed by the use of the full faculty as a deliberative body on such general issues as an increase in the size of the college, the addition of a department, and the revision of curricular requirements.

Value consensus and informal integration, however, rendered the formal scheme of the campus something less than commanding. The chief administrators and senior faculty remained in close agreement; clearly neither Nason nor Smith intended to proceed in directions that would threaten the basic commitments of the faculty. Hence their authority was not to be feared. With faculty paranoia thereby reduced and with the Quaker norm of muted comment, faculty criticism of the administrators was usually made in sorrow rather than with the thrust of a knife. Also, the administration did not possess the means to buck the faculty. Informal consultation and persuasion is a two-way street: It controls arbitrary administration as much as it does faculty interest-group politics.

Therefore, to be effective, the Swarthmore presidents have had to work with the faculty as much as presidents at Antioch and Reed have had to.

In sum, then, the central values and high degree of integration of Swarthmore have shaped the expression of authority within it. The presidents shared with the faculty the wish to hold to traditional character. Objectively, it would have been exceedingly difficult to proceed in ways counter to the desires of the faculty. It would have been bad form even to try. The faculty, if need be, could defend its deeply held definition of Swarthmore. Its size, prestige, and confidence greatly exceeded that of the faculty into which Aydelotte stepped as an agent of change in 1920, and most important, it possessed a binding belief. The "legend" of the college had become the fundamental determinant of interaction in the campus system.

## The Viability of Program

Along with the personnel structure of Swarthmore, the curriculum also remained relatively stable. The distinction between honors and course continued largely without change; the proportion of juniors and seniors taking the honors route had leveled off at around 40 per cent in the thirties and had remained there. In 1940 the honors students organized their efforts around two seminars a semester; twenty years later they still had two seminars each term. Similarly, for those in course, the program of study in 1960 differed little from what it had become in 1940.

Two features of this stable program had special impact on Swarthmore as a social system. One was the intense participation induced by the competition in honors; the other was the pluralism provided on a small campus by two major tracks in the curriculum.

### THE EXCITEMENT OF HONORS

However routinized and stable it may have become, the curriculum possessed features that continued to excite faculty and students. The give-and-take of the honors seminars surprised faculty members because of the quickness and astuteness of an unusual undergraduate mind. Throughout the array of courses, the mix of bright students with able, teaching-oriented scholars guaranteed liveliness in thinking and discussion. And, capping it all was the traditional excitement of the end of the road in honors work. The oral examination by outside professors in late May or early June on two years of work was an event that could not be missed by anyone on campus.

By the time the day arrived for the orals, the honors student had already sat for written examinations prepared and graded by the outside examiners. The writtens were handled through the mails, with the bluebooks going back and forth between Swarthmore and the examining professors at their home institutions, such as the University of Pennsylvania, Cornell, Harvard, Yale, Columbia, Princeton, Oak Ridge National Laboratory, Washington Center for Foreign Policy, Johns Hopkins, Emory, and Michigan State. The examiners then arrived on campus for three days of oral testing. The students were commonly examined for about one and one-half hours in one major and two related minor subjects, e.g., English literature, fine arts, and philosophy; economics, philosophy, and political science. This testing required a small army of examiners, about sixty men in the early sixties, and an elaborate scheduling of students and panels of examiners.

With some variation by department, the student sitting for an oral examination ordinarily faced three to five examiners and had at his back, listening at a suitable distance to the rear, some of the faculty with whom he had studied. The department chairman of his major field and some faculty members sat or stood outside the room, quietly directing traffic and talking with the upcoming candidates. For the weaker students, several faculty members would ease into the room to listen; for strong candidates, the ones likely to sparkle and to gain highest or high honors, more of the faculty would move into the back of the room. Thus, the student had quite an audience of adults—the visitors unknown to him as persons but often well known as scholars and his own professors. In one natural science oral examination, observed in 1961, the student had a large panel of eight visitors in front of him and six to eight of his own professors behind him to hear it all! Rare would be the graduate student under examination for the Ph.D. degree who would find himself so outnumbered.

In their performance some students normally appeared weak, with a few seriously cowed by the situation, but most handled the questions to the reasonable satisfaction of their examiners, and on the whole, the students appeared impressively mature in attitude, committed to the intellectual life, and well versed in their specialties. A few always performed brilliantly, demonstrating not only unusual intellectual poise for undergraduate American students but also great grasp of and originality in their disciplines. These stars had not only read the spots off the books, as their peers had, but also worked their way through to the basic ideas and problems of a field—performing the way professors hope Ph.D. candidates will perform, although they so often do not, after several years of graduate school. These outstanding performances delighted the visiting examiners, usually sending them away as believers in the program, and they were immensely rewarding to the instructors with whom the students had worked and whose self-esteem was also partly on the line. The half dozen to a dozen top student performances in these culminating encounters dramatically validated the honors program.

After the oral sessions were finished, the examiners then met together for several hours in clusters of related disciplines to decide on the awarding of highest honors, high honors, honors, and failure. The faculty and students stood by. The lists were then prepared and posted. Perhaps a half dozen were awarded highest honors; a much larger number, perhaps a half of those taking the examination, found they had been awarded high honors. Nearly all the rest received honors; very few failed since the faculty at the end of the junior year usually weeded out the students who did not belong in honors and moved them to course. The few who did fail had their performance reviewed by the regular faculty and were usually voted a degree in course. Whatever the outcome for the individual, the afternoon when the lists went up was a time of high excitement. There were shouts of laughter and crying, strong feelings of pride and disappointment, many congratulations to give and receive—and many condolences to be socially managed. The last day of the honors competition was dependably the most intense day of the year on campus. By itself it spoke volumes about the transference of student attention from social to academic matters. There were exciting days in track and lacrosse, football and baseball, but none to rival seriously the day in early June when the scores went up on the best minds on campus.

THE TWO-TRACK DIVISION

As discussed in Chapter 8, the pass man was gradually wiped out at Swarthmore as the upgrading effort of the twenties and the thirties brought a brighter group of entering students, but the college kept the two tracks originally designed for a difference in ability and motivation. This basic differentiation had two important effects.

The primary effect was to offer two major, alternative ways of taking an undergraduate education. Small liberal arts campuses, in contrast to universities, are plagued with the problem of narrow alternatives. Most such campuses have a single set of general course-distribution requirements and then a single way of taking courses in a major and in related fields in the last two years. The single way commonly fits some students but not others. If everyone takes a sedate round of lecture courses, the independent students are bored. If all have to demonstrate great capacity to work independently as little dons, many are not emotionally or otherwise prepared to so perform. The Reed program is an excellent example of the single-track approach to high academia, with every student treated as an honors student. This system is basic to the academic sternness of Reed, but as discussed earlier, it fails to provide any alternative other than dropping out for those students who, however bright, either will not or cannot yet work as quasi-independent scholars, preparing a thesis and going through broad written and oral examinations.

At Swarthmore, the bright nineteen-year-old student who is not ready for a total diet of seminar papers or who wishes to spread himself around among a number of interesting subjects, with a lecture course here and a lecture course there, can go the regular course route. The lecturing is good; one's peers are bright and lively. One is freer to select courses than is the case in the honors program, and one has available the over-all atmosphere and extracurricular resources of the campus. Then, too, since most of the very best students choose or feel compelled to enter the honors route, those who are on the other track gain some lightening of the academic competition. The worst of the rate-busters are gone from one's classrooms, allowing academic breathing space and hence time to run a track or throw a ball or sit quietly. Hence, course provides another way, a more normal way, that will likely fit somewhat better than honors those who are in the bottom half of the student body in academic ability—and there is always a bottom half—or those who simply are not psychologically equipped at this age for the life of the Ph.D. candidate. This curricular pluralism adds considerably to the capacity of Swarthmore to accommodate different kinds of students, to hold them and see them through, and to reduce somewhat the cruelty inherent in the internal competitiveness of the brightest student bodies in the country.

A subsidiary result of the honors-course system is the specter of inequality. The college has done better than outsiders would think possible in reducing the stigma of second-class citizenship for those not brought into honors work. Many students in course are secure about their own ability and their place in the college. The college has eased matters with such devices as granting the degree in course "with distinction" for work of high quality and giving a number of special awards for excellence in fields as diverse as poetry and engineering. Yet the problem of second-class status is always right beneath the surface, inherent in the attention and resources given to the honors effort and in the prestige of the honors symbols. This problem has been a point of minor vulnerability in an otherwise serene arrangement since at any time the status of course, as compared with honors, could be seized as a defect, by outside critics, unhappy faculty members, or—most likely—a group of students seeking an activating issue in campus affairs.

## Student Values

The life of the student at Swarthmore in the forties and fifties was more structured than that at Antioch and considerably more than that at Reed. There were traditional expectations about student conduct and a willingness on the part of administration and faculty to stand with rules. Student marriages were discouraged by a rule that one or the other of the wedded pair would have to withdraw from the college. Premarital sex relations were hindered by rules that restricted dormitory intervisitation to fewer hours than those permitted at the other two colleges and that prescribed open doors during the visiting hours. Drinking on campus remained formally forbidden. An automobile could not be maintained without special permission. The adults of the campus preferred to have academic work and social life "governed by good taste and accepted practice rather than by rules."[10] With this general guideline, and such specific rules as those above, the students were not as free as their counterparts at Antioch and Reed.

They were also under less psychological strain. The academic work was hard and the competition severe, but the stress thereby occasioned was not, as at Antioch and Reed, exacerbated by the need to decide so much about one's behavior outside the classroom. Individual students were in a relatively firm social structure.

The greater structure and integration at Swarthmore reduced student mortality. The dropout rate was never anything like the 50 per cent and over that we noted as characteristic of the other two colleges. Some 75 to 90 per cent of an entering class would persist and graduate on schedule, e.g., over 80 per cent in the 1936–41 period,[11] about 75 per cent in the classes around 1960.[12] This high retention rate is typical of those at the best private colleges and universities on the East Coast. Swarthmore shares in the high status that makes admission alone terribly important to many. Once in, students are not readily inclined to transfer or otherwise to terminate before the degree. There was never at Swarthmore any inclination on the part of students to use it as a junior college, as had happened at Reed. In addition, the secure and stable social structure of campus life encouraged staying. With entering students intending to complete the four years, with the expectations by faculty and peers that one should stay, and without the personal stress occasioned in some students by permissive individualism, Swarthmore did not develop a serious dropout problem.

The restrictions on student freedom imposed by the rules and the lingering norms of Quaker morality, in any event, were not severe. Students increasingly viewed them as annoying symbols of adult-imposed authority. When students were asked in the early sixties whether they thought their campus should have more permissive regulations, 78 per cent answered yes at Swarthmore, compared to 32 per cent at Antioch and 23 per cent at Reed.[13] In actual behavior, however, there was much leeway. Here, an ample physical plant helped greatly. Swarthmore had three hundred acres (compared to one hundred at Reed) for its eight hundred to nine hundred students, with a mile of woodland along Crum Creek

10. "Student Activities Handbook," *Swarthmore College Bulletin*, Vol. 58, No. 3 (October, 1960), p. 42.
11. Swarthmore College Faculty, *op. cit.*, p. 68.
12. Unpublished study of student development, Center for the Study of Higher Education, University of California, Berkeley.
13. *Ibid.*

rimming the western edge of the center of the campus. Its several dozen buildings were set well back from the front of the campus, along which ran the railroad tracks of a suburban commuter train, and the whole effect, as one came up a long main walk, was one of traditional buildings in an open and peaceful setting. Lawns and playing fields covered nearly eighty acres. Although students often felt cramped in the dormitories, some of the parlors, lodges, and meeting rooms not generally used for classes could be reserved for special occasions, and many could be used quasi-privately on an unplanned basis. As a result, students wishing to be by themselves could find a cozy spot. This "social space" took the edge off many rules and constraints and helped to drain away the tensions generated in students by the confines of dormitory, cafeteria, and classroom in a small college.

THE ALTERNATIVE STYLES OF LIFE

The Swarthmore two-track program of honors and course, as indicated, served both as a highly visible point of distinction and as a way of accommodating the interests of different students. Outside the classroom, several alternative styles evolved that even more importantly accommodated a range of students. The impulse induced by Aydelotte to bring sports to an amateur level and social activities to a minor status did not go so far as to drive out sports and dating. As also indicated earlier, the wish was for a Rhodes Scholar type of excellence in amateur sports; once sports were brought to an amateur level, the administration was interested in promoting them. This interest became reflected in the attitude and behavior of one wing of the student body—a moderate, serious-student version of the old Joe College subculture. Here students were interested in intercollegiate sports to the point where they not only would suffer the loneliness of the long-distance runner—as some of their tall and thin intellectual peers were willing to do—but also would make the lung-bursting effort and take the physical punishment that goes with lacrosse and football. Such students manned the teams that made Swarthmore respectable in the intercollegiate games of its small-college leagues. This commitment to sports was qualitatively different from the disdain institutionalized at Antioch and Reed. These students also helped keep the fraternity system going, maintaining lodges to which they could repair with coat, tie, girl friend, and whatever beverages could be managed. Such students often came from the families of alumni, and the old and most visible applied field of the college, engineering, was a popular major with them. This part of the student body was linked to the past, to alumni nostalgia, and to conservative money. Usually somewhat on the defensive, the students involved have nevertheless been able to maintain a viable tradition. They have not been driven out, by admission selectivity, faculty grading, or the derision of peers. They have been a regular part of the admission mix;

they have had their own physical and social niches on campus; and they have been tolerated by the other students.

At the other extreme, the intellectuality and reputation for liberality and friendliness brought the college, in the fifties, a noncomformist subculture, a fourth or so of the student body that was interchangeable with the nonconformists of Reed. Often very bright, and often very neurotic, such students developed a campus style of life sharply at variance with that of the collegiate group. They wished to listen to a few professors but mainly to be left alone to talk with one another and to develop their individuality more fully. They sought to stay away from campus administrators or sometimes to provoke them with ironic commentary in the student newspaper. Their style of housekeeping tended to turn dormitories into pads. They inclined to folk-singing festivals that littered the front lawn with guitars, blankets, beards, and bare feet—predictably bringing cries of outrage from the townspeople and no little shock in some quarters of the faculty and administration, but many were so pure and serious in their concern with ideas or artistic work that they were admired on campus by those not prepared to imitate their habits of dress and deportment.

The majority of Swarthmore students were found neither in the lodges of the fraternities nor in the pads of the nonconformists. They were a part of an academic-intellectual subculture that fit the dominant values of the college. They were the devoted students of the classrooms and seminars; their ranks included science majors who spent all their time in laboratories and students in the humanities already equipping themselves with careful habits thought appropriate to lifelong scholarship. They participated, along with the collegiates, in the regular institutions of student government, student publications, and student clubs. They were often interested in national and world affairs. The students in this academic middle would have been quite visible on average campuses as a very bright, studious minority. At Swarthmore they were not so visible because they were right at home—the regular army of a college that had come to reflect academic intellectuality fully. These students set the main tone of student life; around them the collegiate and nonconformist groups formed as subordinate types.

These student orientations provided alternative homes for students as they came to the college, and therefore they accommodated a wider array of interests and capacities than were accommodated at culturally homogeneous colleges such as Reed. There were not only different ways of meeting formal requirements, as between honors and course, but also choices among informal requirements—the pressures that students bring to bear upon one another.

THE INTELLECTUAL AS HERO

These alternative styles of student life were not sharply set apart. To describe them as three types is to make them appear more autonomous and bounded than they were in practice. The lines between them were blurred; students mixed the several styles, and it was easy to slide from one to another. Most important, any division within the student body took place within an overwhelming consensus about the primacy of academic labor and the goodness of intellectual virtues. The collegiates at Swarthmore were only a half step away from their serious academic peers, resembling them more than they resembled those who belong to fraternities and sororities at a state university. The Swarthmore chapters of fraternities were important in their opposition to discriminatory provisions in national fraternities, and several disaffiliated themselves, adapting to the values of the college by going local. The nonconformists at the college exchanged respect with most of their peers and usually honored the institution rather than trying to pull it down. They did not drop out in rank disgust with the establishment but stayed sufficiently integrated to do the work, meet the requirements, and graduate, even with one of the higher levels of honors.

The glorification of academic work gradually established in the two decades under Aydelotte continued to develop after World War II, fixing the leading student as the hero of the student body, which by 1960, was about as bright as any in the country. The social life was low key. The majority were preparing themselves for graduate education. As described above, the competition for highest honors, coming to a climax in the oral exams, was a focus of excitement. And long before the climax, students were well aware of who among them was doing exceedingly well and was likely to perform brilliantly on the orals—or likely to receive special commendation in the nonhonors program. Esteem was handed out accordingly. The student culture articulated well with that of the faculty and the administration in its acceptance of the primacy of academic intellectual values.

## Success and the Future

Swarthmore was, thus, in 1960 a clear case of success in the making of a college, a success clouded by only relatively minor problems. Its daily habits reflected academic ideals long cherished in England and the United States. Its faculty was able, its students bright and lively, its financing substantial and secure. Its trustees, administrators, and faculty had something approaching a community of values, taking pleasure together in what the college had become. Conflict among these major parties had little of the character of interest-group bargaining or confrontation politics but took softer, more muted form in personal exchange. Some strains were present, but internal and external stresses had little of the depth and danger present at Reed, which, having become successful through conflict, had discord inherent in it; or at Antioch, which was still trying to convince the outside world of the value of its heady combination of activism and work-study. No college is ever free of problems, especially in the turmoil and change of the mid-twentieth century, but Swarthmore was one of the dozen or so campuses in the United States—along with its Quaker neighbors, Bryn Mawr and Haverford—whose problems were the derivatives of quality and success, the problems that several hundred other colleges would be pleased to have. The nearest thing to a genuine concern was a feeling expressed here and there within and outside the college that the senior faculty and administration should be more sensitive to the dangers of complacency and ossification.

But by 1960, as set forth in the introduction to this study, the place of the detached liberal arts college was being questioned. Higher education, at a rapid rate, was becoming expensive, public-supported, and centered on large, comprehensive campuses. The natural sciences were the dominant disciplines nationally, and they especially required big money and large facilities. The place of the small private campuses, committed as they were to undergraduate education alone, was problematic, and the small colleges were clearly going to be squeezed by fast-moving competition. They would not necessarily go out of business but would find themselves in such a marginal role that decline in quality would be inevitable. So went the refrain. One could wonder whether the Swarthmore character would stand up to these fundamental trends; if its possibilities for doing so were minimal, then the liberal arts college was in a bad way.

Although Reed has proved that money is not absolutely necessary, its presence normally enhances viability. Swarthmore had the capacity to find this resource. A second and clearly essential element to the character and role of Swarthmore was good students. Swarthmore was attracting bright boys and girls and could count on a continuation of this resource. The third element was a good faculty—the big question for small, undergraduate-centered campuses, the resource they might well fail to attract. The more the rewards of academia swung toward research and publication, the more likely it was that the university would grow in attractiveness for faculty over the college. In this critical matter in 1960, Swarthmore was effectively holding its own.

The American academic market place contained thousands of good scholars willing to consider taking up residence in a small undergraduate college if they could find attractive conditions of work, which, for the best men, increasingly meant conditions conducive to productive scholarship. The Swarthmore character met these conditions. Teaching loads were modest and partly composed of seminars. The students were intellectually stimulating, more so than many graduate students. If the faculty spent more time with students than they would at the university, they spent less time in the labyrinths of bureaucratic structure and formal committee consultation. The nearness of Swarthmore to eastern universities and cities was a special advantage, allowing convenient contact with extended academic circles, government, and business. A Swarthmore professor could sit with government as readily as one shuttling to Washington from Princeton, Ithaca, or Cambridge, and much more easily than a counterpart in Bloomington, Denver, or Seattle. And salaries were competitive. One great lack was the graduate student, who, for the university professor, can be protégé, colleague, and worker combined. In compensation, Swarthmore offered the simplicity of personal commitment and the modest encouragement for scholarship that allows a man to brood about his book for a number of years, if he so wishes, rather than rush its publication for purposes of promotion.

In 1960, then, the conditions of work for the faculty were still sufficiently attractive to recruit and hold a scholarly group. This capacity resulted considerably from the successful embodiment of the Aydelotte values. If the first critical function of the honors effort (in the twenties and thirties) had been to change the students, the second critical function (in the forties and fifties) had been to hold together an appropriate faculty. The reputation and self-concept established by the honors program and then increasingly the conditions of academic work created around it gave Swarthmore a competitive advantage in an academic market fast becoming adverse to small liberal arts colleges. This was no mean effect. Under the conditions of 1960 it was perhaps the most important function of distinctiveness in the character of small colleges.

In the face of university growth and the dominance of public higher education, Swarthmore was able not only to maintain a strong and distinctive place but also to demonstrate that teaching and scholarship could be coupled in the small college. Its character gave it a formula that was still "right"; its aura and success added to its durability. But the need to compete with leading universities in attracting and holding first-rate scholars was the obvious wedge in the side of the organization, one that might later, if struck with heavier blows, force Swarthmore to major change and another stage of development.[14]

14. At the time of the final writing of this study, Swarthmore entered into a major self-study, the first since the early years of Aydelotte's tenure. "In the immediate background were a number of local issues: some anxiety about the loss of faculty to graduate schools and institutes; a concern about the adequacy of research support for faculty members in terms of facilities, teaching loads, and summer compensation; some dissatisfaction with the curriculum of the first two years; growing doubts about the Honors program and the adequacy of the Course program to meet the needs of the other upperclassmen; and a less tangible sense of uncertainty, as the College grew and its traditions lengthened, about the efficiency of its internal structure and its receptivity to change." *Critique of a*

Whatever the sources and forms of future change and durability, the college in the early sixties was a full-fledged case of an organization that had become a saga. Somewhat quieter in daily tone than Antioch or Reed, somewhat less stimulated by direct and open conflict, this social institution had a strong collective sense of having an eminent, unique history and a noteworthy present character. This feeling added considerable emotional meaning to the lives of many participants. In it, as in the first two colleges, we see the blending of organizational, group, and individual identities that occurs when a college has first sought and then achieved, through several decades of work, a distinctive character and a particular hold on social esteem.

---

*College* (Swarthmore, Pa., Swarthmore College, 1967), p. 9. The investigation was intensive, the recommendations extensive. Some change seemed likely; how much, only time would tell.

# PART IV

# The College As Saga

# Chapter 10. The Making of an Organizational Saga

ANTIOCH, REED, AND SWARTHMORE in 1960 had organizational faces that stood out in the crowd of small colleges, and they were continuing to make their mark in a system of higher education increasingly dominated by large universities. Their reputations of success, although often inflated, reflected their capacity to come closer than hundreds of other colleges to certain educational ideals connected with the vision of turning out the liberally educated man. When these colleges are held sternly against the ideal—Do they give the world men of learning, sophisticated understanding, and critical intelligence?—they are defective, leaving much to be desired; but when their accomplishments are compared with those of others in the pursuit of the same ends, they are effective, achieving sufficiently more than the average to warrant the designation of excellence.

From the study of these three campuses we can draw ideas about the distinctive expression of values in the organized tools of education. What are the conditions for moving effectively toward a unifying and noteworthy emphasis in the organization as a whole? If a group wishes to travel the road to distinctive character, to what organizational features must attention necessarily flow? What is the place of the great leader, and how much does his influence explain organizational distinctiveness?

Among all their specific historical and structural differences, what developments do distinctively excellent colleges perhaps have in common? Can any feature of their natures be grasped hypothetically as central to all others?

Our analyses of Antioch, Reed, and Swarthmore have pointed to a strong organizational saga or legend as the central ingredient of the distinctive college. As reviewed briefly in the Introduction, this concept can be related to and distinguished from the ideas of organizational role and mission. Organizations, like individuals, have roles, ways of behaving associated with defined positions in a social system. An organizational role entails both a basic method or way of performing and a place among organizations that carry on related activities.[1] A role may be assigned to an organization by superior authorities or outside groups with power to tell it what to do; it may accrue to an organization by drift, without much conscious control by an internal or external group. In role assignment or role accrual, those inside the organization are relatively passive, a posture enjoined by dependency on others or lack of will.[2] Officials work at means and have little to say about ends. In contrast, roles may be actively sought by those reponsible for an organization. They may attempt to define for themselves its working character and its place in the larger setting. When the leaders attempt to seize a role (or have forced upon them a dynamic social assignment that requires strong effort to define and establish purpose), we may usefully speak of an organizational mission.[3] When roles are fought for and actively assumed, the organization has the plan, the will, and then finally the capability to perform in certain ways that allow it to develop a niche in a larger social mosaic.

In these terms, all colleges have roles, but only some have missions. Only in some have an internal group and an internal dynamic played an important, even dominant, part in determining performance and place. Only in some has a man or a group of men had the opportunity and the will to devise a plan, test and reform it actively over a number of years, and have it reflected in the thought and style of the organization.

Successful missions in time become transformed to some degree into organizational sagas. Initially, the mission is simply purpose, something

1. Philip Selznick, *Leadership in Administration* (New York, Harper & Row, Publishers, 1957), pp. 82–89.

2. Public adult schools and public junior colleges are types of educational organization in the United States that, because of heavy dependency on controlling authorities and consumer demands, generally have their organizational roles determined by assignment or drift. See Burton R. Clark, *Adult Education in Transition: A Study of Institutional Insecurity* (Berkeley, Calif., University of California Press, 1956); and Burton R. Clark, *The Open Door College: A Case Study* (New York, McGraw-Hill, Inc., 1960).

3. Selznick, *op. cit.*, Chap. 3, "The Definition of Mission and Role," pp. 65–89. This use of "mission" is considerably broader than the military usage. It is similar to what we mean when we speak of a man with a mission or a group determined to define its future.

men in the organization hold before themselves. But the mission tested and successfully embodied through the work of a number of years does not remain a statement of intent, a direction, a guidepost. It becomes a saga that tells what the organization has been and what it is today—and hence by extension what it will be tomorrow. In the mission we look to create a performance and a place; in the saga or legend we look to the history and presence of the successful, willed creation. The institutional saga is a historically based, somewhat embellished understanding of a unique organizational development. It offers in the present a particular definition of the organization as a whole and suggests common characteristics of members. Its definitions are deeply internalized by many members, thereby becoming a part, even an unconscious part, of individual motive. A saga is, then, a mission made total across a system in space and time. It embraces the participants of a given day and links together successive waves of participants over major periods of time.

The most important characteristic and consequence of an organizational saga is the capturing of allegiance, the committing of staff to the institution. Emotion is invested to the point where many participants significantly define themselves by the central theme of the organization. The organizational motif becomes individual motive, much more than a statement of purpose, a cogent theme, a doctrine of administration, or a logical set of ideas. Deep emotional investment binds participants as comrades in a cause. Indications of an organizational legend are pride and exaggeration; the most telling symptom is an intense sense of the unique. Men behave as if they knew a beautiful secret that no one outside the lucky few could ever share. An organizational saga turns an organization into a community, even a cult.

An organizational legend, located between ideology and religion, partakes of an appealing logic on the one hand and sentiments similar to the spiritual on the other. However rational the choice of words, however clear the articulation of means and ends in the minds of the believers, a sense of romance and even of mystery helps turn a cold organization into a beloved social institution. We often charge those who love a college with becoming religious about it. If "religious" means having fervent spirit, they do indeed. Many college sagas, even modest ones, have the capacity to make strong men cry in the bright glare of the afternoon gathering as well as in the darkness of the lonely hours.

At Antioch, Reed, and Swarthmore institutional themes became powerful legends. On the Antioch campus the philosophy of the whole man, expressed in the unique combination of work, study, and community participation and embossed with principles of nonconformity, became motif and motive. Around the specific doctrines and the efforts and practices that define and help realize them, a sense of a beautiful secret and an intense loyalty developed. Antiochians come to think of themselves as a special breed. Many never rid themselves of the urge to go home again—to take up residence in Yellow Springs—and quite a few have been unable to leave. At Reed the idea of uncompromised academic devotion, spelled out in a unique set of practices, and the traditions of student freedom, also uniquely expressed, together deeply engaged the hearts of many. There, too, those who have strolled the campus commonly feel that the participants have a secret. The way of life is held to be very special; and selection and socialization work powerfully to create a Reed type, one frequently remarked on by professors in many of the best graduate schools. At Swarthmore the symbols and practices of the honors program gave specific definition to the claim of excellence, and men steadily acquired a faith in the unique nature and special value of the collective effort. Here, too, one finds pride and exaggeration. For those who believe, there is a Swarthmore saga. And here, also, to marry a graduate is often to find that one has married a college. In all three cases, the original missions, as worked-out central themes, became captivating to the point where men felt their enterprise was a special one, with its uniqueness based not on the romantic beauty of buildings and trees and other such common grounds of alumni and faculty nostalgia, but on the academic and intellectual virtues of the campus as a group of men. In each case, the history of the college was invested with the qualities of an epic, and some men became cultists.

Participants within many colleges easily overlook the importance of a unifying and motivating theme when they think of improving the positions of their colleges in society. Faculty and administrators commonly pay attention to their courses and their bookkeeping, the bread and butter of college affairs, and assume that road is the one to salvation. Men outside colleges, on the other hand, can easily sit apart from day-to-day operations and offer grand designs. Reformers who advise others usually pay attention to the logic and elegance of their educational plans, the bread and butter of abstract argument, and hope therein to provide the keys to the doors of success. What is so difficult, so hard as to occur infrequently, is to put it all together: to realize the necessity of a unifying theme; to formulate one feasible in a given social context; to build the organizational conditions and structures that allow and help a mission to get under way; and to develop and continue the structures that elaborate a mission into a rich and encompassing definition of the institutional self.

These steps should not be viewed neatly since the making of a distinctive college is rarely a definite sequence of clear purpose and stubborn pursuit. Typically, there is a complicated interaction between what appears possible, what is thought desirable, and what is done. Those who pursue distinctiveness in an established college cannot ignore its geographic location, traditional clientele, entrenched personnel, and fixed reputation. They must gradually evolve and specify a theme, rather than grasp it boldly and clearly, as they test the tolerances of the context; they must gradually build the means that support the idea and restructure the internal and external constraints. Such was the case of Frank Aydelotte at Swarthmore.

In other times and places, the purpose of a man may strongly dominate the interaction from the beginning. Once Arthur Morgan was on the scene at Antioch, his educational ideas marched boldly to the front, and all else, for awhile, was entourage. His efforts were a violent attack designed to hook environment and organization to purpose. Compromises took their toll within a decade, but not before the vision had had its day and had set the main drift. In short, there are different dynamics and emphases when colleges attempt to construct consistent and fruitful themes. What is common to success is that out of the interplay of purpose, structure, and setting comes a powerful legend.

To examine the processes through which sagas are constructed, it is useful to look first at the conditions under which and the means by which they are first instituted. Initiation can take place under widely varying conditions, and since it occurs within a relatively short period of time, unique features of the time and place make generalization hazardous. Here we shall specify several sets of conditions. We shall then conceive as systematically as possible the means by which unifying themes are extensively developed and sustained. Sustenance, having to do with tools of action that endure, is a more regular matter than initiation, and here the paths of development converge on certain inescapable features of organization.

## Initiation of the Saga

### THE CONDITIONS OF ACTION

An institutional innovation leading to distinctiveness may be attempted under three main conditions: new organization, crisis in an established institution, and evolutionary openness in an established institution. These conditions are different forms of structural permissiveness and conduciveness to change.[4]

*The New Context.* To start with a new organization is widely considered the preferred condition for innovating leadership. The restraints of the past are usually then minimal. Old preferences may be brought to bear, imported and impressed from the surrounding society, but at least the men with new ideas do not have to cope with an established organizational structure and the rigidities of organizational custom. New organization also heightens choice and consciousness of choice, forcing men to

---

4. On structural conduciveness in the causation of social change, see Neil J. Smelser, *Theory of Collective Behavior* (New York, The Free Press, 1963).

think about the rationale and consequences of different arrangements and to deliberate the wisdom of imitating current practices. Reform-bent administrators and professors gravitate toward new organizations—the new campus, the new subcollege, the new department.

William T. Foster at Reed was a clear case. Unhappy with the college practices of his day, wary of being trapped in the administering of a traditional eastern college, as we have seen, he waxed lyrical about the opportunity to escape the restraints of the past in the openness of the new ground in Portland. At Reed he faced none of the encrustedness that comes from old lecture notes, established powers of faculty, student traditions, and alumni memories. Once he established a strong position for himself in relation to the trustees, there were no beliefs, structures, or groups to stay his hand. The environment stood back, the means were his to build. Even if thus free for only a few years, he was able to initiate the structures that would soon bring certain ideas to an intense expression in organizational performance.

*The Revolutionary Context.*   For those who wish to innovate boldly, to form a college with a difference, the principal alternative to organizing a new college is to pick an established college that appears ready for change. One condition of readiness is exemplified by the Antioch of 1919—the condition of intense failure, of unsuccess. Crisis in the organization, intensified to the point at which survival is questionable to those in charge, is the great eraser of prior commitments. By forcing those in charge to give up established ways or else to give up the organization, the deep crisis re-creates some of the conditions of new organization. It also calls for the man who can help conditions and events to conspire in lifting the hand of tradition. Morgan at Antioch was such a man, determined to build in line with his vision of the educational road to the good society. Thrown into contact with the perishing college, he estimated that the physical assets were a great advantage over building a new campus from the ground up. He seized the unstable setting as one in which to break continuity with old forms and to institute a new set of means of education for this college and, in hope, for American higher education.

In short, in ongoing organizations as in political regimes, the opening to radical transformation lies in lack of success. The unsuccessful situation, by dramatizing the failure of old methods and the weakness of existing organization, tends to catch the wandering eye of outside reformers or to offer certain attractions when the reformer is approached. The would-be leader, in turn, must estimate whether the situation will make him or bury him—a calculation made by dozens of men every year in American higher education as they consider the presidency or deanery at a struggling, low-grade college. The situation of organizational failure or crisis can be a great danger, more a trap than an opportunity. The key is whether the state of the system has been accepted by the ancient regime as impossible or otherwise unwanted.

*The Evolutionary Context.* A third, and perhaps the most common, area in which institutional sagas are initiated is that of the established and reasonably successful college—a place that is at least paying the rent and satisfying the expectations of some students and faculty and that has sufficient reputation and alumni tradition to stabilize resources now and in the foreseeable future. At first glance, this condition is an unnatural one for leadership. With commitments made and patterns set, where is the leeway for change? It is common in educational reform circles to believe that existing colleges are stuck in a rut, but commitments and patterns vary widely in rigidity. If relatively flexible, they can be sometimes used as a platform, a base camp, for deliberate and fairly rapid evolutionary movement.

Aydelotte judged that Swarthmore in 1920 was a case in point. The place had its rigidities—the alumni tradition that sons and daughters would be admitted; an established, reasonably contented faculty; a definite student collegiate subculture—but the place also had relatively liberal Quaker thought on top of general financial health. For Aydelotte that combination was an opening to flexibility. He proved over a period of fifteen years, during which his major changes were made, that his judgment of the situation for embodying his own emphasis was correct, even though the opening was narrow at times, the margin of tolerance was slim, and a less forceful man might not have squeezed through. The personal capacity for leadership thus also entered the equation. Swarthmore was neither new nor in crisis, but, within the constraints of an old organization, a reformer was able to introduce a new mission, to build the supports to turn the mission into a legend, and in general, thereby to make the Swarthmore experiment into a transformation of national note and influence.

Thus, in the initiation of fruitful college legends, the most favorable states of the system are newness of organization and the shattering of restraint occasioned by crisis or anticipated decline. But a self-defined and publicly-perceived effort can be initiated also in established, stable, and partly successful institutions. In these latter places, we must then distinguish between closed and open stability. The internal features and the external relations of established campuses vary in disposition to tolerate new thought and practice. Even in a single college at different times in its development there are critical differences in closed and open campus ethos and in social bases tolerant and intolerant of change. Established colleges often appear so set in present character that they tempt only the foolhardy reformer with an instinct for tilting with windmills. But apparently solid structures of commitment and action may be routine structures continued in the absence of alternatives. To put it only a little differently: The zone of acceptable policy may often be much wider than we commonly expect.[5] The institutional leader is then the one who conceives a convincing alternative to established policy; e.g., a new plan with the inducements of higher organizational status and public acclaim to outweigh the sacrifice of traditional ways. One key to change here is the state of organizational ambition.

Common to the three conditions of change is a normative as well as a structural openness in which a new man with a new plan has the leeway, at least for a few years, to bring his ideas to operational viability in the context of existing constraints.

CHARISMA AND CHANGE

These three cases of the initiation of an institutional legend each entail a heavy contribution by one man and raise the issue of the great man versus institutional dynamics and group contribution in organizational change. The great-man theory of history has a specific version in education in the frequent claim that the institution, especially the noteworthy one, is the lengthened shadow of a man. In the history of the successful college, so the interpretation goes, lurks the forceful president (or regent) who made it what it is today. Therefore, the personality of an individual is the ultimate factor in institution-building; the key to success is to find the strong leader.

Sociological study of strong leadership has been oriented largely by the concept of charisma made popular by Max Weber in his attempt to accommodate the personal and unusual elements of leadership to categories of social structure. In contrast to bureaucratic and traditional structures of authority, which we may see as institutions of the routine, leadership sometimes resides in a man who holds "specific gifts of the body and spirit." [6] Such a man is obeyed neither because of an office from which he draws authority nor because of a traditionally legitimized status, but because others are attracted by his unusual qualities and devote themselves to his person. The striking examples of this nonroutine form of leadership have occurred in embryonic religious and political movements, outside the formal institutions and organizations or before the movement has become organized and established. Also, charisma occurs, usually in

5. The idea of the zone of acceptable policy introduced here is, at the level of organizational purpose, somewhat analogous to Chester I. Barnard's "zone of indifference" in the acceptance of authority within organizations. Barnard sees the width of the zone of indifference determined by "the degree to which the inducements exceed the burdens and sacrifices which determine the individual's adhesion to the organization." *The Functions of the Executive* (Cambridge, Mass., Harvard University Press, 1953), p. 169.

6. *From Max Weber: Essays in Sociology,* trans. by H. H. Gerth and C. Wright Mills, eds. (New York, Oxford University Press, Inc., 1946), p. 245.

modest form, in organizations where personal magnetism combines with the normal authority of a position to give a man uncommon influence.[7]

The sociological understanding of charisma has moved only slowly toward consideration of group and situational determinants. As an exceptional form of leadership, charisma has remained linked with exceptional events and conditions. When, where, and how seem mysterious, although perhaps crisis-related in many instances, and charisma still seems determined by the unpredictable intrusion of the uncontrolled man. Our materials can be used to reflect on the relation of this man to the group and the situation. At least in organizations (which are relatively deliberate and structured social systems), conditions cause high and low probabilities of the occurrence of both intense and concentrated charisma as well as its attenuated and dispersed expressions. Through various processes the rank and file in an organization help to create and to destroy the personal components of leadership. Regular organizational authority depends on the consent of subordinates. Charismatic authority depends also on the views of subordinates and, behind their views, on the situations in which they currently find themselves and their organization. Thus, charisma is a function of the social situation and the perspectives of the rank and file as well as of a man's personal qualities.

The occurrence of charisma is controlled and enhanced in systematic ways. It is partially controlled through the deliberate avoidance of charismatic figures. In higher education, men who appear strongly charismatic are not commonly selected by boards of trustees and faculties to be presidents of colleges, not primarily because of a shortage of supply, but because such men are inappropriate for the stability, continuity, and maintenance of the existing power structure. Such men seize and demand, rather than follow rules and respond to others. In normal times they are judged too disruptive. They wish to break with historical reality when others see little need to shatter the tried and true. Those who do the hiring, therefore, avoid charisma by anticipating a radical and unneccessary disjunction between leader and setting. Avoidance is the most important way by which routine actors control the occurrence of charisma in organizations.

If by mistaken impression or deliberate gamble, a man of great personal force is brought in as president of a stable college, we enter a second situation in which charisma is commonly reduced. The man becomes an unwanted intruder who comes to blows with the faculty, the other administrators, the trustees, or some combination of these groups. When important interests in the organization do not consider the personal gifts valu-

7. Edward Shils, "Charisma," in *International Encyclopedia of the Social Sciences*, Vol. 2 (New York, The Macmillan Company and The Free Press, 1968), pp. 386–90; Reinhard Bendix, *Max Weber: An Intellectual Portrait* (Garden City, N.Y., Doubleday & Company, Inc., 1960), Chap. 10.

able, many are hard at work circumscribing and denying the personal force. Charisma, in short, must be seen and valued by those manning the college. If others do not attribute charisma, then *in that context* the man does not have it. In most normal situations of organization life,[8] others are led to withhold a major grant of charisma.

As we turn from the control to the enhancement of charisma in organizations, the three paths of innovation exemplified by Reed, Antioch, and Swarthmore suggest facilitating conditions. A new organization has a relatively high probability of creating and enhancing charisma. Those who hire the first top administrator are often looking for a man who will attract others and who has the will to build and shape. Once upon the scene, the president is in a position to build from the top down, especially to select men for the top echelons of the administration and faculty by personal effort and choice, and thus to begin with personal lieutenants rather than with men voted up from the rank and file. The Reed trustees, wanting a builder, took unto themselves a stern and uncompromising young man, one who established much presidential autonomy as a condition of employment. Foster personally hired the faculty and for a few critical years personally selected the students. For a time all echelons in the organization were a direct expression of his will. He also sought to build the ethos of difference by acting differently, with Simplified Spelling an eye-catching instance, on top of the Portland reform crusade and the World War I pacifism. He had some specific gifts of the body and spirit to offer, and for awhile he also had considerable leeway in their exercise. When troubled descended, after the first five years, he still had the personal gifts, but he no longer had the leeway. His personal leadership was soon deemed dysfunctional for the college, his charisma was situationally denied, and he was encouraged to take his capacities elsewhere.

The condition of unsuccessful organization—Antioch among our cases —also has a high probability of exercising charisma. Decline spells crisis, and crisis shows the regular agents of the situation directly that they and their methods are now incompetent, that despite all wishes and intentions, the past is not an adequate guide for the future. Crisis calls out for charisma because old rules do not work and someone must try to devise new patterns. The old Antioch trustees, giving up, handed the mantle of leadership to the new man among them, the boldest by far, a man quick to promise action, assume command, and begin with a plan.

Since Morgan was extremely charismatic in personal qualities and that situation of crisis at Antioch an extreme one, the juncture produced one of

8. One important exception to the suppressing of charisma in stable organizations is when charisma is vested in certain offices so that any incumbent is defined to have unusual power, e.g., the priest. See Amitai Etzioni, *A Comparative Analysis of Complex Organizations* (New York, The Free Press, 1961), Chap. 9.

the more extreme cases in American higher education of conditions and the man leading to radical transformation. The transformation in character of Antioch College came about through the following sequence, which links crisis, charisma, and abrupt transformation:

1. The college became increasingly weak in its ability to relate to its environment, losing its capacity to gain resources, particularly money.

2. The objective weakness became subjectively accepted. The incumbent leadership developed a sense of the possible collapse of the institution.

3. The sense of imminent organizational death lifted the heavy hand of tradition. A feeling developed that "we cannot go on this way," past performance was suspended as a guide to action, and routine procedure was thrown into question. Years of incremental adjustment had not solved the problem of organizational survival.

4. As adjustment along old paths was ruled out, the choice was between institutional death and a wrenching effort to change. Radical change was preferable to the demise of the organization, especially since original purpose had been seriously eroded and the staff was largely attached to the organization as an end in itself. For men who tried but could not cope, the preference for survival meant a preference for new leadership, even if it meant a surrender of authority.

5. The organization lay open for the entry of strong leadership. It was ready to welcome the man with a charismatic bent to originality,[9] one whose characteristics promised a new mobilization of effort and resources. Crisis thus made charisma organizationally appropriate.

6. The charismatic leader brought new purpose and sought to specify that purpose in new programs and new forms of organization. Many persons inside and outside the organization subscribed to the man and his ideas and became followers, encouraged by his convincing forcefulness and dedication. They were encouraged also by the excitement and promise of a new collective effort born of crisis. For a while, the leader was the center of organization and authority.

7. As the organizational change became institutionalized, the charismatic relation attenuated, and the charisma became routinized in a collegial group. The followers developed personal investments in the organization, aside from attachment to the leader, and reduced their appreciation of his qualities. The leader, in turn, interacting with the growing denial of his special gifts of body and spirit, dimmed his gifts by taking on the additional characteristics of disappointment, resentment, and fatigue.

The realization of charisma in a new college and especially in a college in crisis is congruent with our general understanding that unusual men will likely connect with unusual times and places. More difficult to under-

9. Shils, *loc. cit.*, p. 389.

stand is the situation at Swarthmore that led to the Aydelotte era. Was Aydelotte a historical accident? As previously stated, some trustees and many alumni favored his appointment and then got more than they had expected. He was known as a forceful scholar and came highly recommended to a college where opinion was at least somewhat sympathetic to scholarly leadership in the president's chair. For himself, Aydelotte had looked at other colleges and judged this one promising. The change-minded leader came to an organization where modest ambition to improve allowed for the introduction of some new ideas.

The Swarthmore case shows that the situation favorable to the work of the unusually forceful and magnetic leader need not be bound tightly by time, existing within a month or year, but rather can be a set of evolving conditions in which the charismatic figure picks up support, gains in power, sets the direction of change, and extends the leeway for personal influence on policy and events. This procedure is chancy and is not promising in the closed, stable colleges where no initial leeway is available in which to chart a course and gain the momentum of personal loyalty; but in a relatively open, stable college, one looking for improvement, an evolving situation can be set in motion. Aydelotte found the initial leeway; he persistently and patiently built supports for himself and his policies. When the battle was joined with the defenders of the *status quo*, he was able to fall back on much personal devotion. At a crucial time in his attempt to change Swarthmore, he crowned his leadership with success by bringing to the college from the foundations and a few private donors, *on the basis of faith in him,* such major resources that he could not be denied.

Leadership has many faces, and charisma comes in long-lasting and relatively quiet administrative containers as well as in the messianic fervor that bursts upon a scene and quickly stirs the passions of men. Foster at Reed was in the presidency for nine years, Morgan at Antioch for about twelve, and both were disappointed men before the end of their tenure. Aydelotte persisted through two decades, shaping conditions as he went and remaining to consolidate a major change. He too had his disappointments, but they did not cut deeply when weighed against the pleasures of success. The style of personal leadership evidenced in the change at Swarthmore seems closer than that at Reed and Antioch to what is possible in the larger and more complicated colleges and universities of the mid-twentieth century.

Thus new organization is open to charisma, and crisis helps to create it, but neither is a necessary condition. Potentially charismatic men can enter successful and relatively stable organizations and encourage the conditions that realize their charisma. What is initially required is an opening for leadership, usually manifested by a willingness to improve. The potentially charismatic figure who works without the benefit of new organization or organizational crisis is usually forced to string out his break with tradition. His charisma is shielded by patience. However, that his impact is more evolutionary need not diminish the magnitude of the change or the effect upon others and upon the initiation of a legend.

Finally, the stages of organizational development can make complicated and delicate the relationship between strong personal leadership and innovation. Charisma may serve an institutional innovation in one stage and subvert it in another. It commonly serves when critical change is being introduced and given momentum and even onward into the stage of embodiment. But it is not likely to serve when the earlier change is being so fully worked out and expressed that it becomes an organizational saga. During the years of necessary persistent and consistent effort, charisma, generally appearing in the form of new presidents brought in from the outside, becomes an unsettling force, a potential source of institutional deflection. Charisma realized in that stage can destroy the major change already under way. The new charismatically inclined president who is not part of the cult and manages not to be controlled by it institutes his own program, hires his own kind of man, and otherwise manipulates the major components of the organization to realize a new plan. In the process, the development of the previous change into a major institutional innovation is aborted.

The strong president who appears too soon, as suggested earlier, is usually fought by the established staff, with the result that his potential for leadership is situationally denied, and he looks for a place more congenial to his talents. In such conflicts, we find vested interests, careerist motives, and the manipulation of organizational ideology. The established staff defends its own power and belief. The forceful new president seeks to leave his mark on the institution, one by which he will be honored by offers of higher positions and eventually by history. Those who resist the new agent of change defend themselves with the ideology of their successful experiment; the new president maintains that he proposes more effective paths to the old ideals of the college. But whatever the motives of the participants and the nature of their ideological weapons, we can study the effect of the conflict upon charisma and the effect of charismatic leadership on the realization of institutional innovation. We may then encounter the paradox of the strong leader working to weaken an organizational change, particularly one that tends toward distinctiveness, while routine actors, obeying the norms of community and cult, proceed to enhance the change.

## Fulfillment of the Saga

The conditions for introducing a distinctive theme into a college are varied, subject in important degree to the accidents of history and the unique features of particular contexts, but the means of institutionalizing the theme are more regular and predictable. The main features of organization portrayed in the case histories of Antioch, Reed, and Swarthmore are inescapable. Although emphasis differs and idiosyncratic habits catch the eye, we can observe certain elements common to the building and maintenance of an organizational legend. First, believers collect in the faculty and gain the power to protect their cherished ideals and practices. Second, features of the curriculum, determining everyday behavior, reflect and express the saga. Third, a social base of external believers provides resources, including moral support, and interests a certain kind of student in the college. Fourth, the students develop a strong subculture that significantly incorporates the central idea of the college. Fifth, the saga itself—as ideology, self-image, and public image—has forceful momentum. Personnel defense, program embodiment, supporting social base, allied student subculture, ideological force—these are the essential carrying mechanisms.

### THE PERSONNEL CORE

Faculty dedication seems the key component in the making of a college saga. When a faculty is hostile to a theme, its attenuation is ensured. When a faculty is passive, the theme is anemic. When a faculty is devoted to the idea, the making of a saga is probable. A single leader, a college president, can initiate change, but the idea does not go far unless ranking and powerful members of the faculty swing into line and remain committed while the initiator is present and especially after he is gone.

The core group develops in part through internal persuasion. Men already on the staff may, especially in the throes of a charismatic relationship, come over to a new conception of the institution and plunge into the effort of making it a living reality. A more important means is selective recruitment and retention, where men come and stay because they find a new plan congenial and because those already upholding the plan think them appropriate. This procedure involves selection on grounds of personality and personal values, as well as of professional competence, and works through official channels, unofficial assessments, and self-selection. When administrators and senior faculty are sensitive to the issue of fitting men to the college on more than their technical competence, they may seek to make the fit in the official acts of selection. They inform prospective faculty members about what the college is committed to and what kind of faculty member is appropriate to it. On the basis of this information the recruit may withdraw his application if he thinks he is inappropriate, or the college may openly select or reject him. Recruiting men appropriate to the central idea is also done by informal and less explicit means, with a member of a faculty drawing the prospective applicant to one side and giving him the low-down on the place, or with faculty members expressing their judgment, unknown to the recruit, that he will not fit in with what they are trying to do.

The most sensitive aspect of selecting faculty members for support of certain values is the retention of men already brought to the faculty, especially the younger men at the critical points of first reappointment and decision on tenure. They have been part of the system and have had a chance to test it and to be tested by it. Senior personnel know them much better than they know applicants; a more critical decision must be made, especially at the time of decision on tenure, for then the faculty member is invited to permanent membership and moves into or close to the centers of power; and the men who are being judged know the system more intimately than the outsider and are aware, usually acutely, of coming to a critical point in their careers.

During and especially after the development of a faculty core, its capacity to help effect a legend depends on its power. In the presence of the innovating leader, the faculty may need only believe and work, but the years soon come when they need to believe and work *and* have the muscle to ward off pressures to deflect the college from its chosen path. The leader tires, or his capital of influence is spent, or he is gone from the setting. Then, faculty authority comes into its own, serving creatively while serving conservatively. It protects the experiment, the plan, the idea from the quick erosion that could otherwise take place after the early years of trial as a new president comes sweeping into office or as members of the board of trustees start listening to new forces in a fast-changing environment. It is not institutionally creative to have an imaginative, strong president devise a new program during the course of a decade in office and then to have it frittered away, essentially lost from sight, before it is fully worked out and so fixed in a college that it becomes a model for others, adding to the leverage for change in the system of education as a whole.

The board of trustees may well help protect the experiment after the innovator is gone: The board at Swarthmore after Aydelotte's departure is a good illustration. But the board may not carry on: The trustees at Reed did not hold to the same cluster of values as the faculty did and, buffeted by financial worries and outside conservative opinion, would have preferred a path tangential to the institutional thrust established by the mid-twenties. Similarly, the follow-up president (and his successor in turn) may help protect and develop the new plan, as did Algo Henderson at Antioch and John Nason and Courtney Smith at Swarthmore, but the next president may not. He may have his own plan, he may be pulled aside by trustees in the hiring process and be told that the next president should make changes, he may be thinking of a visible organizational mark that will lead to a bigger and better job elsewhere. The board and the president are relatively exposed to outside pressures; the president's office is relatively exposed to the hopes and rewards of change.

The faculty is least exposed and can afford, when it desires, to be the least caring about change. The faculty also has a great capacity to support or sabotage a new plan because it is the full-time staff that does the work. Therefore, faculty commitment is essential, more so than that of the board or of the succeeding president. The faculty is also the most dependable element, the one least likely to change its mind in the succeeding decade or two. Thus, faculty authority conserves essential commitments and perpetuates the innovation. The strong faculties that developed at Antioch, Reed, and Swarthmore largely controlled the instructional program, the selection and retention of faculty, and the policy on student life. Beyond that, they usually were in a position to influence heavily the selection of presidents. When they were not consulted or when the man they had agreed to turned out to be a mistake, they could ward off his efforts at change and shorten his stay on campus. When they and the trustees were in disagreement, they went on operating the college as they saw fit, while the trustees grumbled.

Thus, the role of a strong faculty is an imposing one in the forming of an organizational legend and the making of a distinctive college. The extent to which faculty authority serves or opposes institutional innovation is more complex than has been commonly understood, depending very much on the stage of development of a college and on the stage in the duration of a particular over-all character in that college. The creativity of doggedly seeing through an innovation to maximize its development on one campus and its influence upon thought and practice elsewhere has been readily overlooked. Strong faculties are able to see it through.

THE PROGRAM CORE

Of all the elements of college organization through which a saga develops, the program is the easiest to identify and understand. College administrators and professors do not feel their campus is distinct unless they see special courses, unusual general education requirements, extraordinary modes of evaluation, unique ways of concentrating and spreading student effort. When claims of distinctiveness are made, we hear most about the program. Reed professors who write about Reed write neither of the ways of their colleagues nor of the public image and social base of the college, but of its curricular practices. The protagonists of Antioch point above all to the work-study scheme, community participation as a vehicle of education, and particular general education requirements. One does not mention Swarthmore without calling attention to the honors curriculum. If we send ten professors to a college to determine whether it is distinctive, nine will proceed to study the curriculum; the tenth man may seek to investigate the administrative structure, or if by some chance he is a psychologist, he will yearn to determine student personality, or if a sociologist, he will wander into the cafeteria and through the dormitories in search of student subcultures. The regular and dependable men, in any event, will study the catalogue and schedule of courses and will converse knowledgeably about distribution requirements, the array of courses in the major, and the formal means of teaching and testing students.

The program, as we have seen, is indeed not a bad place to begin, for a well-embodied general idea shows through there in specific forms. One cannot long gaze at the requirements of the Junior Qualifying Examination and the senior thesis at Reed, for example, without getting a hint that Reed is committed to academic toughness. What is more difficult for outsiders to grasp, even to have in mind to look for, are the unannounced, latent ways in which the regular program of teaching may express and support an organizational legend.

One form of subtle expression in the program is the common model of academic effort presented by a number of professors in the way they work. At Reed there was the long-emulated style of the latter-day Socrates, shrewdly and systematically questioning students to force independent thinking and logical formulation. This teaching method was taken at Reed as an expression of academic toughness and individualism. At Antioch there was the much-prized style of the life-aims philosopher who could take any dull, specialized lecture topic and, in a few minutes, plunge into an exciting discussion that students would remember for years after. This method was taken as an expression of the desire to treat the student as a whole and to engage him at the level of basic personal values. At Swarthmore there has been the style of the graduate seminar leader, guiding a student in intense pursuit of a topic, moderating a critical discussion of his paper, and grading it with further suggestions on sources, conceptualization, and integration of argument. This style has been taken as an expression of academic excellence.

Second, the program core is subtly interconnected with other major components of the organization that carry the organizational idea. Its most essential connection is to the beliefs of the faculty, for they define whether a given practice or recommended new course is appropriate. The committed faculty believes in the rightness of a number of program practices, that in turn, help to shape the faculty core, as men react positively and negatively to what they see are becoming and have become the dominant styles. Young faculty men have left Reed precisely because of the way senior men handle the humanities course; they have chosen to leave Antioch because its general education modes were too loose for their specialized tastes; they have departed from Swarthmore because they believed the honors seminars were not so special after all.

Third, the program is a set of symbols and rituals. Academic men point to their decorated spears, their village totems, their bracelets signifying honor and beauty, as they speak proudly of the courses they have long embellished, the curricula they have lovingly fashioned by hand, and the trials they have devised for students to give great meaning to what otherwise would be only a paper credential. When they do so and do it so effectively that they convince themselves, the students, and many outsiders, the curriculum becomes rich with cultural meaning. Mundane matters become partly mystified. Culturally, value is added to the practices themselves, to the organization as a whole, to those who spend their lives there, and to those who are there for only four years. The practice at Reed of not reporting grades to the student, as reviewed earlier, did not remain simply a grading scheme. It became a symbol to prospective students as well as to those on campus of a curriculum, a faculty, a student body, and a college that cared about learning for learning's sake. This invested meaning is the important part of the practice. Taken straight, this policy is not much different from policies elsewhere; claims about its import are much ado about nothing, but the practice as symbol is very important. It is then a cultural artifact as well as an instructional technique, part of the general institutional legend.

THE SOCIAL BASE

Colleges inevitably must find groups and aggregations in the larger society from which they draw money, moral support, personnel, and students; and the nature of the external footing, whether developed deliberately or by accident, heavily influences the nature of the college. A financial constituency expresses approval and disapproval as money is handed over; and a student constituency tailors itself around images of the institution. A college must willy-nilly commit such bases; a college seeking distinctiveness must make believers out of thousands of people on the outside whose lives are not directly bound up in the fate of the college. To the extent that outsiders believe in it, the college achieves a differentiated, protected position in the markets and organizational complexes that allocate money, personnel, and students.

An important change in the character of a college involves attending to the limitations of the given social base and to the necessity and means of changing it. Small colleges typically find themselves on a relatively monolithic base—the active and powerful members of the alumni who share a common definition based on past experience. These outsiders "belong" to the particular college and to no other and hence are invaluable, paying the annual tithe and making the annual pilgrimage to the hallowed halls. They are necessary to viability, but if the college has nowhere else to go for finance and defense except to them, then it can easily become dependent, with the outside group calling the shots. Thus a change in character entails either winning their support for the internal change or so altering the base with new supporters that the college can make its way around the traditional group. The key device here is diversification—multiplying the sources of financial support. When a private foundation chooses to back a new program in a college, it becomes an alternative to alumni support, thereby reducing alumni influence. When the federal government contributes large funds to a state university, the university becomes less dependent on the officials and legislature of its own state for financial backing for certain changes. A strongly diversified financial base is helpful for a high degree of autonomy. When the guardians of one financial drawer shake their heads "no," the administrator needs another into which he can dip his hand. An innovating president's best friend, in a sense, is the unearmarked account on which he can draw at his own discretion.

Small American colleges have in the past also found themselves on a narrow, local student base, which overlaps extensively with the monolithic financial base of alumni. The key device here, in a change toward distinction, has been nationalization of the student body, recruiting from other states and distant parts of the country. Reaching toward distant populations is done in the name of improving the caliber of the student body, but it is often also intended to and nearly always does reduce the control of the traditional social base and increase the control of the personnel of the college. A national social base is less monolithic and less organized than a local one. Outside influence is diffused rather than concentrated. Thus, basic differences in control by social base follow from the narrowness or the generality of the catchment area—the sources of money and students.

In their major changes, Antioch and Swarthmore had to alter their social bases. Swarthmore is the more instructive in this regard. The social base at Antioch was weak and ineffectual, and Morgan had simply to ignore it. The traditional base at Swarthmore, however, was strong and effective, and Aydelotte, as we have seen, had to maneuver with care and patience. The financial base was significantly altered by the addition of foundation support; the influence of traditional clientele through the input of students was gradually curtailed as the student base was broadened from local to national. Out of it all came bases that allowed a high degree of administrative autonomy and that were deeply supportive of and appropriate to the change that had been made. The newer alumni, graduates of the altered college, together with those in the old alumni who had come to support the change, became an extended external family of believers, second to none in sentimental attachment to the general visions and the specific symbols of what the college had become.

No matter how radical their political and religious beliefs, the alumni of a college are likely to be deeply conservative about changing its character. Of all the major groups who must believe in the special nature of a college if it is to become distinctive, the alumni are the best located to hold beliefs enduringly pure; the students come next, then the faculty, then the administration. The administration is up close to trouble, to the specific strains encountered in a changing environment. The faculty also tune in to the troubles, but most do so at a first remove. Some in the faculty are so much in their own tunnel of specialization that they cannot even see new campus-wide problems. The students experience some of the current tensions of the campus but are usually too far outside the channels of information and decision and too transient and inexperienced to understand well what is going on. Responding at a second remove from gritty administrative problems, they hold to true beliefs and act to protect them. The alumni are, of course, much further removed. For them the idea of the college, the warm legend, can be everything. They demand that those who are on the campus act to ward off the changing environment and to shut off internal deviations.

The social base of the distinctive college, then, is no cold matter of money and students. The central ideas and the defining theme tend most toward the qualities of an untouchable saga precisely in the minds of the committed, external beholders.

### THE STUDENT SUBCULTURE

The social base of the college, with some assistance from the admissions office, defines the participating clientele upon which the organization works or to which it offers its services. The students are important to the character of the system in that they are the material for much of its work, they define for insiders and outsiders what the enterprise is largely about, and they can usually manipulate the system. When we compare them with persons in other people-processing institutions, they are relatively free, with many options for action. Persons defined as sick in some form, and thereby confined in a general or mental hospital, usually have little room to maneuver; they are constrained by the debilitating effects of the illness, the sanctioned and respected professional decisions and rights of the doctor, the close control of the hospital staff, and sometimes the force of legal commitment. Those defined as lawbreakers, and thereby placed in a prison, usually have some room in which to manuever, since "good" or "bad" behavior in the system can affect early or late release under the terms of the original assignment; an inmate subculture offers definitions of the situation independent of the official system and helps the individual manipulate the guards and other officials. Students, much more than inmates, are free to form their own structures and to bring their own values to bear upon the rest of the institution. Students can change their majors as well as their courses, voting with their physical presence for and against different professors, courses, programs, and departments. They can alter the intensity of their participation, seeking to move close to a professor or to flee contact with him. And they have the ultimate step, taken frequently in American higher education, of dropping out altogether and transferring to another place. Most important is that they come with personal inclinations and then informally relate to one another in patterns that uphold the predispositions or alter them. As a result of the inputs, options, and self-maintaining structures, the student body becomes a major force in defining the institution.

An important change in a college, then, depends upon acceptance on the part of the students. They must be brought in line. For the change to become a legend, the dominant student subculture must forcefully support it, integrating significantly with the central ideals of the administration and faculty. When most of the students or a vigorous, substantial minority define themselves as personally responsible for upholding what the college has become and are ready to take on enemies, real and imagined, then an organizational mission has become to some degree an organizational saga.

In all three of the colleges under analysis, student subcultures have been powerful mechanisms for carrying the institutional legend from one generation to another and over several decades. Reed students have been unexcelled believers in the uniqueness and power of their campus, constantly on the alert for any administrative action that would alter the place, ever fearful that some men in the administration and faculty might succumb to pressures of the day and seek to make Reed into a college just like all the others. The academic and the nonconforming students have generally joined hands in this regard. They can detect a possible change very quickly and man the battlements even before it is presented for discussion. Students at Antioch have been only a little less pure in the clarity of their vision and only a shade weaker in the intensity of their wish to help protect the character of their campus; they, too, long offered unstinting support for the institutional idea. The Swarthmore student body, as we have seen, was brought from a collegiate definition of student life to a severely academic one between 1920 and 1935 by a change in both the input of students and the structures and practices of their lives on campus. The student subculture at Swarthmore, as at Reed and Antioch, then steadily and dependably transferred campus ideals from one generation of students to another. And they, too, became largely a conservative force, committed to the central ideals, convinced that Swarthmore was unique, and eager to protect the college as the subculture defined it.

THE IDEOLOGY

The role played by quiet fanaticism is often not perceived in the history of colleges. The academic world contains more than its share of ideologues, for academics live amidst ideas, argue over them, and make their living by them. They work with the ideas of their particular discipline, they are self-defined critics of society, and they are likely to have a strong opinion about the proper purpose and shape of their own campuses.

When a college has developed or is developing a distinctive theme, the committed professor can become ideologically a very stubborn man. As we observed at Antioch, Reed, and Swarthmore, particularly in the character-forming or transforming decade, men were willing to sacrifice personally for ideas and to have the organization live dangerously. They were willing to protect the faculty radical whose actions dried up gift money, took food from the mouths of faculty children, and brought to campus the turmoil of the congressional investigating committee. They were willing to diminish sports, suffering the consequences of hostile public opinion. They were willing to permit students much discretion, in full awareness that some would find their way to behavior that shamed the college and placed it on the brink of public scandal. Such willingness was called irresponsibility by some, courage by others. Whatever the judgment, the will stemmed from doctrine, not from opportunism, from stubborn belief that the ideals of the college were right and that the outside world was wrong.

For a particular theme to have much scope and effect in a college, it clearly needs such faculty dedication and, as we have seen, the emerging legend is also reflected in student values, administrative perspectives, and alumni sentiments. But the saga is even more embracing than that. It includes a generalized tradition, a set of statues and ceremonies, an "air about the place" felt by participants and some outsiders. Colleges are prone to a remembrance of things past and a symbolism of uniqueness. The more special the history or the more forceful the claim to a place in history, the more intensively cultivated are the ways of sharing memory and symbolizing the institution. Antioch is an excellent example. For those who know it well, the word "Antioch" sets up intense vibrations: It is Morgan and community government and not firing anyone in the depression and paying off the mortgage and the fire in the Science Building and folk dancing in Red Square and personnel counselors and the crazy antics of the last genuine "character" among the students, and always the ceaseless exchange of on-campus and off-campus students in the co-op program. So much is symbol of a unifying theme, of the meaning of living one's years at the college, and of the potency of the college in society. Ideology is carried in a generalized memory culture expressed in dozens of ways in everyday life. The legend initiated at Antioch in the twenties is found in the sixties in the beliefs expressed in catalogues and at commencements, in the repetitious cry of students and faculty that the college is not living up to what it has always stood for, in the sustained meaning given to certain buildings and patches of sidewalk, in the interpretation assigned to the faces and figures of retired deans who still stroll the grounds. The self-image is imposing and unified.

The idea of the distinctive college is also present in its public image, in the impressions held by outsiders, although often, as we have seen, in distorted, unanticipated, and unwanted ways. Self-image and the practices that support it and give it credence spill over the boundaries of the campus, offering a picture of the institution to which outsiders react before forming their own definition. The Reed self-image of a unique combination of academic sternness and nonconformity, fully credited by campus practices, is at the root of its powerful public image—an image that appeals to a few and repels so many, that makes it a favorite of intellectuals and an object of distaste in nonintellectual strata. The outside impressions distort the details, often seriously, but at the heart of the public image is what the institution has become and what it thinks of itself. Similarly at Antioch and at Swarthmore, in public image, as in self-image, we find a root and a global presentation of the institutional legend.

Since the public impressions mediate in so many of the contacts of the college with its environment, they strongly affect, as we have seen in all three cases, the gathering of financial and human resources. Who the college wants to reach is set in its developing self-image. Who is willing to reach toward it becomes set primarily in the developing public impressions. Formally and informally, deliberately and in unplanned ways, the symbolic expressions of the college contribute to the assembling of an external social base that, in turn and in close integration with other parts of the institution, embodies the central idea.

Finally, then, a saga is reflected in nearly all segments of an organization in a highly integrative way. For discussion and analysis, we have detached certain supporting components, given them separate labels, and spoken of them as essential. But the whole rather than the parts is to be emphasized since a saga produces unity. It binds together the structural elements, it links internal and external groups, and it merges, as we have emphasized, individual and organizational identities.

## The Leader, the Group, and the Community

The three case studies and the foregoing discussion suggest how distinctiveness is achieved in an American college. It is initiated by a single individual, or a small band, in a setting conducive in normative and structural openness. It is sustained by a much larger number of people, on and off campus, through many interlocking components of durable organization.

When we look for how distinctive emphasis gets under way, we find typically a single individual, usually the president, or a very small group. The innovator formulates a new idea, a mission; he has, with varying degrees of deliberateness, found his way to a particular college that is in a particular stage of development and that is structurally open, and he starts to design appropriate means of embodying his idea in the organization and to enhance the conduciveness of the setting. Although this is the function of the strong president, it can likely be performed also by a unified junta.

When we look for the way distinctive emphasis is maintained in a college, we find it typically firmly expressed in interlocking stable structures. The key structure is usually a tenured faculty armed with power. The senior faculty members are personally committed to the emphasis, are collectively the center of power or are so powerful that they can veto attempts at change, and are replaced over time in such a way as to continue the embodiment of the historic purpose in faculty values.

The question of who is most important in the making of a distinctive college, one raised often in educational circles, becomes then not a useful question. It leads toward simple answers and polarized arguments that obscure more than they reveal. For example, if we ask: "Is not Antioch the lengthened shadow of Morgan, a creature of his ideals and introduced practices?" the answer "yes" is a partial truth that overlooks the essential work of full development and institutionalization that took place under Henderson in the thirties; the essential, permanent commitment of the senior faculty; and the essential expression of an Antioch legend in student subculture, public image, and social base. If we answer the same question with a flat "no," we underestimate the great impact of one man in designing a change and getting it under way. The question requires an answer informed by an awareness of the stages of development in a college; the differing roles of the leader and the group in initiating and sustaining a distinctive style; and the complicated, ongoing interaction of purpose, leadership, environment, and the means of organization. The question of how distinctiveness is achieved must at least be broken into the two parts of how it was initiated and how it is sustained. That the question can be further specified and fruitfully posed in other ways has been demonstrated in earlier discussion.

We may note particularly that distinctiveness in a college involves and encourages those characteristics of group life commonly referred to as community. It offers an educationally relevant definition of the difference of the group from all others. And salient elements in the distinctiveness become foci of personal awareness and of a sense of things held in common with others currently on the scene, those who have been there before, and those yet to arrive. Distinctiveness captures loyalty, inducing men to enlist and to stay against the lures of careerism. And it arrests the most transient members, the students, extending their devotion for years to come.

In turn, the conditions most favorable to the existence of a community assist in the development and maintenance of distinctive character. One such condition in a formal organization is singularity of purpose. Group integration is promoted when all are headed in the same direction. A second condition is smallness of size, which allows informal as well as formal links across the specializations and internal divisions inherent in formal organization. An aggregate of strangers brought together to pursue a common purpose within a small organization is more likely to develop a community than is an aggregation set to multiple purposes in a large enterprise. These conditions favor frequent and intense interaction across the system and encourage convergent rather than divergent personal experiences leading toward a sense of oneness. They then obviously can be put to the service of distinctiveness.

However, other conditions can sometimes compensate. Multipurpose universities of the size of ten thousand can still have a relatively strong sense of community and a distinctive character, e.g., Harvard and Yale. Here, long tradition, slow growth, high status, and units promoting intensive interaction combine to combat the structural and subjective fragmentation inherent in largeness and multiplicity of purpose. Tradition contributes an aura. Slow growth helps preserve a sense of unity, by granting time for the assimilation of newcomers into established staff and of new thought into traditional conceptions. High status encourages close identification with the institution: Harvard professor and Yale man are terms usually seized rather than resisted by those entitled to them. Structures promoting interaction—the Harvard residential houses, the Yale residential colleges—help students cope psychologically and socially with the potential stress of individual detachment among thousands of strangers. But these conditions are in short supply in American colleges and universities. The common situation is one of little tradition, rapid growth, modest status, and weak structures for promoting interaction. With these conditions, large size and multiple purpose sharply diminish the possibilities for a sense of community and for distinctive character in the whole.

We may also reflect on the achievement of distinctiveness by asking about its failure to occur. The explanatory scheme here suggests three main sources of nonoccurrence. One is lack of will, or essentially no man with a mission. The second is the absence of structurally conducive conditions for the introduction and early working-out of the mission. The third is weakness or breakdown in the structures of institutionalization, the major components of the organization highlighted earlier, whose embodiment of the mission to an important degree turns it into a saga. Thus we have the denial of distinctiveness when the mission-oriented leader cannot be found or induced to come to the organization; or having arrived, cannot loosen the organization from its web of traditional expectations and commitments; or having broken tradition and established the mission, the mission does not endure because one or more major structural supports develop weakly or give way. The latter problems include weakness in the social base, as nonbelievers stiffen their resistance and withhold support; attenuation of belief in the faculty, as nonselective recruitment introduces nonbelievers; fragmentation of the student subculture, as a growing student body becomes more heterogeneous and draws from the youth of a new age; and loss of unity and distinctiveness in curricular practices, as adaptations are made to placate external and internal interests. Above all, as emphasized, vulnerability lies in weak power of the believing group, for then agents of change can divert the organization to a new course.

## The Risks and Tensions of Distinctiveness

Distinctive colleges, because they attempt to be special and not all things to all men, are likely to have one or more distinctive strains, exhibiting in higher degree tensions found elsewhere. In emphasizing one value, they underplay, oppose, or ignore others. In securing the loyalty of one segment of society, they may secure the hostility of others. In committing the organization strongly to one path of action, they find it difficult at a later time to take another route or otherwise to adapt as new demands are made upon them.

Among the three colleges of this study, we have seen a number of tensions and risks: the strain between adult responsibility and the freedom of students; the struggle between specialization and general education; the split between teaching and research; the risk of being a cult in a hostile countryside; the danger of getting cut off from ordinary funding sources. At Antioch, as we have seen, the freedom of students was a persisting source of institutional strain, presenting problems with which only a true believer would willingly live. The salient commitment to general education also produced a severe problem when the more specialized interests of modern academic men demanded to be served. And for decades the general liberality, nonconformity, and political action have produced local disdain and hostility, complicating severely the task of raising necessary funds. To become distinctive the college lived through two decades of being heavily in debt. After the retirement of the debt, the college continued to find its fund-raising efforts heavily mortgaged by its reputation. Antioch has had only a few quiet years since 1920, and it has had very few financially easy years.

Reed has shared with Antioch a deep institutional strain over student freedom. The internal anxiety and the external antipathy have been an enduring part of institutional affairs. One president after another has found student behavior his cross to bear, and trustees could hardly help resting uneasy, no matter how strong their pride in accomplishments. The college proved better oriented than Antioch for an age of specialization in that its posture was not rooted in an equally broad version of general education; but its dogged commitment to teaching meant stubborn resistance to the interest in research growing everywhere in the academic world. And no other college of similar national standing has had such a problem of fund-raising. In its business affairs, it was a shoestring operation, with all that that entails in administrative anxiety, lack of physical plant, and underpayment of faculty. The strain and the risk have been high, again only tolerable to determined men who are sure they are right.

Of the three colleges, Swarthmore has been least subject to strain because of distinctiveness. To effect a major change it did not undergo the uncertainties of new organization or the difficulties of crisis. The change was more evolutionary and considerably better funded than was the case in the other two colleges. But Swarthmore could have lived an easier life if it had stayed more in the normal mold. The many changes of the twenties and thirties had to be fought out; alumni resistance made the whole effort a precarious one for several years and a matter of some stress for a longer period. Although the college was well oriented (for its size) for the growing interests in specialization and research, it, too, had to struggle to attract and hold an appropriate faculty against the lures of the universities. Even more than Antioch and Reed, the college could not make do with faculty members whose job alternatives were in average small colleges. Student brightness alone would make this foolhardy, and the self-concept and national leadership role of the college made it highly inappropriate. As a result, the college pitted itself against Ivy League universities in recruitment, not a soft road for any small college to travel. And then, too, the college found student freedom and nonconformity a steady source of strain within its membership and especially with the surrounding community.

The ultimate risk of distinctive character is that of success in one era breeding rigidity and stagnation in a later one. Commitments are precise rather than diffuse, sharply made rather than dully connected, articulated rather than unspoken; in short, they constitute a formula for later trouble. But in such matters, involving stages of organizational development and degrees of openness to later change, we know little about compelling restraints and open options. Surely the organization that turns a mission into a saga, a good idea into a fruitful legend, moves, in the full flush of success, toward the possibility of its distinctiveness becoming an antiquated mode, one from which it cannot unhook itself until torn by trouble. But surely, just as ordinarily routinized colleges can vary in degree of openness to change, distinctively fixed colleges can also vary. Among the three colleges, for example, one can speculate that Reed is the least open to change. The Reed capacity, one may say the Reed necessity, to endure through sheer stubbornness gives it a sharp problem of adaptability. Swarthmore appears in a middle ground, conservative in habit but with possible flexibility within its open Quaker ethos and its general institutional health. Antioch appears the most open to change, even to diffusion of hard-won character. Its central educational values leave the curriculum exposed: To believe that the young learn from work in jobs off campus and from campus experiences outside the classroom is to unbutton things.

for then why not this and why not that, why not course credit for making pottery or for living and working three months with a farm family in France? The ideals of social reform, strongest at Antioch, also spill over into a sense that one's own campus can stand improvement. The values institutionalized at Antioch have, in general, left the college somewhat experimental-minded, with a passion for self-study and for leadership in experimental-college circles.

In the face of the common institutional danger that distinctiveness may lead in time to rigidity and stagnation, we may note several features that are favorable to change and that are likely to be present in all distinctively excellent colleges. One feature is the challenge of bright students. To have a bright student body is to have a steady infiltration of critical minds. The faculty and administration then come under heavy pressure to remain alert, first in the performance of traditional practice, and second to the possibilities of altering practices to meet the changing needs and demands of the students. In the best colleges, the students tend to become brighter than the faculty. Many faculty members must then struggle to maintain their credibility as teachers, reading widely and critically, staying abreast of the latest perspectives and findings of the discipline so that they at least know more than the students even if their mental gears do not go around so fast. On affairs that engage the whole campus, the bright students offer rational arguments that are qualitatively different from those of students at average small colleges. At an Antioch or Reed or Swarthmore, time and again one can observe students getting the best of an administrator in an argument, driving him back against the wall as he tries to give a rational explanation for traditional controls over student behavior. In such settings, effective administrators not only must be intelligent and quick but also must be capable of adapting to the changing nature of sophisticated youth.

A second feature favorable to change is the expression of new views that occurs when the authority structure is relatively democratic and when discussion is relatively open. The students, faculty, and administrators who flow in from the outside, not as well socialized to what the college has been, as are the old-timers, are often the source of new thought. In time, on the average, they become socialized or they go away. The chance for them to express themselves in influential ways while they are young in the organization becomes an important factor in change. Forms of organization at Antioch, for example, have allowed young faculty members to have influence. The young ones do not sit in hushed silence, in awe or fear of their elders, as young men do in many small colleges. With the faculty meeting allowing a reasonable chance for men to be equal, Young Turks cannot be ignored. Community government, in addition, has allowed the voices of students to be heard. As a result, the oligarchs are not completely in control. There is always a group with a new plan that must be considered and in some cases adopted. Other leading colleges, in somewhat lesser degree, usually possess this source of adaptation.

Finally, sources of openness to change are found in the tensions and risks, described earlier in the section, that inhere in distinctive character. The tensions force small crises in organizational viability; the risks generate anticipation that present character may not be able to cope with future pressures. The small crises and worries about the future are commonly generated by problems of finance and retention of faculty. The frequent annual deficit shocks everyone when, in the current year, it jumps to a new high. The normal loss of faculty members to other places becomes abnormal and threatening when four associate professors leave in a single year. Such events can be taken as signs of a gathering storm, for if repeated because the college has become out of joint with the times, then the institution, beloved character and all, will decline in health and quality.

## The Rewards of a Saga

When we hold educational ideals in mind, the making of a college is much more than raising money, erecting buildings, recruiting professors, organizing courses, and enrolling students. Past minimal competence lies the problem of whether the operations of the college will reflect to a significant degree certain educational and social values. To build effectively is to incorporate purpose effectively, and not any purpose but purpose congruent with the general ideals of a class of organizations and of a large social institution; e.g., the ideals of the liberal arts college and the ideals of excellence in higher learning. The reflected purpose can be a specific imitation of what the leading colleges of a given period are doing; and that is hard to do, requiring as it does supportive settings that are in short supply and organizational means that must be obtained in a competitive market. Even more difficult is to find the specific formula that allows the college to reflect general values in a new, highly productive, and esteemed form. The vision that drives the best educational leaders is to approach a general ideal of man by developing new organizational devices and practices.

Antioch, Reed, and Swarthmore are among the handful of colleges that, through ingenuity and persistence in the four decades of 1920 to 1960, came to reflect most fully distinctive excellence in liberal education on the American scene. Their stories tell us how they did it and suggest what is essential and what may be accidental to doing as well in other efforts. Optimistically, we see elements of organizational development that could be widely replicated. The common elements discussed here can at least inform the images of the future held by college administrators and faculties. Pessimistically, however, we see conditions, men, and events that have rarely conspired. No one should suggest that it is easy to get purpose and men together under conditions that permit effective expression of cherished educational ideals.

Either way, we find at root in these successful cases a willingness to risk much, personally and organizationally, to try a different route. The personal commitment required of many actors in the situation can be set in motion by the charisma of a single man. It can be fully invested and steadily carried over the years, however, only by a fusing of an idea and the organization. Careerist motives are not enough; an embodied idea is the institutional chariot to which individual motive becomes chained. When the idea is in command, men are indifferent to personal cost. They often are not even aware of how much they have risked and how much they sometimes have sacrificed. As ideologues, as believers, they do not care. They are proud of what they have been through, what they have done, and what they stand for. They feel highly involved in a worthwhile collective effort and wish to remain with it. For the organization the richly embellished institutional definition that we call a saga can then be invaluable in maintaining viability in a competitive market. It is also invaluable as a foundation for trust within the institutional group, easing communication and cooperation.

The individual and group returns are thus considerable. In offering so much thrill and pleasure, a saga maximizes for the individual the esthetic rewards of administration and group membership. The organizational means become beautiful ends in themselves. In turn, in binding and motivating the individual, even in fusing personal and organizational identities, the legend becomes a precious resource for those who fashion the enterprise, a resource created out of the social components of organization. In such efforts, the task—and the reward—of the institutional leader is to create and initiate an activating mission. The task—and the reward—of the institutional group is to have purpose and organization become a saga.

*Appendices*

# *Appendix 1.* The Research Opportunity

THIS STUDY BEGAN in 1958 as part of an interdisciplinary effort at the Center for the Study of Higher Education, University of California, Berkeley, to study the impact of college on the personalities and values of students. In the first year the study involved Antioch, Reed, Swarthmore, and San Francisco State College; in the second year, it turned also to St. Olaf, University of the Pacific, University of Portland, and our own campus in Berkeley. The research encompassed a number of methods, particularly repeated interviews of students and repeated use of personality scales and social-data questionnaires with the students. The field work was completed between 1958 and 1964. The unpublished results of the analysis of student development are available from the Berkeley Center.

While my colleagues attended primarily to characteristics of the students, I focused principally on characteristics of the colleges. My effort entailed two- and three-week visits each year to the four colleges with which the study began in 1958. During this time I was free to interview, observe, and read college documents and records. I also spent much shorter periods in observation at the second four colleges. In the course of the field trips of the first two years, one question became increasingly interesting and insistent: How had the colleges developed the characteristics that defined them in 1960 and that seemingly affected their students? While other analyses went forward, I undertook also to pursue this question for the three highly distinctive liberal arts colleges in the study. The result of that exploration is this volume.

The question of historical development led me primarily to administrators and faculty members most acquainted with the affairs of past years and to administrative records and library documents. Informal, conversational interviews were the best source of general information about past events and trends, giving potential insights that could then be pursued in the written records. In nearly every case, however, information obtained by interview has been considered dependable only when it appeared also in documents, and in cases of conflicting information between personal recall and written record, the record was taken as primary.

Thus, on the days of research when this historical question was uppermost in the apportioning of time, I was usually in the basement or tower or special room of the college library where in varying states of order and disarray one might find papers about the college—the official series of bulletins, newspaper clippings, old trustees' minutes, student term papers concerning the college—or in the offices of the registrar, admissions officer, and whatever official had the file of minutes of meetings of the whole faculty and key committees. The records differed considerably from one college to another in ways somewhat paralleling their differences in general character. Swarthmore has long had annual reports by presidents, documents that are orderly and, over the long run, informative in tone and substance, but it has had a minimum of loose documents of self-analysis. Antioch has not had an orderly series of published annual reports but has mimeographed intracampus reports of self-analysis stuffed in one file drawer after another in Antiochiana and administrative offices. Reed was parsimonious on both scores; but since its character and conflict occasioned so much outside attention, there are reams of local newspaper and magazine description and comment, some of it written by reporters considered eminently informed and fair. Determination of the documents used as basic sources in Chapters 1 to 9 was based considerably on these differences in style of public reporting and intracampus discussion.

# *Appendix 2.* Faculty Questionnaire Data

As PART of the Berkeley study of the impact of college on students (Appendix 1), a brief questionnaire of forty-six items on personal background and attitude was sent to the faculties of the eight colleges in the spring of 1963. The questionnaire went to a one-fourth sample (every fourth name in a faculty listing) at the University of California, Berkeley, and to the entire faculty at the other seven institutions. One follow-up letter and questionnaire were sent to nonrespondents. The final response rate was, in descending order: Swarthmore, 93 per cent; St. Olaf, 92 per cent; Antioch, 88 per cent; Reed, 87 per cent; University of Portland, 87 per cent; University of the Pacific, 85 per cent; San Francisco State College, 83 per cent; and University of California, Berkeley, 67 per cent. Thus, for a questionnaire, the rate of return was very good for the three colleges of this volume and for all the other colleges other than the university campus. The lower return rate for the Berkeley faculty seemed one indication among many others that although the research was based on that campus and most members of the research group were members of that faculty, the research was less well known and less valued there than at the other seven institutions.

The questionnaire is available at the Berkeley Center. Table A2-1 reports information from the questionnaire that has been referred to at one or more points in chapters one to nine.

TABLE A2-1. *Faculty Questionnaire Data: Antioch, Reed, Swarthmore, and Five Other Colleges, 1963, Percentages*

| | Antioch | Reed | Swarthmore | University of California, Berkeley | San Francisco State College | St. Olaf | University of the Pacific | University of Portland |
|---|---|---|---|---|---|---|---|---|
| *Have doctoral degree* | 56 | 61 | 74 | 70 | 61 | 46 | 57 | 27 |
| *Publication record* | | | | | | | | |
| Published one or more books | 20 | 19 | 36 | 40 | 25 | 16 | 15 | 16 |
| Now writing a book | 38 | 43 | 51 | 52 | 48 | 25 | 29 | 23 |
| Published three or more articles | 42 | 34 | 54 | 74 | 41 | 28 | 38 | 24 |
| *General feeling about the college* | | | | | | | | |
| It is a very good place for me | 76 | 65 | 80 | 68 | 61 | 71 | 63 | 63 |
| Could not be equally satisfied anywhere else | 51 | 38 | 38 | 33 | 24 | 29 | 20 | 29 |
| It is one of the top ten colleges | 68 | 72 | 92 | 90 | 5 | 4 | 2 | 0 |
| *Estimate of faculty teaching commitment and capability* | | | | | | | | |
| Over half the faculty are superior teachers | 76 | 68 | 90 | 38 | 30 | 44 | 26 | 29 |
| Over half the faculty are strongly interested in the academic problems of students | 86 | 89 | 87 | 34 | 51 | 75 | 61 | 58 |
| Over half the faculty are strongly interested in the students' lives outside the classroom | 36 | 6 | 27 | 5 | 9 | 40 | 18 | 24 |
| *Academic freedom of faculty and students* | | | | | | | | |
| Faculty should be free to publish the findings of all investigations | 92 | 92 | 88 | 91 | 86 | 85 | 83 | 72 |
| Faculty should be free to present any and all ideas in regular classes | 85 | 82 | 72 | 76 | 77 | 68 | 65 | 45 |

| | | | | | | | | |
|---|---|---|---|---|---|---|---|---|
| Faculty should be free to participate in any public controversy | 89 | 84 | 70 | 73 | 73 | 70 | 68 | 48 |
| Student publications should be free, subject only to the censorship exercised by the United States postal authorities | 73 | 64 | 38 | 59 | 47 | 36 | 35 | 22 |
| *Civil liberty issues* | | | | | | | | |
| Legislative committees should not investigate the political beliefs of university faculty members. *Strongly agree* | 83 | 85 | 70 | 67 | 63 | 49 | 53 | 31 |
| Present members of the Communist Party should not be allowed to teach in a college or university. *Strongly or moderately disagree* | 64 | 63 | 49 | 50 | 45 | 30 | 21 | 10 |
| *Political party* Identification | | | | | | | | |
| Republican | 9 | 9 | 17 | 19 | 23 | 44 | 47 | 31 |
| Democrat | 42 | 49 | 46 | 57 | 51 | 34 | 28 | 46 |
| Independent or Socialist | 45 | 42 | 33 | 20 | 23 | 21 | 22 | 20 |
| Voted for Stevenson (1956) | 74 | 85 | 68 | 70 | 66 | 41 | 38 | 34 |
| Voted for Kennedy (1960) | 78 | 88 | 76 | 76 | 72 | 51 | 40 | 65 |
| *Religion* Present religion | | | | | | | | |
| None | 53 | 51 | 38 | 50 | 40 | 3 | 15 | 5 |
| Protestant | 30 | 31 | 47 | 33 | 43 | 96 | 78 | 21 |
| Jewish | 9 | 5 | 6 | 7 | 5 | 0 | 2 | 1 |
| Catholic | 5 | 7 | 3 | 4 | 6 | 1 | 2 | 68 |
| Consider oneself moderately or deeply religious | 49 | 34 | 58 | 45 | 55 | 96 | 85 | 86 |
| N = | 78 | 74 | 90 | 286 | 480 | 114 | 120 | 107 |

# *Appendix 3.* Student Questionnaire Data

THE INFORMATION in the following table is drawn from a much larger set of questions posed to students at Antioch, Reed, Swarthmore, and the five other colleges and universities of the Berkeley study in repeated questionnaires in the years 1958–1963. The ten questions reported here illustrate the differences consistently found among the student bodies. Students at Antioch, Reed, and Swarthmore, compared with the other institutions, were more liberal in political attitude, more secular in religious practice, more socially conscious, and more sophisticated in cultural matters.

The methods and findings of the attitude research, including change in attitudes over the college years, are available from the Center for the Study of Higher Education, University of California, Berkeley, California.

TABLE A3–1. *Student Questionnaire Data: Antioch, Reed, Swarthmore, and Five Other Colleges (Freshman Students), 1958–1959, Percentages*

| Attitude or Preference | Antioch | Reed | Swarthmore | University of California, Berkeley | San Francisco State College | St. Olaf | University of the Pacific | University of Portland |
|---|---|---|---|---|---|---|---|---|
| Prefer Republican Party in politics | 21 | 20 | 28 | 44 | 36 | 68 | 65 | 39 |
| Preferred Republican candidate (Eisenhower) in 1960 presidential election | 34 | 26 | 35 | 63 | 53 | 87 | 79 | 69 |
| Agree that a former member of the Communist Party who refuses to reveal the names of Party members he had known should not be allowed to teach in a college or university | 20 | 14 | 14 | 43 | 52 | 56 | 61 | 71 |
| Agree that the government is acting properly in refusing a passport to a Socialist | 8 | 8 | 9 | 25 | 37 | 23 | 35 | 44 |
| Strongly disapprove of the methods used by the late Senator McCarthy in his investigations | 57 | 70 | 61 | 23 | 19 | 11 | 15 | 7 |
| Agree that there is too much conformity among American college students | 69 | 79 | 51 | 38 | 33 | 50 | 40 | 33 |
| Attend religious services only once or twice a year or never | 41 | 61 | 33 | 34 | 25 | 2 | 14 | 4 |
| Greatly interested in national and world affairs | 33 | 42 | 33 | 26 | 15 | 20 | 19 | 19 |
| Enjoy poetry very much | 43 | 46 | 39 | 21 | 22 | 20 | 19 | 19 |
| Like classical music very much | 58 | 64 | 58 | 40 | 45 | 48 | 38 | 27 |
| N (approximate*) = | 375 | 185 | 260 | 2,675 | 740 | 570 | 360 | 360 |

* The number of responding students varied slightly from one question to the next.

# Bibliography

Adamic, Louis, *My America*. New York, Harper & Row, Publishers, 1938.

Allen, Rev. Ira W., *A History of the Rise, Difficulties and Suspension of Antioch College*. Columbus, Ohio, J. Geary & Son, 1858.

*American Universities and Colleges*, 2nd ed. Washington, D. C., American Council on Education, 1932.

*American Universities and Colleges*, 8th ed. Washington, D. C., American Council on Education, 1960.

Aydelotte, Frank, *Breaking the Academic Lock Step: The Development of Honors Work in American Colleges and Universities*. New York, Harper & Row, Publishers, 1944.

—— *The Oxford Stamp and Other Essays*. New York, Oxford University Press, Inc., 1917.

Babbidge, Homer D., Jr., *Swarthmore College in the Nineteenth Century: A Quaker Experience in Education*. Unpublished Ph.D. dissertation, Yale University, 1953.

Barnard, Chester I., *The Functions of the Executive*. Cambridge, Mass., Harvard University Press, 1953.

Bendix, Reinhard, *Max Weber: An Intellectual Portrait*. Garden City, N. Y., Doubleday & Company, Inc., 1960.

Chatterjee, Manmatha Nath, *Out of Confusion*. Yellow Springs, Ohio, The Antioch Press, 1954.

Clark, Burton R., *Adult Education in Transition: A Study of Institutional Insecurity*. Berkeley, Calif., University of California Press, 1956.

—— *The Open Door College: A Case Study*. New York, McGraw-Hill, Inc., 1960.

—— "Organizational Adaptation and Precarious Values." *American Sociological Review*, Vol. 21, No. 3 (June, 1956), pp. 327–36.

Cremin, Lawrence A., *The Transformation of the School*. New York, Alfred A. Knopf, Inc., 1962.

*Critique of a College*. Swarthmore, Pa., Swarthmore College, 1967.

Doherty, Robert W., *The Hicksite Separation: A Sociological Analysis of Religious Schism in Early Nineteenth Century America*. New Brunswick, N. J., Rutgers University Press, 1967.

Earnest, Ernest, *Academic Procession*. Indianapolis, Ind., The Bobbs-Merrill Company, Inc., 1953.

Etzioni, Amitai, *A Comparative Analysis of Complex Organizations*. New York, The Free Press, 1961.

Flexner, Abraham, *The American College*. New York, Century Company, 1908.

Foster, William T., *Administration of the College Curriculum*. Boston, Houghton Mifflin Company, 1911.

*From Max Weber: Essays in Sociology*, trans. by H. H. Gerth and C. Wright Mills, eds. New York, Oxford University Press, Inc., 1946.

Henderson, Algo D., and Dorothy Hall, *Antioch College: Its Design for Liberal Education*. New York, Harper & Row, Publishers, 1946.

Hunt, Everett Lee, *The Revolt of the College Intellectual*. New York, Human Relations Aids, 1963.

Hutchins, Robert M., *The State of the University, 1929–1949, A Report by Robert M. Hutchins Covering the Twenty Years of His Administration*. No place or publisher given, 1949.

Johnson, Emily C., *Under Quaker Appointment: The Life of Jane P. Rushmore*. Philadelphia, Pa., University of Pennsylvania Press, 1953.

Johnson, Owen, *Stover at Yale*. Collier Books. New York, The Macmillan Company, 1968. (Originally published in 1912.)

Keezer, Dexter Merriam, *The Light That Flickers*. New York, Harper & Row, Publishers, 1947.

Knapp, Robert H., and Hubert B. Goodrich, *The Origins of American Scientists*. Chicago, The University of Chicago Press, 1952.

Knapp, Robert H., and Joseph J. Greenbaum, *The Younger American Scholar: His Collegiate Origins*. Chicago, The University of Chicago Press, 1953.

Learned, William S., *The Quality of the Educational Process in the United States and in Europe*, Bulletin No. 20. New York, Carnegie Foundation for the Advancement of Teaching, 1927.

Le Duc, Thomas, *Piety and Intellect at Amherst College, 1865–1912*. New York, Columbia University Press, 1946.

McGrath, Earl J., ed. *The Humanities in General Education*. Dubuque, Iowa, Wm. C. Brown Co., 1949.

Magill, Edward Hicks, *Sixty-five Years in the Life of a Teacher, 1841–1906*. Boston, Houghton Mifflin Company, 1907.

Mann, Mary Peabody, *Life of Horace Mann.* Washington, D. C., National Education Association of the United States, 1937. (Centennial Edition, *in facsimile.* Originally published by Walker, Fuller and Company, Boston, 1865.)

*Max Weber: The Theory of Social and Economic Organization,* trans. by A. M. Henderson and Talcott Parsons. New York, Oxford University Press, Inc., 1947.

Morgan, Arthur E., *A Compendium of Antioch Notes.* Yellow Springs, Ohio, Kahoe and Company, 1930.

—— *Edward Bellamy, A Biography.* New York, Columbia University Press, 1944.

—— *Nowhere Was Somewhere.* Chapel Hill, N.C., The University of North Carolina Press, 1946.

—— *The Philosophy of Edward Bellamy.* New York, King's Crown Press, 1945.

Morgan, Joy Elmer, *Horace Mann at Antioch.* Washington, D. C., National Education Association of the United States, 1938.

Mulhern, James, *A History of Education.* New York, The Ronald Press Company, 1946.

Parrish, Edward, *Education in the Society of Friends.* Philadelphia, Pa., J. B. Lippincott Company, 1865.

Rudolph, Frederick, *The American College and University.* New York, Alfred A. Knopf, Inc., 1962.

Schmidt, George P., *The Liberal Arts College.* New Brunswick, N. J., Rutgers University Press, 1957.

Selznick, Philip, *Leadership in Administration.* New York, Harper & Row, Publishers, 1957.

Shils, Edward, "Charisma," in *International Encyclopedia of the Social Sciences* (New York, The Macmillan Company and The Free Press, 1968), Vol. 2, pp. 386–90.

Smelser, Neil J., *Theory of Collective Behavior.* New York, The Free Press, 1963.

Straker, Robert L., *Horace Mann and Others.* Yellow Springs, Ohio, The Antioch Press, 1963.

—— *The Unseen Harvest: Horace Mann and Antioch College.* Yellow Springs, Ohio, The Antioch Press, 1955.

Swarthmore College Faculty, *An Adventure in Education: Swarthmore College Under Frank Aydelotte.* New York, The Macmillan Company, 1941.

Tewksbury, Donald G., *The Founding of American Colleges and Universities Before the Civil War.* Hamden, Conn., Archon Books, 1965. (Originally published by Teachers College, Columbia University, New York, 1932.)

Thomas, Russell, *The Search for a Common Learning: General Education, 1800–1960.* New York, McGraw-Hill, Inc., 1962.

U.S. Bureau of the Census, *Historical Statistics of the United States, Colonial Times to 1957.* Washington, D. C., 1960.

U.S. Department of Health, Education, and Welfare, *Higher Education,* Vol. XVII (January, 1961).

Waller, Willard, *The Sociology of Teaching.* New York, John Wiley & Sons, Inc., 1932.

# Index

277